ROUTLEDGE LIBRARY EDITION:
SYNTAX

Volume 6

THEMATIC THEORY IN SYNTAX AND INTERPRETATION

THEMATIC THEORY IN SYNTAX AND INTERPRETATION

ROBIN CLARK

LONDON AND NEW YORK

First published in 1990 by Routledge

This edition first published in 2017
by Routledge
2 Park Square, Milton Park, Abingdon, Oxon OX14 4RN

and by Routledge
711 Third Avenue, New York, NY 10017

Routledge is an imprint of the Taylor & Francis Group, an informa business

© 1990 Robin Clark

All rights reserved. No part of this book may be reprinted or reproduced or utilised in any form or by any electronic, mechanical, or other means, now known or hereafter invented, including photocopying and recording, or in any information storage or retrieval system, without permission in writing from the publishers.

Trademark notice: Product or corporate names may be trademarks or registered trademarks, and are used only for identification and explanation without intent to infringe.

British Library Cataloguing in Publication Data
A catalogue record for this book is available from the British Library

ISBN: 978-1-138-21859-8 (Set)
ISBN: 978-1-315-43729-3 (Set) (ebk)
ISBN: 978-1-138-69809-3 (Volume 6) (hbk)
ISBN: 978-1-138-69810-9 (Volume 6) (pbk)
ISBN: 978-1-315-51989-0 (Volume 6) (ebk)

Publisher's Note
The publisher has gone to great lengths to ensure the quality of this reprint but points out that some imperfections in the original copies may be apparent.

Disclaimer
The publisher has made every effort to trace copyright holders and would welcome correspondence from those they have been unable to trace.

Thematic Theory in Syntax and Interpretation

Robin Clark

ROUTLEDGE

London & New York

First published 1990
by Routledge
11 New Fetter Lane, London EC4P 4EE

Simultaneously published in the USA and Canada
by Routledge
a division of Routledge, Chapman and Hall, Inc.
29 West 35th Street, New York, NY 10001

© 1990 Robin Clark

Typeset in 10/12pt Times, Scantext by Leaper & Gard, Bristol.
Printed in Great Britain by T.J. Press, Padstow

All rights reserved. No part of this book may be reprinted or reproduced or utilized in any form or by any electronic, mechanical, or other means, now known or hereafter invented, including photocopying and recording, or in any information storage or retrieval system, without permission in writing from the publishers.

British Library Cataloguing in Publication Data
Clark, Robin
  Thematic theory in syntax and interpretation — (Croom Helm linguistics series)
  1. Grammatical relations. Lexical aspects
  I. Title II. Series
  415

ISBN 0-415-01942-7

Library of Congress Cataloging-in-Publication Data
Clark, Robin Lee, 1957–
  Thematic theory in syntax and interpretation / Robin Clark.
    p. cm. — (Croom Helm linguistics series)
  Revision of the author's thesis (Ph.D)—University of California, Los Angeles, 1985.
  Includes bibliographical references.
  ISBN 0-415-01942-7
  1. Grammar, Comparative and general—Syntax. 2. Generative grammar. 3. Lexical grammar. I. Title. II. Series.
  P295.C57 1990
  415—dc20   89-10981
                                                            CIP

Contents

Preface	vii
1 Introduction	1
2 On a certain class of nominals	19
Some preliminaries	21
Some properties of retroactive nominals	26
Operator binding in retroactive nominals	31
Some inadequacies of operator binding in retroactive nominals	36
'Move NP' inside NP	41
Generalizing across categories	43
Transparency and categories	51
PRO in NP	52
Thematic properties and proper government	57
Affixation and retroactive nominals	67
Affixation and external thematic roles	74
A note on 'worth'	76
Summary	79
3 Thematic domains and bounding	81
Thematic domains	82
Subject and adjuncts	88
Barriers and transparency	101
Extensions to transparency	114
Summary	131

4 Control and non-overt operators	133
Approaches to control	134
A theory of non-overt operators	147
Non-overt operators and control	161
LF representations and the interpretation of arbitrary control	200
Conclusions	236
Notes	242
References	254
Index	260

Preface

This book is a revised version of my UCLA doctoral dissertation. I would like to thank the members of my committee: Hagit Borer, Ed Keenan, Carlos Otero, Eric Wehrli, and Ken Wexler. Particular thanks go to Tim Stowell, the chair of my committee. I have a special debt to Joseph Aoun and Tom Roeper. Ken Safir gave me particularly detailed comments on an earlier draft of the book. Any errors and mistakes in the result are, of course, my own.

Finally, I want to thank my wife, Maryellen MacDonald, to whom I dedicate this book with love.

Chapter one

Introduction

The lexicon has come to play an increasingly important role in generative grammar. The first widely read monograph on generative grammar, Chomsky's *Syntactic Structures* (1957), lacked a lexical component in the current sense. The analysis of what are now regarded as lexical properties had to be analyzed in the syntactic component of the grammar; even the insertion of lexical items into a syntactic representation was handled by phrase-structure rules. The lexicon and the study of lexical properties are relative newcomers to the generative scene, although the importance of the lexicon and lexical semantics is uncontroversial.[1]

I will consider some aspects of the role played by lexical argument structure in syntactic representations. I mean, by argument structure, the array of thematic roles encoded on a word as a function of its lexical interpretation. For example, the verb *hit* minimally involves a two-place relation between an agent (the one who hits) and a patient (the individual on the receiving end of the blow). Intuitively, the thematic roles associated with a lexical item give some cognitive content to the parts that that item's arguments play in the relation named by that item. The examples in (1) should serve to clarify what I mean:

(1)   a. John hit Bill.
       b. John saw Bill.

In (1a) John is the agent of the action denoted by *hit.* He is actively engaged in the hitting. Bill, on the other hand, is a patient who is the target of John's hitting. Example (1b) is quite different, although at first glance it seems syntactically quite analogous to (1a). John, in (1b), is experiencing the seeing; unlike (1a), there is

Introduction

no implication that John is acting upon Bill. Since John is not an agent in (1b), there is no implication that Bill is a patient; rather, Bill is the source of John's perception.

I will argue, throughout, that thematic roles constrain the syntax in a number of other ways. In the first part of the book, I will propose that the relation 'X assigns a thematic role to Y' serves to define the domain out of which a syntactic element may be moved. A constituent is an island to extraction if that constituent is not related to a head under thematic-role assignment. The examples in (2) form a class under this approach since the wh-phrase at the beginning of the clause has been extracted from a constituent that does not enter into the proper sort of thematic relation. As is standard, t marks the gap related to a wh-phrase at the beginning of the clause:

(2) a. *Who did pictures of t annoy Bill?
 b. *What did John scold Bill because he took t?
 c. *Which company do you consider employees of t unfortunate?

In (2a) the wh-phrase, *who*, has been extracted from the subject of a tensed clause; since the subject is not thematically related to a lexical head in the proper way, the acceptability of (2a) is lessened. In example (2b) the wh-phrase, *what*, has been extracted from a sentential modifier which, again, is not related thematically to a lexical head. Finally, in (2c) a subpart of the subject of the predicate *unfortunate* has been extracted; I will argue that the explanation of (2c) is the same as that of (2a–b).[2] If the approach advocated here is correct, then thematic relations form part of the foundation for grammatical locality ('bounding'). This conclusion is by no means obvious; until recently (for example, Chomsky 1986), thematic relations have not played such a direct role in syntactic locality.

In the second part of the book, I will investigate the relationship between argument structure and control structures:

(3) a. John$_i$ took the aspirin [PRO$_i$ to get rid of his headache]
 b. John$_i$ tried [PRO$_i$ to get rid of his headache]
 c. Bill persuaded John$_i$ [PRO$_i$ to take aspirin]

The element 'PRO' in (3) marks the cite of a non-overt subject; the subscripting relation indicates coreference. It has long been recognized that control relations involve lexical argument structure (see Chomsky 1980; Nishigauchi 1984, and the references cited there). I will first outline a syntactic treatment of the element PRO in terms of phonologically null operators and then show how the theory of binding and predication can give a unified treatment of control. I will be particularly concerned with the contrast shown in (4):

(4) a. John$_i$ tried [PRO$_i$ to take aspirin]
    b. [PRO taking aspirin] often cures headaches

The PRO in (4a) has an overt syntactic antecedent, *John*; the type of structure exemplified in (4a) is often referred to as an 'obligatory control structure'. The PRO in (4b) has no overt antecedent; (4b) exemplifies a structure of 'arbitrary control'. I will argue that the same principles operate in both obligatory and arbitrary control; the distinction between the two types of control structure follows from the level of syntactic representation at which the principles apply. If they apply at one level, then the PRO is interpreted as obligatorily controlled by a syntactic antecedent. If they apply at a different level, then the PRO is interpreted as arbitrarily controlled. Finally, I will put forward some proposals on the relationship between control and syntactically complex predicates.

Throughout the course of this book, I will adopt the formalisms and methodology of Government–Binding theory (see Chomsky 1981, 1986 and the references cited there). Government–Binding theory guarantees the syntactic realization of lexically required arguments in the form of the Extended Projection Principle and the θ-Criterion, both of which act to ensure that lexically required elements and subjects have a syntactic manifestation.

(5) *The Extended Projection Principle*
Lexical requirements must be satisfied and the subject of S must be represented at every level of syntactic representation.

(6) *The θ-Criterion*
(i) Every argument must be assigned one and only one thematic role.
(ii) Every thematic role must be assigned to one and only one argument.

Introduction

The interaction of the Extended Projection Principle and the θ-Criterion allows us to differentiate among the following examples:

(7) a. John hit Bill.
    b. *Hit Bill
    c. *John hit

Examples (7b) and (7c) are ruled out because at least one thematic role fails to be assigned in each example. In example (7a) both the agent and the patient thematic roles are assigned.

Given the above, it seems very natural that argument structure should play a central role in syntactic representation. The argument structure of a particular lexical item determines the number of arguments that the item may take and the way in which these arguments may be interpreted relative to the lexical item. Hence, one would expect that the syntactic licensing of elements must take into account the argument structure of the lexical items involved in the representation.

Government–Binding theory has a number of properties which distinguish it from other theories of grammar: first, it assumes a number of distinct levels of representation; second, it has a modular character in that it assumes a number of independent sub-theories which interact to derive representations; finally, it places a great emphasis on the role that constraints on representations play in filtering the set of possible sentences in a given natural language. A natural result of the emphasis that Government–Binding theory places on constraints is a de-emphasis of the role of language-particular rules. This point has important consequences for the relationship between linguistic theory and learning theory (see Borer 1984, and Borer and Wexler 1987 for a discussion of the relationship between parameters and language learnability). In this introductory chapter we will discuss some of the ramifications of each of these properties of the theory, albeit at a somewhat superficial level.

To say that the theory assumes distinct levels of representation is roughly equivalent to saying that, for each well-formed string in a language, the grammar assigns an ordered n-tuple of labeled bracketings, minimally consisting of a D-Structure representation, an S-Structure representation, a Phonetic form (PF) representation and a Logical Form (LF) representation:

(8) ⟨D-Structure, S-Structure, PF, LF⟩

The labeled bracketings are related by means of a general rule component (the syntactic movement rule is normally referred to as 'move alpha'; the rule component may possibly contain some language-particular rules involving the deletion of some specified element(s) and 'stylistic' movement; see the discussion of 'local transformation' in Emonds 1976). Each level of representation must obey certain constraints on representation placed on it by the grammar. We can take the above ordered quadruple to be a derivation for a sentence in the language.

The relationship between levels of representation can be represented visually by means of the diagram in (9).

(9)
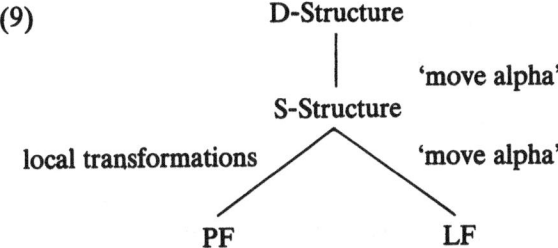

The form of the grammar restricts the possible dependencies between levels of representation. Notice, for example, that PF representations cannot interact with LF representations, both being derived independently from S-Structure representations (see Aoun 1979). Thus, a rule applying in the mapping to PF should be completely irrelevant to the treatment of LF representations. Furthermore, the relationship between D-Structure representations and LF representations is mediated by the presence of S-Structure.

The rule 'move alpha' can be stated as 'move an element in a labeled bracketing anywhere in that labeled bracketing, the output being subject to the constraints placed upon representations by the grammar'. It is standard to restrict the application of 'move alpha' to phrases and words that head phrases (see the discussion of X̄ theory, below). The rule, then, applies quite freely to syntactic representations, although the distance between the point of origin and the destination ('landing site') of the moved element may be strictly bounded. Notice that this generalized view of movement rules may allow for a number of different (but presumably equivalent) derivations for a particular string. In order to demonstrate that a particular string is not in the language, it must be shown that no well-formed derivation exists for that string. Grammaticality of a particular example, on the other hand, requires only that we show that a single well-formed derivation for the string exists.

To say that the theory has a modular character means that the theory of grammar is divided into a number of modules, each of which operates independently of the others. Chomsky (1982) gives the following set of modules:

(10) a. $\bar{X}$ theory
b. θ-theory
c. Case theory
d. Binding theory
e. Bounding theory
f. Control theory
g. Government theory

Each of the above modules may be in operation at one or more of the levels of representation. We will be most concerned with this last fact in this chapter, since Government–Binding theory derives much of its theoretical interest and explanatory power from the relationship between levels of representation and modules of grammar.

Let us begin by hypothesizing the existence of an infinite set of labeled bracketings (trees). For convenience, we will call this set 'T*'. The set of possible D-Structures for a given language will be just those labeled bracketings in T* that obey $\bar{X}$ theory, obey θ-theory (in particular, the θ-Criterion) and obey the Extended Projection Principle. Let us consider, briefly, what it means for a labeled bracketing to obey $\bar{X}$ theory. $\bar{X}$ theory is, roughly, a filter on labeled bracketings; schematically, it can be stated in the following way (substituting primes for the number of bars above the X):

(11) a. X″ → Spec X′
b. X′ → X Comp

The 'X' in (11) is a variable that ranges over grammatical categories like nouns ([+N, −V] in feature notation; see Chomsky 1970; Jackendoff 1977, and Muysken and van Riemsdijk 1985 on feature notation), verbs ([−N, +V]), adjectives ([+N, +V]), and prepositions ([−N, −V]). 'Spec' (Specifiers) and 'Comp' (Complements) are also variables that range over grammatical categories. So, for example, determiners and noun phrases may appear as the Spec of N″ (= NP), as shown in (12) (irrelevant details omitted):

(12)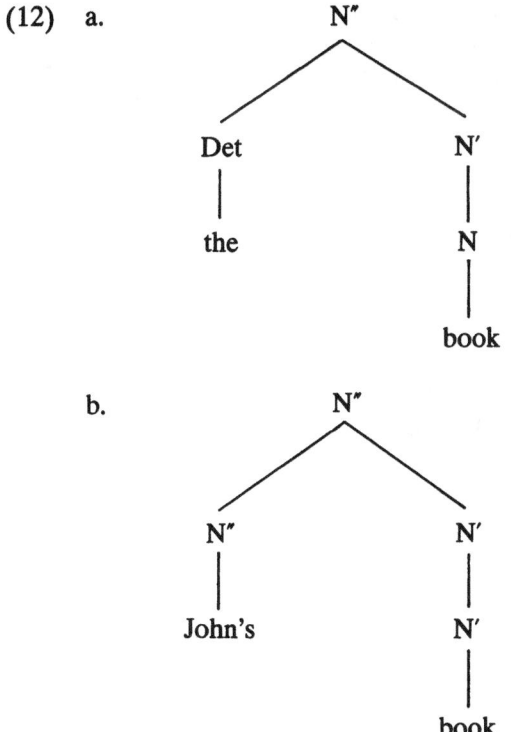

Crucially, since (11) can be taken as a template of well-formed parse-trees, each well-formed phrase in a tree must have a head, so a representation like (13) will be ruled out at D-Structure as ill-formed, since the N″ lacks a head:

(13)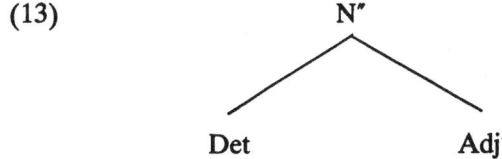

Introduction

For any given language, it is part of the task of the language learner to determine, on the basis of experience, whether X' precedes or follows Spec and whether X precedes or follows Comp and, to a certain degree, exactly which items may instantiate Spec and Comp.

For English, it appears that Spec precedes X' and X precedes Comp. Thus, taking the category 'determiner' to be a possible Spec for N', we can assign the following tree structure to the NP, *the destruction of the city* (irrelevant details again omitted):

(14)

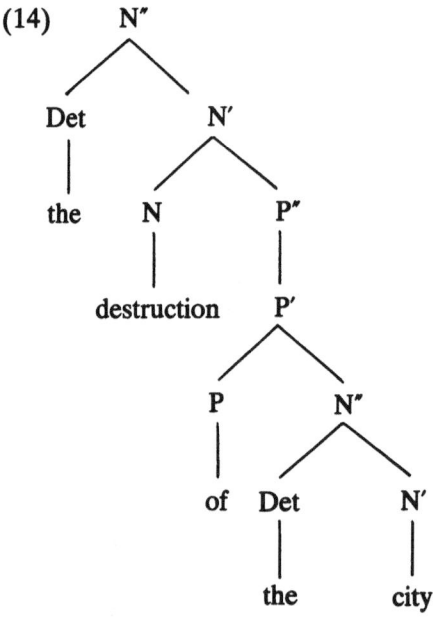

which can be mapped onto the following, equivalent, labeled bracketing:

(14') [$_{N''}$[$_{Det}$ the] [$_{N'}$ [$_N$ destruction] [$_{P''}$ [$_{P'}$ [$_P$ of] [$_{N''}$ [$_{Det}$ the] [$_{N'}$ [$_N$ city]]]]]]]

Notice that the determiner (Spec of N) always precedes N' and the head noun, *destruction*, precedes its complements. Notice also that Spec and Comp may be null. Fortunately, we rarely need to present labeled bracketings in such detail as the example in (14') during the course of a theoretical discussion.

We will take the category S (clause) to be a projection of an abstract element Infl (inflection), the Spec of which must be instantiated by an NP.[3] Given what we have said about English, the expansion of S will be as in (15):

(15) a. Infl" → N" Infl'
b. Infl' → Infl Comp

I will assume that the Comp of Infl is generally instantiated by VP, although it may be instantiated by an adjective phrase, a prepositional phrase, or a noun phrase in copular sentences.

It is important to note that the phrase-structure rules in (15) should not be taken as having an independent existence; while the phrase-structure rules in (15) may correctly characterize the structure of S, their effects may follow from independently required subtheories of the grammar (see Chomsky 1981; Farmer 1984; and Stowell 1981). If this is indeed the case, then the phrase-structure rules are epiphenomenal, having no status in the theory of grammar.

Consider, now, the following set of labeled bracketings (I have eliminated irrelevant details under the assumption that the internal structure of the NPs and VPs obey $\bar{X}$ theory):

(16) a. [$_{Infl"}$ [$_{Infl'}$ [$_{VP}$ ate the food] Infl] [$_{NP}$ the dog]]
b. [$_{Infl"}$ [$_{Infl'}$ Infl [$_{VP}$ ate the food]] [$_{NP}$ the dog]]
c. [$_{Infl"}$ [$_{NP}$ the dog] [$_{Infl'}$ [$_{VP}$ ate the food] Infl]]
d. [$_{Infl"}$ [$_{NP}$ the dog] [$_{Infl'}$ Infl [$_{VP}$ ate the food]]]

The examples in (16) show the possible orderings of the constituents which are internal to Infl" and Infl'. Given the relative ordering of Spec and Comp with respect to the head in English, it follows that only (16d) is a potential candidate for being an element of the set of D-Structures for English. The example in (16a) is ruled out because the Spec of Infl' precedes its head (i.e. Infl') and the Comp of Infl precedes its head (i.e. Infl). Example (16b) is ruled out because the Spec of Infl' precedes its head. Finally, example (16c) is ruled out because the Comp of Infl precedes its head. Notice that since Government–Binding theory is modular and contains distinct levels of representation, we could exempt D-Structure from obeying $\bar{X}$ theory, in which case all of the structures in (16) might be well-formed D-Structures of

Introduction

English. We should note that many of the properties ascribed to X̄ theory in this chapter may well follow from other modules of the grammar.

To say that D-Structures are those elements of T* (the set of possible labeled bracketings) which obey θ-theory and the Extended Projection Principle means, roughly, that every element in the labeled bracketing occurs in a position that receives one and only one thematic role and, furthermore, that Infl″ must have a subject position. Returning to the example, above, of *hit*, we know that *hit* takes an object (an internal argument), to which it assigns the patient thematic role; thus, the following subpart of a labeled bracketing is well-formed at D-Structure:

(17) $[_{V''} [_{V'} [_V \text{hit}] [_{N''} \text{Bill}]]]$

while the labeled bracketing in (18) is not a possible subpart of any D-Structure, given *hit*'s argument structure:

(18) $^*[_{V''} [_{V'} [_V \text{hit}]]]$

Furthermore, the VP *hit Bill* assigns a thematic role (agent) to a subject position (an external argument). From this fact and the Extended Projection Principle, it follows that the labeled bracketing in (19) is a well-formed D-Structure:

(19) $[_{\text{Infl}''} [_{N''} \text{John}] [_{\text{Infl}'} \text{Infl} [_{VP} \text{hit Bill}]]]$

Notice that the Extended Projection Principle requires that Infl″ have a Spec position even if that position does not receive a thematic role. If we take a VP like *seems that John is sick*, then the labeled bracketing in (20a) is a well-formed D-Structure for English while the labeled bracketings in (20b) and (20c) are not (note that *e* represents the empty string):[4]

(20) a. $[_{\text{Infl}''} [_{N''} e] [_{\text{Infl}'} \text{Infl} [_{VP} \text{seems} [_{\bar{S}} \text{that John is sick}]]]]$

b. $[_{\text{Infl}''} [_{\text{Infl}'} \text{Infl} [_{VP} \text{seems} [_{\bar{S}} \text{that John is sick}]]]]$

c. $[_{\text{Infl}''} [_{N''} \text{Bill}] [_{\text{Infl}'} [_{VP} \text{seems} [_{\bar{S}} \text{that John is sick}]]]]$

The structure in (20b) violates the requirement placed on representations by the Extended Projection Principle, since Infl″ lacks a Spec position. The structure in (20c) has a Spec position, but this position is occupied by a referential NP, *Bill*, which does not receive a thematic role; hence, (20c) violates the θ-Criterion since at least one argument lacks a thematic role.

Consider, in the light of what we said above, the status of the representation of passive sentences at D-Structure. According to the analysis of passives found in Chomsky (1981) and Jaeggli (1986), the thematic-role assignment to the subject position (Spec of Infl″) is blocked by the passive morphology. Of the following set of labeled bracketings, only one, the bracketing in (21a), is a possible candidate for the D-Structure representation of *Bill was hit*:

(21)   a. $[_{Infl''} [_{N'} e] [_{Infl'} [_{Infl} \text{was}] [_{VP} \text{hit} [_{N'} \text{Bill}]]]]$
       b. $[_{Infl''} [_{Infl'} [_{Infl} \text{was}] [_{VP} \text{hit} [_{N'} \text{Bill}]]]]$
       c. $[_{Infl''} [_{N'} \text{Bill}] [_{Infl'} [_{Infl} \text{was}] [_{VP} \text{hit} [_{N'} e]]]]$
       d. $[_{Infl''} [_{N'} \text{Bill}] [_{Infl'} [_{Infl} \text{was}] [_{VP} \text{hit}]]]$

In (21a) *Bill* occurs in the object position of *hit* and receives the 'theme' role from *hit*; the Spec of Infl″ is present, but is lexically empty, as required by θ-theory. In (21b) the Spec of Infl″ is not present and, hence, the Extended Projection Principle is violated. In (21c) *Bill* is present in the Spec of Infl″ position, which does not receive a thematic role; θ-theory is violated since a referential NP is not incorporated into the argument structure of the predicate. Furthermore, the empty string, *e*, is in the object position of *hit*; since the empty string is non-referential, it cannot bear the patient role and θ-theory is violated.[5] In the final example, (21d), *Bill* does not receive a thematic role and there is nothing after the verb *hit* to receive the theme role; example (21d) is a double violation of the θ-Criterion since one argument does receive a thematic role and one thematic role cannot be assigned to an argument. Hence, θ-theory will rule out (21d) as a possible D-Structure representation.

We can see from the above examples that $\bar{X}$ theory, θ-theory and the Extended Projection Principle work together to limit the labeled bracketings that can count as well-formed D-Structures for any given language. Thus, as noted above, argument structure (in the guise of θ-theory) plays a profound role in the theory of Universal Grammar since it drastically restricts the set of possible syntactic representations. However, since the theory is modular, we can imagine that any of the above subtheories might not apply to D-Structure representations. As the reader can easily verify, any such change would significantly alter the character of the set of

Introduction

D-Structures, allowing more structural descriptions into the set of well-formed D-Structures.

We will say that S-Structure results from the application of 'move alpha' to elements in the set of D-Structures. This means that for any element of the set of D-Structures, application of 'move alpha' to any subpart of the labeled bracketing results in a potential S-Structure. 'Move alpha' may be applied any number of times to a D-Structure, including 0 times and the result is a potential S-Structure. The set of S-Structures for a given language are just those S-Structures that obey a number of constraints. A well-formed S-Structure must obey the Binding theory, Case theory, and the Extended Projection Principle, in addition to the previously mentioned constraints. We will discuss the Binding theory extensively in later chapters; for the moment, I will restrict my attention to an informal version of Case theory (Rouveret and Vergnaud 1980; Chomsky 1981).

Case theory requires that NPs which are realized phonologically must bear abstract Case. An NP bears abstract Case only if it stands in a particular structural relationship with some other element in a labeled bracketing. The exact nature of this structural relationship is the subject of Government theory, so I will put off further discussion of it here. Instead, I will state the environments of abstract-Case assignment in the following way:

(22) a. An Infl with the feature [+tense] assigns Nominative Case to its subject.
b. A verb assigns Accusative Case to its object.
c. A preposition assigns Oblique Case to its object.
d. The Spec of N" may receive Genitive Case.

Consider the following representations:

(23) a. [$_{Infl"}$ [$_{N"}$ Bill] [$_{Infl'}$ [$_{Infl}$ to] [$_{VP}$ see Mary]]]
b. [$_S$ for [$_{Infl"}$ [$_{N"}$ Bill] [$_{Infl'}$ [$_{Infl}$ to] [$_{VP}$ see Mary]]]]
would be a mistake
c. John believes [$_{Infl"}$ [$_{N"}$ Bill] [$_{Infl'}$ [$_{Infl}$ to] [$_{VP}$ have seen Mary]]]

The representation in (23a) is not a well-formed S-Structure representation because there is no tensed Infl to assign Nominative Case to the subject, *Bill*. Hence, the representation violates the constraint that phonologically realized NPs must bear abstract Case. In (23b) the subject of Infl″ will receive Oblique Case from the preposition, *for*; (23b) will count as a well-formed S-Structure representation since it does not violate Case theory. Finally, the subject of the embedded Infl″ in the S-Structure in (23c) will receive Accusative Case from the verb *believe*, so it too counts as a well-formed S-Structure representation.

Let us return, for the moment, to the issue of passive sentences. The well-formed D-Structure of a passive sentence is shown in (24):

(24)   [$_{Infl''}$ [$_{N'}$ *e*] [$_{Infl'}$ [$_{Infl}$ was] [$_{VP}$ hit [$_{N'}$ Bill]]]]

The subject position is not assigned a thematic role in passive sentences, forcing the presence of an empty non-referential NP in the Spec of Infl. Passive morphology in English prevents the assignment of Accusative Case by any verb bearing this morphology (see the references cited on p. 11). From this fact, it follows that (24) is not a well-formed S-Structure representation, although it is a well-formed D-Structure representation. The only way in which we can map (24) onto a well-formed S-Structure representation is if we place the object NP in a position that will receive case. The grammar provides us with only one mechanism for doing this: we must apply 'move alpha' to the NP *Bill* in such a way that it lands in a Case-marked position. Hence, the following is an image of the D-Structure representation in (24) that will count as a well-formed S-Structure:

(25)   [$_{Infl''}$ [$_{N'}$ Bill]$_i$ [$_{Infl'}$ [$_{Infl}$ was] [$_{VP}$ hit [$_{N'}$ *e*]$_i$]]]

(Notice that I have included indices on the moved NP, which is required by the Binding theory and θ-theory.) In (25) *Bill* will receive Nominative Case from the tensed Infl.[6] Since this position does not receive a thematic role at D-Structure, *Bill* bears one and only one thematic role, as required by the θ-Criterion. Hence, (25) counts as a well-formed S-Structure, since it does not violate any of the constraints placed on the set of S-Structure representations.

The account of passive sketched above nicely illustrates some of the properties of a modular constraint-based theory of grammar. The mechanism which we used to rule out (23a) from the set of S-Structure representations is exactly the same mechanism which we used to rule out (24) from the set of S-Structure representations, and is also the same mechanism which 'forced' *Bill* to move to the subject position in (25). There is no sense in which we have had to state an obligatory passive rule to generate the representation in (25). Suppose that we had no subtheory concerned with Case to which we could make appeal in deriving the above facts. We would, therefore, be forced to state explicitly that an overt (i.e. phonologically realized) NP may occur in the subject position of an infinitival clause just in case it is immediately preceded by the preposition *for* or by a verb like *want*. Furthermore, we would be forced to make a special provision concerning passives: namely, an NP obligatorily moves from the object position of a verb bearing passive morphology to the Spec position of Infl". These special provisions do not make any generalization about the mechanism underlying the derivation of passive sentences and the distribution of overt NPs in the subject position of infinitival clauses.

By exploiting the subtheory of grammar concerned with Case, we were able to state a generalization concerning the distribution of NPs that is not otherwise available to us. Furthermore, in our imaginary theory which lacked this subtheory we were forced to state a special rule which was concerned only with the derivation of passive sentences. Thus, by assuming the existence of Case theory, we may state rules in their most general form – 'move alpha' – and, furthermore, we need not assume that rules apply obligatorily, since we can use the various subtheories of grammar to filter out ill-formed representations. The ability to state rules in their most general form benefits the field of comparative linguistics and makes it possible to pursue the problem of specifying the possible limits of variation within the class of possible grammars for natural languages. For example, rather than concentrating on the form that the rule of passivization takes in various languages – an impossibility, given that there is no such rule in any natural language – emphasis would be placed on studying the principles of grammar (including, of course, the various modules responsible for the derivation of passive constructions in these languages). The term 'passive' takes on a taxonomic nature. In short, a modular grammar provides an extremely reasonable research program for a theory that seeks to give an account of what it means to be a possible human language: I will assume that a modular grammar is the null hypothesis.

Returning, now, to the various levels of representation, LF representations are derived from S-Structure representations under the rule of Quantifier Raising. Quantifier Raising is a form of 'move alpha' which applies to NPs having a quantifier or wh-elements that have been left in place in the syntax and adjoins them to some (maximal) projection (see May 1985 for some further discussion). Intuitively, LF is a level which represents the scope relationship between various logical operators, where the scope of an operator is defined as the set of nodes which it c-commands.[7] Thus an S-Structure like the one in (26a) will be mapped onto an LF like that in (26b):

(26) a. [$_{Infl''}$ [$_{N''}$ John] [$_{Infl'}$ Infl [$_{VP}$ saw [$_{N''}$ every student]]]]
b. [$_{Infl''}$ [$_{N''}$ every student]$_i$ [$_{Infl''}$ [$_{N''}$ John] [$_{Infl'}$ Infl [$_{VP}$ saw [$_{N''}$ e]$_i$]]]]

Naturally, we must place a number of constraints on the set of possible LF representations. Among these constraints is the Empty Category Principle (ECP) (Chomsky 1981, 1986; Lasnik and Saito 1984; Pesetsky 1982a), which concerns itself with the distribution of the empty string, *e*. While I will return to a more precise formulation of the ECP in subsequent chapters, we can informally state some relevant consequences of this principle here:

(27) a. An empty string in the object position of a verb obeys the ECP.
b. An empty string in the subject position of a tensed S obeys the ECP only if the adjacent Comp exhaustively dominates an element that is co-indexed with the subject position.

The statement of the ECP in (27) is technically incorrect, but it will serve our purposes for the moment.

As a consequence of (27a), the following (partial) labeled bracketings are well-formed at LF:

(28) a. [$_\bar{S}$ [$_{Comp}$ who$_i$] [$_{Infl'}$ did John [$_{VP}$ see t_i]]]
b. [$_\bar{S}$ [$_{Comp}$ who$_i$] [$_{Infl'}$ Bill think [$_\bar{S}$ that [$_{Infl'}$ John [$_{VP}$ saw t_i]]]]]

The empty string in each of the examples in (28) is in object position, and so obeys the ECP. Consider now, empty strings left in the subject position of a tensed S:

(29) a. [$_\bar{S}$ [$_{Comp}$ who$_i$] [$_{Infl''}$ t_i saw Mary]]
 b. [$_\bar{S}$ [$_{Comp}$ who$_i$] [$_{Infl''}$ did Bill think [$_\bar{S}$ [$_{Comp}$ t'_i]$_i$ [$_{Infl''}$ t_i saw Mary]]]]
 c. [$_\bar{S}$ [$_{Comp}$ who$_i$] [$_{Infl''}$ did Bill think [$_\bar{S}$ [$_{Comp}$ that] [$_{Infl''}$ t_i saw Mary]]]]

The empty category in the matrix-subject position in example (29a) is adjacent to a Comp which exhaustively dominates an element bearing the index, i. According to (27b), this empty element obeys the ECP and, all other things being equal, the labeled bracketing in (29a) should be a well-formed LF representation. In example (29b), the empty category in the subject position of the embedded clause is again adjacent to a Comp which exhaustively dominates the trace left by its antecedent (i.e. t'). Again, the labeled bracketing in (29b) should count as a well-formed LF representation. Finally, consider the labeled bracketing in (29c). Here, the trace left in the subject position of the embedded clause is not adjacent to a Comp which exhaustively dominates an element with the proper index since the Comp also dominates the complementizer, *that*. The labeled bracketing in (29c) is, therefore, not a possible LF representation since it violates the ECP. This is the correct result, given the ungrammaticality of

(30) *Who did Bill think that saw John.

Earlier, I accepted the stipulation that the ECP applies only to LF representations as opposed to S-Structure or D-Structure representations. Notice, however, that example (30) could be accounted for if the ECP applied to S-Structure representations; the offending trace is already present at S-Structure, although not at D-Structure. Examples like (30) can show that the ECP cannot apply (exclusively) to D-Structure representations, but they cannot be used to distinguish between S-Structure and LF representations.

To settle the question, consider the case of a wh-element that has not been moved in the mapping from D-Structure to S-Structure:

(31) *[$_\bar{S}$ who$_i$ [$_S$ t_i knows [$_\bar{S}$ if [$_S$ who left]]]]

Following standard assumptions (Chomsky 1981; May 1985; and references cited there), suppose that the wh-element left *in situ* is assigned a scope by moving it to a Comp; then (31) maps onto either of the following LF representations:

(32) a. *[$_\bar{S}$ who$_j$ who$_i$ [$_S$ t_i knows [$_\bar{S}$ if [$_S$ t_j left]]]]
 b. *[$_\bar{S}$ who$_i$ [$_S$ t_i knows [$_\bar{S}$ who$_j$ if [$_S$ t_j left]]]]

In (32a) the *who* in embedded subject-position has been assigned scope over the entire clause, and in (32b) it has been assigned scope over only the embedded clause.

Both representations in (32) violate the ECP as informally defined in (27). That is, the empty category in the subject position of the embedded clause is never adjacent to a Comp which exhaustively dominates an element co-indexed with it. Crucially, this property holds only of the LF representations in (32) and not the S-Structure representation in (31). Application of the ECP to the S-Structure in (31) would not rule out the representation, since there is, as yet, no offending trace. By stipulating that the ECP applies to LF representations, the account of the unacceptability of (31) collapses with the account of (30); both types of examples violate the ECP.

The above examples indicate how the assumption that there are several distinct levels of representation involved in the derivation of sentences contributes to the nature of the generalizations we can make about the human language-faculty. Because we assumed an abstract level of representation, LF, at which wh-elements are assigned a scope, we could collapse the explanation of the ungrammaticality of structures like that in (30) with the explanation of the effects found in wh-*in-situ* constructions like (31). It is not at all obvious how a theory of grammar which assumes only a single level of representation could provide so general an account of these phenomena (for further discussion, see Clark 1985a).

The informal discussion of Government–Binding theory in this chapter was intended to highlight the deductive nature of constraint-based theories which involve multiple levels of grammatical representation. Assumptions about how the various constraints on representations are arrayed across the possible levels of representation are directly reflected in the kinds of languages our theory can account for. As we have seen, the assumption that the ECP, for example, applies to LF representations has significant effects upon the potential analyses of various constructions.

The far-reaching effects of the modularity hypothesis and the hypothesis that various levels of grammatical representation exist has led to a deductive character in grammatical analysis which has great appeal, given the problem of language acquisition. The problem of the possible variation in natural languages is, naturally, of central concern. This concern has led to the assumption that Universal Grammar is made up of a set of parameterized principles; in other words, the principles of Universal Grammar contain variables which must be instantiated in deriving the grammar of a particular language (for some discussion, see the papers in Hornstein and Lightfoot 1981). That is, we may assume that a child acquiring a particular language does not induce rules that account for particular grammatical constructions but, rather, deduces the properties of these grammatical constructions from principles of grammar. In particular, the hypotheses that the child can consider are severely limited, since there are a finite number of parameters, each of which has only a finite number of possible values. The hypothesis space that the child can search in discovering the adult grammar is finite. This approach contrasts sharply with inductive approaches, where the child must combine predicates in a hypothesis language to generate rules. Such inductive procedures admit an infinite number of different hypotheses about the adult grammar. While learnability might be guaranteed for the latter approach, depending on the particulars of the learning procedure, the parameterized approach seems quite attractive.

Learnability, of course, is not immediately guaranteed even in a parameterized approach to natural language. We can only investigate learnability in the light of substantive proposals regarding the various principles and parameters of Universal Grammar. This is only to say that we must have some characterization of the target of developmental change before we can profitably theorize about the process of development itself. Bearing in mind the ultimate goal of providing an account of linguistic development, I will now turn to some syntactic investigations of the adult state.

Chapter two

On a certain class of nominals

In this chapter, I will examine the properties of a small class of constructions in English:

(1) a. My room needs a thorough picking up.
b. His criticisms don't merit worrying about.

Despite the limited distribution of this construction, an examination of its properties has some rather interesting ramifications for the theory of empty categories and the way in which this theory interacts with thematic (θ-) theory. The theory of the distribution of empty categories is sufficiently constrained to give us a relatively small hypothesis space in which to operate. The theory of the distribution of empty categories, the theory of movement, and the theory of binding act in such a way as to leave very few choices about the possible representations associated with a particular sentence.

Government–Binding theory makes strong predictions about the representation of examples like those in (1). The mechanisms governing the relationship between argument structure and the syntax force us to hypothesize an empty category inside the nominal; I will argue that the empty category must be a PRO which is controlled by the subject of the matrix predicate. This result follows from general constraints on syntactic representations. The Binding theory and θ-theory force the empty category to be a pure non-overt anaphor. A pure non-overt anaphor must be bound from a position which does not receive a thematic role (a so-called θ-position) which receives a grammatical function (e.g. subject or object). This requirement is neatly illustrated in the contrast between (2a) and (2b).

(2) a. It$_i$ seems [t_i to rain alot here]
    b. *It$_i$ tries [t_i to rain alot here]

Notice that both (2a) and (2b) involve the presence of a special expletive which is restricted to appear in the subject position of weather verbs. We may assume that this expletive, 'weather *it*', may not occur in a position which receives a thematic role like AGENT or EXPERIENCER, and so on. The contrast between (2a) and (2b) follows if there is a trace in the subject position of the embedded clause. In (2a) the matrix verb, *seem*, does not assign a thematic role to its subject. Hence, the binding relation between weather *it* and its trace is well-formed, since *it* occupies a θ-position at S-Structure, In (2b), on the other hand, weather *it* occupies a θ-position at S-Structure, since *try* assigns a thematic role to its subject. Hence, the binding relationship between *it* and the trace is impossible. Since the thematic role assigned to weather *it* by *try* is incompatible with *it*'s status as a non-argument, there is no well-formed representation associated with the string in (2b).

The requirement that pure anaphors must be A-bound from a θ-position will force us to assume that these nominals contain a subject as well as an object; both the subject position and the object position will contain empty categories. Given the presence of a subject inside the NP, it will follow from independently motivated constraints on binding and argument structure that the pure anaphor in object position inside these nominals must be related to the empty category in the subject position of NP either by movement or a co-indexation process that mimics the effect of movement. The representation of (1a) is (1a'):

(1) a'. [$_S$ [$_{N'}$ My room]$_i$ needs [$_{N'}$ PRO$_i$ a thorough picking t_i up]]]

Since the NP-internal movement is similar to passivization, without any overt marking (such as passive morphology or a postposed *by* phrase), I will refer to this construction as a retroactive nominal.[1]

Of particular interest is that retroactive nominals which involve preposition stranding (as in (1b)) are restricted to gerundive nominals (I will refer to these as *-ing* nominals). A nominal without the proper morphology cannot license preposition stranding. Example (1b) should be compared with:

(3) a. *This legislation could use some arguments about.
    b. *His criticisms don't merit any worry about.
    c. *This guy doesn't deserve any conversation with.

I will argue that this asymmetry between -*ing* nominals and other kinds of nominals follows as a systematic fact about the interaction between the -*ing* affix and the syntax. This conclusion lends support to the view that morphological processes are not restricted to the lexicon, but may pervade the syntax (S. Anderson 1982; Baker 1988).

2.1 Some preliminaries

One of the fundamental organizing principles underlying syntactic representations is the Projection Principle (see Chomsky 1981). The content of the principle can be formulated quite simply as in (4) (see also the discussion in Chapter 1):

(4) Lexical requirement must be satisfied at every level of syntactic representation.

Despite its simplicity, the Projection Principle has far-reaching effects. For example, it provides the foundation of the theory of empty categories; the Projection Principle can be taken as an axiom with which to explore the properties of a variety of syntactic constructions.

By way of illustration, consider the problem of how to represent wh-questions in English:

(5) Who did John see?
(6) a. [$_{\bar{S}}$ who$_i$ [$_S$ did John see]]
    b. [$_{\bar{S}}$ who$_i$ [$_S$ did John see [$_{NP}$ e]$_i$]]

The simplified labeled bracketings in (6) represent two *a priori* possible S-Structures for the sentence in (5). In (6a) the verb *see* is not followed by an NP; despite the fact that *see* is a transitive verb, (6a) represents it as an intransitive. By contrast, (6b) preserves the information that *see* is a transitive verb, since it is followed by an NP; this NP, however, lacks phonological content. The bracketing in (6a) violates the Projection Principle because a lexical feature of *see*, namely its transitive subcategorization feature, is not satisfied

21

by an NP in the syntactic representation. Thus, the Projection Principle unambiguously forces us to select (6b) as the only possible representation of (5) since only (6b) represents the subcategorization feature of *see* as satisfied.

The assumption that the representation in (6b) contains an empty category makes it possible to account for a number of (apparently) unrelated facts:

(7) a. *Who$_i$ did he$_i$ see e_i
  b. *Who$_i$ did you think that e_i left

In (7a), the pronoun *he* binds[2] the empty category left by wh-movement; if the trace left by wh-movement must be locally bound by an element in a non-argument position, like Comp, then an account for the ungrammaticality of (7a) follows immediately. If such an empty category must be locally identified and the complementizer *that* is not sufficient to identify the empty category in the subject position of (7b), then an account of the ungrammaticality of (7b) also follows (see the discussion of the ECP in Chapter 1). The assumption that syntactic representations contain empty categories can carry a great deal of explanatory weight, providing a unifying property for a variety of apparently different phenomena.

Given that the empty category left by movement must be bound by the moved element, we have a strong constraint on possible movement operations. No rule may move a constituent to a landing site which does not c-command the original position of the constituent. Thus, the structure in (8b) cannot be derived from (8a) because the moved element, *Mary*, does not c-command its trace; (8c) is well-formed since no movement occurs:

(8) a. It bothers Mary [$_{\bar{S}}$ that [$_S$ [*e*] would apear that John is lying]]
  b. *It bothers t_i [$_{\bar{S}}$ that [$_S$ Mary$_i$ would appear that John is lying]]
  c. It bothers Mary that it would appear that John is lying.

The representations in (6b) and (7) contain an empty category. *Prima facie*, allowing the empty string to occur in syntactic representations appears to invite disaster, since it arms us with a very powerful notational device; the evidential support provided for empty categories in (7) may be because the notation is too powerful. For example, given that an empty category may satisfy lexical requirements, what prevents us from predicting the following sentences to be grammatical?

(9) a. *[$_{NP}$ e] saw him
 b. *He saw [$_{NP}$ e]

How it is possible for a child acquiring English to learn, on the basis of positive evidence, that examples like (9) are ungrammatical?[3] This phenomenon is especially curious when it is observed that examples parallel to (9) are perfectly grammatical in Chinese (Huang 1984):

(10) a. [$_{NP}$ e] kanjian ta le.
 '(He) saw him'
 b. ta kanjian [$_{NP}$ e] le.
 'He saw (him)'

Since, by hypothesis, Chinese and English both obey the core principles of Universal Grammar and since the child cannot reasonably be assumed to have much in the way of direct evidence about things that he or she cannot hear in the speech signal, it would appear that the assumption that syntactic representations contain empty categories is rather difficult to maintain. Notice, however, that the contrast between (9) and (10) does not present a problem for the hypothesis that syntactic representations may contain empty categories. The difference between Chinese and English must be accounted for by any grammatical framework, no matter whether that framework hypothesizes the existence of phonologically null elements. Stating the problem in terms of the potential parametric variation in the licensing mechanisms for empty categories provides a coherent statement of the problem. Thus, the contrast between English and Chinese does not in any sense falsify the hypothesis that empty categories are syntactically relevant. In fact, the examples in (7–8) indicate that empty categories are of great explanatory value. If anything, the contrast between Chinese and English may provide very strong evidence in support of the existence of empty categories.

I will assume, then, that the theory of empty categories and the Projection Principle are correct in their essential details. Furthermore, I will assume, following a number of researchers (eg. Bouchard 1983 and Chomsky 1982), that the Binding theory partitions the class of NPs into four categories. An NP, like *himself*, is an anaphor which must be bound from an argument position contained within some local domain. A pronoun, like *she* or *her*, may not be bound from an argument position contained within some local domain. A name, like *John*, has inherent reference and so may not be bound from an argument position. These differential properties of NPs are illustrated in (11-13):

(11) a. John$_i$ saw himself$_i$ in the mirror
     b. *John$_i$ said [$_S$ Mary saw himself$_i$ in the mirror]
(12) a. *John$_i$ saw him$_i$ in the mirror
     b. John$_i$ said [$_S$ Mary saw him$_i$ in the mirror]
(13) a. *He$_i$ saw John$_i$ in the mirror
     b. *He$_i$ said [$_S$ Mary saw John$_i$ in the mirror]

The differential behavior of NPs with respect to binding suggests the following set of features (see Chomsky 1982):

(14) [+anaphor, −pronominal]
     [−anaphor, +pronominal]
     [+anaphor, +pronominal]
     [−anaphor, −pronominal]

The feature system in (14) predicts the presence of four types of NPs, but examples (11-13) illustrate only three types of overt NPs. Consider the properties of an NP marked [+anaphor, +pronominal]. By virtue of being marked [+anaphor], such an NP must be bound from an argument position in its local domain. By virtue of being marked [+pronominal], it may not be bound in its local domain. Since no element can be both bound and free in any local domain, and since the definition of local domain crucially relies on government, it follows that such an elements may not be governed. A minimal requirement of phonetically overt NPs is that they bear abstract Case. Since assignment of abstract Case is generally contingent on government, we may assume that an ungoverned element will not receive Case (but see footnote 4). Hence, phonetically overt NPs may not bear the features [+anaphor, +pronominal].[4] The requirement that an NP bear Case does not hold for non-overt NPs; the Case filter, which rules out phonetically overt NPs that lack Case, does not apply to empty categories. The theory allows an empty category to bear the features [+anaphor, +pronominal] just so long as that empty category appears in an ungoverned position. Like an anaphor, this empty category could be obligatorily bound in some configurations and, like a pronominal, this empty category has the option of being free in other configurations. Such an empty category is found in the subject position of infinitives and gerunds, as illustrated in (15–16):[5]

(15) a. John$_i$ wanted [$_S$ PRO$_i$ to shave himself$_i$]
     b. *John$_i$ wanted [$_S$ PRO to shave oneself]
(16) a. It is obvious how [$_S$ PRO to boil water]
     b. [$_S$ PRO boiling water] is trivial

Again following Chomsky (1982), I will assume for the sake of discussion that the null hypothesis is that the properties of empty categories are not inherent, but can be determined given the properties of the structures in which the empty categories occur.[6] Specifically, there is only one type of empty category, unmarked for the features [± pronominal, ± anaphor]. The values for these features can be filled in, given information about whether the empty category is bound or free and, if the empty category is bound, information about the nature of the position occupied by the binder. An empty category bears the features [−pronominal, −anaphor] if it appears in an A-position and if its antecedent appears in an Ā-position. Otherwise, an empty category in an A-position is marked [+anaphor]. If the empty category is either free or bound by an element with an independent θ-role, then it is also marked [+pronominal]; otherwise, it bears the feature [−pronominal].[7]

(17) [+anaphor, −pronominal] = NP-trace
     [−anaphor, +pronominal] = pro[8]
     [+anaphor, +pronominal] = PRO
     [−anaphor, −pronominal] = variable

2.2 Some properties of retroactive nominals

We are now in a position to apply the above diagnostics to the following set of examples:

(18) a. John could use [$_{N'}$ a good looking at]
b. These ideas merit [$_{N'}$ some working on]
c. This problem bears [$_{N'}$ a good deal of thinking about]
d. My room needs [$_{N'}$ a thorough picking up]

Each of the above sentences contains a derived nominal in object position and each of the derived nominals contains a stranded preposition, except for (18d) which is a 'noun + particle' construction. The Projection Principle derives the fact that the (transitive) prepositions must have empty nominal complements. The sentences in (18) could be more accurately represented as in (19):

(19) a. John could use [$_{N'}$ a good looking at [*e*]]
b. These ideas merit [$_{N'}$ some working on [*e*]]
c. This problem bears [$_{N'}$ a good deal of thinking about [*e*]]
d. My room needs [$_{N'}$ a thorough picking up [*e*]]

Intuitively, the empty categories in the above sentences are A-bound from the subject position of the clause that contains them. That is, example (19a) indicates that someone should talk to John (and John would benefit thereby), not that John would benefit by talking to someone. For example, we might paraphrase the retroactive nominal in (19b) with a passive, as in (20):

(20) These ideas$_i$ merit [PRO$_i$ being worked on t_i]

As will become apparent, I take this paraphrase relation to be a salient fact about the structure of retroactive nominals.

For the moment, I will assume that there is a single empty category in these nominals; the discussion will show that this assumption is untenable. By applying the functional determination of empty categories to the empty category inside the complement position of retroactive nominals, the marking [+anaphor] is derived for each of the above cases. Assume, for the moment, that the empty category in these structures is a pure anaphor. Minimally, the empty category in this structure must comply with condition A of the Binding theory. In order to test this hypothesis, we need only find a structure in which the subject position of the sentence if outside of the governing category of the putative anaphor. If there is a SUBJECT accessible[9] to the anaphor within the NP, then it should be the case that the anaphor will not be bound by the matrix subject:

(21) a. *John$_i$ could use [$_{N''}$ [$_{N''}$ a competent psychiatrist's] looking at [e]$_i$]
b. *These ideas$_i$ merit [$_{N''}$ [$_{N''}$ Bill's] working on [e]$_i$]
c. *This problem$_i$ bears [$_{N''}$ [$_{N''}$ everybody's] thinking about [e]$_i$]
d. *My room$_i$ needs [$_{N''}$ [$_{N''}$ the janitor's] picking up [e]$_i$]

As the examples in (21) show, it is impossible for the matrix subject to act as the antecedent for the empty category inside the nominal if the nominal contains a SUBJECT accessible to the anaphor.

The ungrammaticality of the examples in (21) cannot be attributed to a semantic restriction on the form of the NP in these constructions, since, although the examples are ungrammatical with an agent in the subject position of the NP, an agent may appear in a postposed *by* phrase, as illustrated in (22):

(22) a. John$_i$ could use [$_{N''}$ a good looking at [e]$_i$ by a competent psychiatrist]
b. These ideas$_i$ merit [$_{N''}$ some working on [e]$_i$ by Bill]
c. This problem bears [$_{N''}$ some thinking about [e]$_i$ by everybody in the class]
d. My room$_i$ needs [$_{N''}$ a thorough picking up [e]$_i$ by the janitor]

The constraint that the NP in these constructions not contain a SUBJECT follows from a purely syntactic constraint on binding relations and not from a constraint on the semantic representation of this construction. *Prima facie*, it would appear that these constructions involve an empty category contained in the complement of the object NP. This NP itself seems to be transparent to binding from without, after the fashion of the overt reflexive in a picture NP:

(23)　John$_i$ saw [$_{NP}$ a picture of himself$_i$]

Having seen some evidence that the empty category in this construction is an anaphor, it is now necessary to determine the value for the feature [± pronominal]. Recall that the empty category is assigned [+pronominal] if it is free or A-bound by an element with an independent θ-role. The empty category in this construction is interpreted as bound by the subject of S, so we can rule out the case of the empty category being free. The question, therefore, reduces to whether or not the subject of S receives a θ-role independently of the empty category inside the nominal; in other words, we must determine whether the subject of S and the empty category form an A-chain.[10]

A-chains are a means of transmitting features from one structural position in a phrase marker to another. They consist, in essence, of an ordered n-tuple of the structural positions occupied by a particular constituent, the first element being the present structural position of the constituent and the tail of the chain being the D-Structure position of the constituent. The tail of the chain will, in the general case, be a θ-position which, by virtue of being a member of the chain, will share its θ-role with the other members. Independent assignment of thematic roles to distinct members of the chain will then result in a violation of the θ-Criterion since the argument at the head of the chain will bear more than one thematic role. Since an argument may occur in the subject position of clauses like those in (22), it must bear a θ-role.

The question, then, is whether the subject of the predicate governing retroactive nominals receives a thematic role directly, or by virtue of heading an A-chain with the empty category inside the object NP as its tail. If the subject position of S is not assigned a θ-role independently of the empty category, then it should be the case that a pleonastic element can occupy this position:

(24)　a.　*It could use[$_{N'}$ a good talking to John]
　　　b.　*It merits [$_{N'}$ some working on these ideas]

      c. *[$_{N'}$ some thinking about this problem]
      d. *[$_{N'}$ a thorough picking up of my room]

Since pleonastic *it* is barred from the subject position in this construction, the conclusion that this position is assigned a θ-role that is independent from the one assigned to the empty category in the NP is warranted, all else being equal. The only conclusion is that the empty category is [+pronominal]. The functional determination of empty categories, therefore, predicts that the empty category is [+anaphor, +pronominal], or PRO.

Identifying the empty category in the complement position of retroactive nominals with PRO has two important consequences. First, the position that it occupies can not be governed. Any element marked [+anaphor, +pronominal] must obey both conditions A and B of the binding, which is a contradiction, since condition A requires that an element be bound in a local syntactic domain while condition B requires an element to be free in that same domain. Since no element can be both bound and free in the same syntactic domain, either the element is not subject to both conditions or the relevant syntactic domain must be undefined for this element. Thus, in order to avoid this apparent contradiction, any element with the feature specification [+anaphor, +pronominal] must occur in an ungoverned position, since government is the criterial feature for defining the syntactic domain in which binding may or may not occur. Second, it is clear that the ability to have a PRO inside the NP is selected for by the head of the matrix predicate. As (25) shows, the retroactive nominal construction does not distribute freely:

(25)   a. *[$_{N'}$ a good looking at PRO] is often necessary
       b. *[$_{N'}$ some thinking about PRO] could be useful
       c. *[$_{N'}$ a lot of working on PRO] would be good

Whatever analysis is given to these nominals must take into account the selectional properties of their governor.[11]

We have seen that the assumption that the empty category in this construction is marked [+anaphor, +pronominal] has led to an apparent difficulty; this empty category stands in a government configuration with some head. Other choices for the empty category fare no better than PRO, as I will show.

Suppose, first, that the empty category in question is a pure anaphor, [+anaphor, −pronominal] (i.e. NP-trace). NP-trace has the property of being locally A-bound by an element that does not receive an independent θ-role; since its binder does not receive a θ-role *in situ*, it must form a chain with the trace and 'share' its thematic role. The ability to share a θ-role with another element is taken as a distinguishing feature of the empty category in raising constructions:

(26) a. It seems that [$_S$ John has left]
     b. John$_i$ seems [$_S$ e_i to have left]

The pleonastic element *it* occupies the matrix-subject position in (26a), indicating that this position does not receive a θ-role from the VP, *seems that John has left*. Hence, the matrix-subject position in raising constructions must be a θ-position. In (26b), on the other hand, a referential NP, *John*, occupies the matrix-subject position. Since, the subject position of a raising predicate is a θ-position, a referential subject must receive its θ-role by virtue of being linked to a θ-position. In order for the representation in (26b) to be well-formed, the matrix subject must form a chain with the empty category in the subject position of the embedded clause; it must be the case that NP-trace always forms a chain with the argument that binds it.

Given the obligatory chain-formation between the NP-trace and its binder, let us reconsider the examples in (24), repeated here as (27):

(27) a. *It could use [$_{N'}$ a good looking to John]
     b. *It merits [$_{N'}$ some working on these ideas]
     c. *It bears [$_{N'}$ some thinking about this problem]
     d. *It needs [$_{N'}$ a thorough picking up of my room]

These examples led us to the conclusion that the subject position in these sentences is a θ-position. But if the subject position receives a θ-role independently of the empty category, then the two positions cannot form a chain, since such a chain would bear two θ-roles, which is impossible. Since NP-trace inevitably enters into a chain relation with some other position, it must be the case that the empty category is not an NP-trace.

I have examined so far two types of empty categories, PRO and NP-trace, and have discovered that the empty category in this construction cannot be identified with either of them. Since PRO and NP-trace form a natural class with respect to the feature system in (17) – the class of nominal elements selected by the feature [+anaphor] – let us assume that this empty category is inherently marked [−anaphor]. The class of non-anaphoric empty categories is exhaustively made up by pro ([−anaphor, +pronominal]) and variable ([−anaphor, −pronominal]).

Suppose that the empty category is a pure pronominal. Thus, the structure in question would have the following representation:

(28) a. John$_i$ could use [$_{N'}$ a good talking to *pro*$_i$]
     b. These ideas$_i$ merit [$_{N'}$ some working on *pro*$_i$]
     c. This problem$_i$ bears [$_{N'}$ a good deal of thinking about *pro*$_i$]
     d. My room$_i$ needs [$_{N'}$ a thorough picking up *pro*$_i$]

As a pure pronominal, it must obey condition B of the Binding theory, and so it cannot be bound in its governing category. Recall, however, that, as the examples in (18) show, placing a subject inside the postverbal NP in this construction invokes a violation of the Specified Subject Condition (SSC). These SSC violations indicate that the empty category must be bound in its governing category. If the empty category must find its antecedent within its local domain, then we cannot identify it with a pure pronominal since we would expect the empty category to be disjoint from the matrix subject in all of the examples in (28) where the pro is, *prima facie*, bound in its local domain. Let us adopt the reasonable assumption that PRO must be locally identified.[12] The empty category in these examples has no local identifier. We must assume that this empty category is not pro.

2.3 Operator binding in retroactive nominals

We have seen that the empty category in examples like (28) cannot be a pronominal. Furthermore, for a variety of reasons, the category cannot be identified with an anaphor, all things being equal. Our remaining option is that the empty category is marked

[−anaphor, −pronominal] (i.e. that it is a variable). It is possible that retroactive nominals might best be accounted for by analogy with 'tough' movement and purposive clauses (see Chomsky 1977, 1980; Bach 1980):

(29) a. John$_i$ is easy [$_{\bar{S}}$ Op$_i$ [$_S$ PRO to dislike t_i]]
     b. This lecture$_i$ is hard [$_{\bar{S}}$ Op$_i$ [$_S$ PRO to follow t_i]]
(30) a. John bought the book$_i$ [$_{\bar{S}}$ Op$_i$ [$_S$ to read t_i to the children]]
     b. A shovel$_i$ is [$_{\bar{S}}$ Op$_i$ [$_S$ PRO to dig with t_i]]

In each of the above examples, an empty category is bound by a phonetically non-overt operator. As argued in Chomsky (1982), these constructions allow parasitic gaps:

(31) This course$_i$ is hard to follow t_i without having done the reading for e_i

If it is true that parasitic gaps may be licensed only by elements in an Ā-position, then examples like (29) are well-formed only if there is a non-overt operator to bind the trace in the object position of the embedded clause.

One possible objection to the hypothesis that this empty category is a variable would be that the empty category is A-bound by the subject of the sentence, which might be taken as a violation of condition C of the Binding theory. Given the existence of examples like (29–31), the condition that variables must be A-free must be weakened to the condition that variables must be A-free in the domain of the operator that binds them (Chomsky 1981).

More explicitly, let us consider the contrast between the examples in (32) and the examples in (33):

(32) a. John$_j$ wonders [$_{\bar{S}}$ who$_i$ [$_S$ Bill met t_i]]
     b. *John$_i$ wonders [$_{\bar{S}}$ who$_i$ [$_S$ Bill met t_i]]
(33) a. John$_i$ is easy [$_{\bar{S}}$ Op$_j$ [$_S$ to please t_i]]
     b. *John$_j$ is easy [$_{\bar{S}}$ Op$_i$ [$_S$ to please t_i]]

The examples in (32) show that an overt operator must be taken as disjoint from other elements in the syntactic representation. The examples in (33) show that a non-overt operator is obligatorily co-indexed with some other element. We might suppose that overt operators have an inherent range (see Chapter 4 for an extensive discussion); in the case of *who*, for example, the operator ranges over the set of humans. The content of condition C of the Binding theory (that referential expressions must be free) is, simply put, that an element with inherent reference (or, in this case, range) cannot be referentially dependent on any other element in the representation of a sentence. Since overt operators have an inherent range, they cannot be referential dependents of a distinct term in the syntactic representation, as is the case in example (32b). The contrast in (32), then, follows from condition C with respect to the binding relation between *John* and the overt operator *who*. The relation between *John* and the variable in the embedded clause, under this analysis, is not crucial in determining the well-formedness of the representation.

I will assume that non-overt operators, being empty categories, lack any inherent range or reference. All things being equal, any variable which is referentially dependent on a non-overt operator will have the status of an expletive element rather than that of a true argument, since the non-overt operator is non-referential. But expletives cannot bear a thematic role according to the θ-Criterion. Thus, unless the non-overt operator is assigned a range, the θ-Criterion will ultimately be violated. A non-argument (the unrestricted variable bound by the non-overt operator) will be assigned a θ-role. As a result, a non-overt operator will generally have the character of an anaphor in that it must be locally assigned some referential content by an independent element. The contrast in (33) follows directly from this account since the non-overt operator in (33b) is free and, as a result, the variable which it binds has the status of an expletive. Let us assume that the construction at hand has the following representation:

(34) This problem$_i$ bears [$_{N'}$ Op$_i$ [$_{N'}$ some thinking about t_i]]

where *Op* is a phonetically null operator that binds a variable.

If this approach to the problem is correct, then the construction bears a superficial resemblance to 'tough'-movement constructions, as illustrated in (35):

(35) a. John$_i$ is easy [$_{\bar{S}}$ Op$_i$ [$_S$ PRO to please t_i]]
 b. John$_i$ could use [$_{N'}$ Op$_i$ [$_{N'}$ a good talking to t_i]]

Like 'tough' movement, the retroactive nominal construction is lexically governed; that is, the adjectives and verbs that may govern a retroactive nominal fall into a semantic class, which we will term 'predicates of requirement'. These predicates include *merit, deserve, could use, need,* among others; the speaker indicates that the subject would benefit from the activity denoted by the retroactive nominal. It is plausible that predicates in this lexical class could trigger some of the special syntactic properties of retroactive nominals by means of subcategorization requirements. The restriction of retroactive nominals to the object position of predicates of requirement is illustrated by the examples in (36) which do not govern the retroactive nominal construction:

(36) a. *John likes some looking at.
 b. *My room looks a little cleaning up.
 c. *This problem appears some thinking about.

Given the apparent similarity between the two constructions, it is plausible that retroactive nominals are a sort of NP version of 'tough' movement. Suppose, for the sake of argument, that NPs may have an internal Ā-position.

The assumption that at least some NPs may have an internal non-argument position, while far from self-evidently true, receives some (very weak) support from a class of NPs which appear to involve movement to some NP-internal first position:[13]

(37) a. [$_{N'}$ how long a book] did Mary write
 b. Mary had never seen [$_{N'}$ so long a book]
(38) a. *[$_{N'}$ a how long book] did Mary write
 b. *Mary had never seen [$_{N'}$ a so long book]
 c. *[$_{N'}$ long a book] did Mary write
 d. *[$_{N'}$ a how long book] did Mary write
 e. *Mary had never seen [$_{N'}$ long a book]

The above examples imply that a suitably operator-modified adjective may be moved to a position preceding the article in some NPs. While it is not our purpose to provide a complete account of the above examples, their existence is suggestive of an NP-internal Ā-position to which certain elements may be moved.[14] I will explore some of the consequences of this assumption in the analysis of retroactive nominals.

Since this construction is lexically governed, it is reasonable to assume that verbs may subcategorize for this non-argument position in much the same way that verbs may subcategorize for a sentential Comp position, as illustrated in (39):

(39) a. I wonder [$_\bar{S}$ [$_{Comp[+WH]}$ who]$_i$ [$_S$ John saw t_i]]
 b. *I wonder [$_\bar{S}$ [$_{Comp[-WH]}$ that] [$_S$ John saw Mary]]

The verb *wonder* subcategorizes for a [+WH] Comp; since the Comp in (39a) contains a wh-word, it satisfies *wonder*'s lexical requirements. The Comp in (39b) does not contain a wh-element and is, therefore, marked [−WH], which cannot satisfy the lexical requirements of the governing verb; so (39b) is ungrammatical.

On this approach, a retroactive nominal would have a D-Structure like (40) (for convenience, I will note this putative NP-internal Ā-position as *NP-Comp*):

(40) John needs [$_{N'}$ [$_{Np\text{-}Comp}$ e] a good talking to Op]

Wh-movement would apply to the non-overt operator to yield:

(41) John needs [$_{N'}$ [$_{NP\text{-}Comp}$ Op_i] a good talking to t_i]

The non-overt operator would then be co-indexed with the matrix subject by predication.

By hypothesis, an NP-internal Ā-position is a marked structure that must be subcategorized for by a lexical item that governs the NP. In the unmarked case, the structure in (42) is impossible:

(42) *[$_{N'}$ ... [$_{NP\text{-}Comp}$ e] ...]

Consider the sentences in (43):

(43) a. *Some thinking about is often necessary.
 b. *A little working on would be useful.
 c. *Looking into appears necessary.

35

The examples in (43) indicate that retroactive nominals exhibit a subject/object asymmetry. The subject NPs in the examples of (43) are governed by Infl rather than a lexical element. The NP-internal non-argument position (NP-Comp) is, as a result, unavailable to these NPs. The D-Structure of (43a), for example, is as in (44):

(44)   [$_{N'}$ some thinking about Op] is often necessary

In order for the non-overt operator to move to a non-argument position, it must move to the matrix Comp. But this movement violates subjacency (or the Subject Condition; see the treatment of left branches in Kayne 1984 and the alternative analysis in Chomsky 1986; see also Chapter 3) and is, therefore, impossible. The non-overt operator must remain *in situ*. Given our assumption, outlined above, that non-overt operators must have their range identified at some level of representation, the non-overt operator in (44) will ultimately violate the θ-Criterion, since it cannot have its range specified; in essence, the above example will be filtered because the non-overt operator lacks a range.

2.4 Some inadequacies of operator binding in retroactive nominals

I have assumed that the non-overt operator is generated in an A-position within the nominal and is moved to an NP-internal non-argument position in the syntax. The operator is then associated with the matrix subject by, say, predication. This analysis makes a number of rather clear predications. First, if the non-overt operator undergoes wh-movement in the syntax, then it should be possible to move the operator successive-cyclically to yield apparently unbounded movement. Second, if the non-overt operator does, in fact, occupy an Ā-position, then it should license parasitic gaps. The ability to move successive-cyclically, licensing of parasitic gaps, and weak cross-over have, over the years, come to serve as diagnostics for operator-variable relations.[15]

Turning to the question of successive-cyclic movement of the non-overt operator, it should be adequate to test nominalizations of verbs that take sentential complements. If the empty category is associated with a non-overt operator, it should be possible to move the operator successive-cyclically, leaving a gap in the embedded clause. The Ā-movement analysis of retroactive nominals predicts that examples like those in (45) are grammatical:

(45) a. *John's paper could use some convincing (of) people that they should read [e].
b. *My office needs some conning (of) the janitor to clean [e] up.
c. *This book deserves some persuading (of) the students to discuss [e] over beer.

The object nominal in example (45a) has the S-Structure:

(46) $[_{N'} [_{NP\text{-}Comp} Op_i]$ some convincing (of) people $[_{\bar{S}} t_i$ that $[_S$ they should read $t'_i]]]$

The non-overt operator first moves into the Comp of the embedded $\bar{S}$. Next, the non-overt operator moves into the NP-internal non-argument position, NP-Comp. Since both steps obey the subjacency condition, derivations such as the one sketched for (46) should be ruled in, since no first principles are violated; in order to prevent sentences such as those in (45), we will be forced to place an otherwise unwarranted constraint on successive-cyclic movement. This result is undesirable in a theory which seeks to give an explanatory account of language acquisition, since the child would be forced to acquire such a restriction on the basis of virtually non-existent evidence, given the limited distribution of retroactive nominals.

The next prediction made by this analysis is that the non-overt operator should license parasitic gaps. According to the analysis of Chomsky (1982), parasitic gaps occur in the environment:

(47) $\ldots Op_i \ldots t_i \ldots e_i \ldots$

Where t_i is the trace left by movement of the operator, Op_i, and e_i is a base-generated gap in a governed position. Recasting Chomsky's analysis into our own terms, if the base-generated gap is left unbound, it will lack any range or reference and, according to the assumptions discussed above, will be taken as an expletive. This will normally result in a violation of the θ-Criterion. If the base-generated gap is taken as locally bound by the wh-trace, then the former gap must be interpreted as PRO, which will result in a contradiction, since the base-generated gap is governed, by hypothesis. Note that the gap cannot be taken as an NP-trace, since either it will form a doubly θ-marked A-chain with the wh-trace, which is impossible, or it will fail to be A-bound in its local syntactic domain, in violation of condition A of the Binding theory. In order for the base-generated gap to be well-formed, it must be bound by the operator and, therefore, treated as a wh-trace, subject to condition C of the Binding theory. Hence, the 'true' gap cannot c-command the base-generated gap since the latter would then be bound in the domain of its operator.[16]

The environment in (47) can be instantiated in structures where the parasitic gap, e_i, is contained in an adjunct. This sort of structure is available in NPs if the NP is headed by a derived nominal:[17]

(48) a. The burning of the tenement after the insurance money had been collected was in very poor taste.
b. The invasion of the country without informing the media was considered a major scandal.
c. Any torturing of the prisoners without getting the president's permission is frowned upon.

Some retroactive nominals are capable of taking adjuncts, although judgements tend to differ from example to example:

(49) a. ??This problem deserves [$_{NP}$ some thinking about t_i [$_{Adjunct}$ without losing any sleep over it]]
b. John could use [$_{NP}$ a good looking at t_i [$_{Adjunct}$ without embarrassing him]]
c. This novel merits [$_{NP}$ rewriting t_i [$_{Adjunct}$ without changing it too much]]

If the structure of retroactive nominals actually involves a non-overt operator, then we would expect the examples in (49) to have counterparts containing parasitic gaps:

(50) ?This problem deserves [$_{NP}$ some thinking about t_i [$_{Adjunct}$ without losing any sleep over e_i]]
(51) a. *?John could use [$_{NP}$ a good talking to t_i [$_{Adjunct}$ without scolding e_i]]

b. John could use [$_{NP}$ a good talking to t_i [$_{Adjunct}$ without PRO$_i$ being scolded]]

(52) a. *?This novel merits [$_{NP}$ some rewriting t_i [$_{Adjunct}$ without changing e_i too much]]
b. This novel merits [$_{NP}$ some rewriting t_i [$_{Adjunct}$ without PRO$_i$ being changed too much]]

The above examples have a rather inconclusive status, rejected by some speakers who otherwise accept parasitic-gap constructions, and accepted by others. The discomfort some have with the above examples may be due to an independent difficulty with true adjuncts on NPs. At any rate, it would be difficult to make any argument on the proper analysis of retroactive nominals hinge on the above examples, given their questionable nature. To the degree that these parasitic-gap constructions are unacceptable, the hypothesis that retroactive nominals involve Ā-binding is not supported.

Beyond the unacceptability of successive-cyclic movement of the putative non-overt operator in retroactive nominal constructions, there is a further inadequacy with the approach that assumes that the empty category in these constructions is a variable; namely, the fact that these NPs may not contain an overt subject. The relevant facts are repeated in (53):

(53) a. *John$_i$ could use [$_{N'}$ [$_{NP-Comp}$ Op$_i$] [$_{N'}$ a competent psychiatrist's] looking at [e]$_i$]
b. *These ideas$_i$ merit [$_{N'}$ [$_{NP-Comp}$ Op$_i$] [$_{N'}$ Bill's] working on [e]$_i$]
c. *This problem$_i$ bears [$_{N'}$ [$_{NP-Comp}$ Op$_i$] [$_{N'}$ everybody's] thinking about [e]$_i$]
d. *My room$_i$ needs [$_{N'}$ [$_{NP-Comp}$ Op$_i$] [$_{N'}$ the janitor's] picking [e]$_i$ up]

If the retroactive nominal construction actually involves an NP-internal Comp position, then it would appear that this Comp is in complementary distribution with the subject of the NP. This apparent generalization does not follow from any principles, however. As in the case of successive-cyclic movement (above), a special stipulation must be made in order for the analysis to be descriptively adequate.

For the sake of completeness, we note that the facts at hand bear a striking resemblance to the construction:

(54) $[_{NP}$ this painting$]_i$ is $[_{AdjP}$ lovely [to look at t_i]]

as discussed in, for example, Chomsky (1977). Like retroactive nominalization, this construction is bounded:

(55) *$[$this painting$]_i$ is $[_{AdjP}$ lovely [to persuade people [to look at t_i]]]

and the embedded clause may not have an overt subject:

(56) *$[$this painting$]_i$ is $[_{AdjP}$ lovely $[_{\bar{S}}$ for $[_S$ John to look at t_i]]]

Notice that this construction, unlike the nominals in question, allows for parasitic gaps:

(57) This kind of painting is $[_{AdjP}$ lovely [to look at t_i $[_{Adjunct}$ without thinking about e_i]]]

The relative acceptability of (57) may be due to the fact that a predicate adjective can more comfortably take a true adjunct than an object NP can. I will put aside the analysis of the above constructions, leaving their proper treatment as an open research question.

We have seen that there are a number of explanatory shortcomings with the operator-binding approach to retroactive nominals outlined above: it cannot account for the locality restrictions on the site of the gap (no long-distance extraction of the operator); it yields no account of the SSC effects (as in (53)); it provides no obvious account for the relative unacceptability of parasitic gaps in these nominals. These inadequacies imply that a different approach to this construction needs to be taken. We have seen that there is some evidence, in the form of apparent violations of the SSC, that the empty category in the retroactive nominal construction is an anaphor. This conclusion was abandoned largely on the basis of the θ-Criterion. If the empty category is an anaphor, then it must form a chain with the matrix-subject position, since an NP-trace may not head a chain; this chain, however, would be doubly θ-marked. If the empty category forms a chain with some element other than matrix-subject position, this problem may not arise. Since PRO, unlike NP-trace, may head a chain, let us assume that the empty category is linked with a PRO inside the NP. If this is indeed the case, the anaphoric properties of the empty category are not inconsistent with thematic theory. Let us turn our attention to some properties of θ-marking and government within NPs.

2.5 'Move NP' inside NP

Since at least Lees (1960), certain parallels in structure between clauses and NPs have been observed. This parallelism between S and NP was one of the factors that motivated the introduction of $\bar{X}$ theory (Chomsky 1970). Subsequent research (for example, Jackendoff (1977) and Stowell (1983)) has supported the assumption that close structural parallelisms exists across all grammatical categories.

One important set of data that has supported the assumption that S and NP have a similar syntactic structure is that verbs which allow passive often have related derived nominals which also have a passive-like form:

(58) a. John narrated the play.
b. The play was narrated by John.
(59) a. John's narration of the play ...
b. the play's narration by John ...
(60) a. John criticized the book.
b. The book was criticized by John.
(61) a. John's criticism of the book ...
b. the book's criticism by John ...

We can account for sentential passives (examples (58b) and (60b)) if we assume that the passive morpheme absorbs the Case assigned by the verb to the object and the θ-role assigned to the subject.[18] Since the subject position is a θ-position, a general rule, 'move alpha', may move the object NP to that position; this movement is, in fact, forced by the Case filter, given that the object position does not receive Case from the verb.

Analogous reasoning may be applied to the 'passive nominals' in examples (59) and (61). Since a noun may not assign Case, we need not consider the Case filter; we must assume, however, that an NP has a subject position and that this subject position is a θ̄-position. This assumption may not be entirely innocent. Williams (1982, 1985) has argued that the subject position of NP always receives a θ-role (see also M. Anderson 1985). In essence, we might assume that the Spec of NP receives a θ-role on the basis of the composition of Ñ, in a manner analogous to the compositional assignment of a θ-role to the subject of S.[19] As a default case, one might argue that an NP in the Spec of NP receives a POSSESSOR θ-role. Witness the contrast between (62a) and (62b):

(62) a. the enemy's destruction of the city . . .
 b. the enemy's tanks . . .

In (62a) *the enemy* receives the AGENT θ-role via composition of the Ñ, *destruction of the city*. In (62b) *the enemy* receives the POSSESSOR θ-role as a default assignment.

At first glance, it would appear that such a system would eliminate NP-movement entirely for want of an appropriate θ-position. Thus, nominals like (59b) and (61b) must be derived from some mechanism other than NP-movement, perhaps the θ-role normally assigned to the nominal's object would be assigned directly to the Spec of NP in these cases. But notice that even if we allow assignment of a POSSESSOR θ-role in the default case, we need not eliminate movement inside an NP entirely. We may assume that the default case is blocked only if the element in the Spec of NP has some independent means of receiving a θ-role. The NP in Spec could either head an A-chain with some other element, as in (63), or receive a θ-role due to lexical specifications of the head:

(63) a. the play's$_i$ narration t_i by John . . .
 b. the book's$_i$ criticism t_i by John . . .

Under the assumption that NP-trace may never head an A-chain, the subject NPs in (63) must enter into the chain relation with the trace and, hence, the subject NPs have a independent means of receiving a θ-role. The default case will be blocked in these constructions, since assignment of POSSESSOR to the Spec of NP would result in a doubly θ-marked A-chain.

The default assignment of a θ-role to the Spec of NP does have the consequence of excluding expletives from this position:

(64) a. the appearance that John was lying ...
b. *its appearance that John was lying ...
c. It appeared that John was lying.

Example (64b) is blocked since the expletive, *it*, would receive the default POSSESSOR θ-role, resulting in a clear violation of the θ-Criterion (M. Andersen 1985). Given this set of assumptions, the object of a derived nominal may optionally move into the subject position of the NP.

2.6 Generalizing across categories

In light of the above facts, I will assume that there are structural similarities across categories and that subtheories of grammar are, in the main, indifferent to grammatical category; 'move alpha', for example, will behave uniformly across categories. This claim should not be taken to mean that grammatical categories are irrelevant to all the various subtheories of the grammar. Case theory, for instance, makes crucial reference to the features $[\pm N, \pm V]$. The hypothesis is that reference to grammatical category should be eliminated where possible. This hypothesis, then, calls into question whether categories like NP or S need to be mentioned in the definition of subjacency and whether the definition of proper government should stipulate the category of proper governors. Our hope is that these (apparently) unrelated stipulations will be derived from some more general principle of core grammar.

Given this type of approach, particular gaps in the paradigms of particular grammatical categories must be derived from independent subtheories of grammar. In order to make the discussion more concrete, let us return to 'passive nominals'. As pointed out above, verbs that allow the passive construction often have derived nominals that have a 'passive' form. This parallelism breaks down systematically, as shown in the following examples:[20]

(65) a. Many people rely on Mary.
b. Mary is relied on by many people.

(66) a. the reliance on Mary by many people (is unwise)
b. *Mary's reliance on by many people (is unwise)
(67) a. Ignorant people laughed at Galileo's ideas.
b. Galileo's ideas were laughed at by ignorant people.
(68) a. the laughter at Galileo's ideas by ignorant people (annoyed the more literate elements of the population)
b. *Galileo's ideas' laughter at by ignorant people (annoyed the more literate elements of the population)
(69) a. Washington slept in this bed.
b. This bed was slept in by Washington.
(70) a. any sleeping in this bed by Washington (will be considered an act of treachery)
b. *this bed's sleeping in by Washington (will be considered an act of treachery)
(71) a. Congress looked into this problem.
b. This problem was looked into by Congress.
(72) a. any looking into this problem by Congress (will be considered a threat to the national security)
b. *this problem's looking into by Congress (will be considered a threat to the national security)

The verbs in examples (65), (67), (69), and (71) all allow pseudo-passive forms, where the object of a preposition may be preposed to subject position. The related derived nominals in (66), (68), (70), and (72), however, do not allow the prepositional object to be preposed. Thus, there is a systematic gap in the pseudo-passive paradigm. If the hypothesis that subsystems of core grammar are largely category-neutral is correct, then we must search for some more abstract principle(s) from which we can derive the fact that derived nominals do not permit pseudo-passive forms.

The pseudo-passive construction is hardly the only construction that, while present with verb forms, is systematically missing from NPs. Kayne (1984) provides a sizable collection of such constructions. To take a few examples, Dative shift, small clauses, tough movement, Exceptional Case Marking, and raising are all absent from derived nominals, although the related verbal or adjectival root may permit such constructions. These facts are exemplified in the following examples:

(73) a. John gave the book to Mary.
b. John gave Mary the book.

(74) a. John's gift of the book to Mary ...
b. *John's gift of Mary of the book ...

(75) a. John considers Bill a threat.

(76) *John's consideration of Bill (of) a threat ...²¹

(77) John is easy to irritate.

(78) *John's easiness to irritate ...

(79) John believes Bill to be incompetent.

(80) *John's belief of Bill to be incompetent ...

(81) John is likely to arrive late.

(82) *John's likelihood to arrive late ...

Kayne (1984) argues that the systematic lack of these constructions by NPs may be accounted for if we assume that nouns may not govern across maximal projections.²² Suppose, for example, that tough movement involves the presence, in the embedded Comp, of a non-overt operator which must be properly governed. Example (78) would have an S-Structure like (83):

(83) $[_{N'} [_{N'} \text{John's}] [_{\bar{N}} \text{easiness} [_{\bar{S}} Op_i [_S \text{PRO to irritate } t_i]]]]$

Since the noun *easiness* may not govern across a maximal projection and the operator is dominated by an S̄, the non-overt operator is not properly governed and, as a result, (83) violates the Empty Category Principle. We can derive the fact that nouns lack some form of Dative shift, Exceptional Case Marking, and small clauses from the fact that nouns do not assign case and that *of* insertion requires government:

(84) *of* insertion
$[_{[+N']} [+N] NP] \rightarrow [_{[+N]} [+N] \textit{of } NP]$
Where $[\underline{+N}]$ governs NP.

Dative shift, small clauses, and Exceptional Case Marking all involve an NP contained in some maximal projection which has no means, internal to that projection, of receiving Case. If the NP is to

45

survive the Case filter, then, it must be assigned Case by an element that is not contained within the projection containing the Caseless NP. In the example at hand, the head noun of an NP would have to govern into some maximal projection in order to trigger *of* insertion. But this is impossible given that nouns cannot govern across a maximal projection.

But why should it be the case that nouns are incapable of governing across a maximal projection? This stipulation about nouns is at odds with the category-neutral hypothesis; optimally, we would prefer to derive the apparent fact that nouns cannot govern across a maximal projection from some component of core grammar rather than, say, by stipulation in the definition of government.

I will assume, as is standard, the following feature system for grammatical categories (see Chomsky 1970; and Jackendoff 1977, who argues that the system is too weak in the sense that it lacks the ability to make sufficiently fine-grained distinctions):

(85) N V
      + + = adjective
      + − = noun
      − + = verb
      − − = preposition

Notice that the inability to govern across a maximal projection does not correlate with the category [+N], since adjectives may so govern:

(86) a. John$_i$ is [$_{adj}$ likely] [$_S$ t_i to win]
     b. John$_i$ is [$_{adj}$ easy] [$_{\bar{S}}$ Op$_i$ [$_S$ PRO to please t_i]]

If adjectives could not govern across a maximal projection, then the trace in (86a) and the non-overt operator in (86b) would not be properly governed (or governed at all); the examples in (86) would then be ruled out by the Empty Category Principle. Since the examples are grammatical, we must assume that adjectives may govern across a maximal projection.

I will hypothesize that the fact that nouns may not govern across a maximal projection follows from some other subcomponent of the theory of grammar and is not simply stipulated by the definition of government. We have already ruled out Case theory as a potential candidate for determining the class of categories that may not govern across a maximal projection; neither nouns nor adjectives may assign Case, but adjectives, unlike nouns, may govern across maximal projections.[23]

If nouns were alone in their inability to govern across a maximal projection, then this inability might well be considered an aberration that is best stipulated, perhaps in the definition of government. There is, however, some evidence that prepositions are also unable to govern across a maximal projection. Let us assume that, following Stowell (1981), that in order for a non-root $\bar{S}$ to have an empty Comp, the Comp must be properly governed. It will then follow that an $\bar{S}$ that is governed by a verb may have an empty Comp:

(87) a. John believes (that) Bill is a spy.
 b. John knows (that) Mary is in Europe.

An $\bar{S}$ in subject position will not be properly governed, since Infl is not a proper governor in English; this treatment predicts that $\bar{S}$s in subject position may never have an empty Comp, which is, in fact, correct:

(88) a. *(That) Bill is a spy is obvious to John.
 b. *(That) Mary is in Europe is quite likely.

In many dialects of English, the preposition *in* may be used to introduce adjunct clauses:

(89) a. In that John treated her so rudely, Mary left early.
 b. You will have to take the exam later, in that you are three hours late.

If prepositions could govern across maximal projections, then we would expect that the Comp of such a clause could be empty:

(90) a. *In [e] John treated her so rudely, Mary left early.
 b. *You will have to take the exam later, in [e] you are three hours late.

Since the sentential object of *in* obligatorily has an overt complementizer, the conclusion is that the preposition does not properly govern the Comp position. This fact is consistent with the hypothesis that prepositions may not govern across maximal projections.[24]

Even in semantically plausible environments, prepositions may not take small clauses, as illustrated in (91):

(91) a. *Mary will always think of John an innocent fool.
b. Mary will always think of John as an innocent fool.

(92) a. *We argued about John guilty.
b. We argued about John's being guilty.

The absence of small-clause complements of prepositions is consistent with the hypothesis that prepositions may not govern across maximal projections.[25]

It would appear, then, that nouns and prepositions form a class with respect to their inability to govern across maximal projections. This class is selected by the feature [−V]. Now we can inquire as to what property, aside from sharing the feature [−V], the class of nouns and the class of prepositions have in common. Following, for example, Jaeggli (1986), let us assume that prepositions may assign a θ-role in composition with some other θ-assignor. Consider, for instance, an indirect object in a Dative construction:

(93) John gave the book to Mary.

By this reasoning, *Mary* receives a θ-role from the verb *give*; the preposition *to* merely acts as an intermediary in the process of θ-role transmission. Similarly, as Jaeggli argues, the head of the *by* phrase in passive constructions acts simply to transmit the external θ-role of the passivized verb; he shows that the θ-role assigned to the object of *by* varies according to the external θ-role on the verb:

(94) a. Bill was killed by *Mary*.
b. The letter was received by *Bill*.
c. The package was sent by *John*.
d. That professor is feared by *all student's*.

The italicized NPs in (94a–d) receive the AGENT, GOAL, SOURCE, and EXPERIENCER θ-roles, respectively; these θ-roles correspond to the external θ-roles assigned by the verbs *kill, receive, send,* and *fear.*

If we examine prepositional phrases more generally, it becomes apparent that if the head assigns a θ-role, it must be a fairly 'schematic' one, open to a variety of interpretations. Consider a preposition like *in*:

(95) a. John was found in the woods.
b. Bill was wounded in the rioting.
c. In some respects, John is anachronistic.
d. Bill made faces at the judge in an act of contempt.

While *in the woods* in (95a) is clearly a locative, the prepositional phrases in (95b–d) are locative in only the most abstract sense. Given the variety of interpretations that a single preposition, in this case *in*, may receive, it is unclear what inherent thematic property, if any, unifies the various roles it may play. It would appear, rather, that their semantic function is determined compositionally on the basis of the lexical properties of predicates which they modify. An exact study of the composition of these lexical properties would take us well away from the topic at hand, so I will leave an exact specification of this compositional process to others. Given the correctness of this line of reasoning, prepositions are not obliged to assign a θ-role directly to their object, but may have the θ-role that they assign determined on the basis of features of the local syntactic context; the preposition then transmits the θ-role to its complement. For example, a preposition subcategorized for by a verb may have the θ-role which it assigns determined by the verb. Similarly, an adjunct PP may have its θ-role determined on the basis of the term which it modifies.[26] In these cases, the θ-role assigned to the prepositional complement is not a lexical property of the preposition; it is computed from the lexical properties of the terms which govern the prepositional phrase.

More concretely, if we are correct in this hypothesis, then prepositional objects pose an apparent problem for the θ-Criterion since we have not yet explicated a method for assigning any θ-role to prepositional objects. As noted above, there are two possible cases: in the first case, the preposition is the head of a subcategorized complement; in the second case, the preposition is the head of a phrase in an adjunct position. We will assume in the first case, when the prepositional phrase is subcategorized by some element, X, that the preposition acts as an intermediary in the transmission of a θ-role from the head, X, to the object of the preposition. Thus, the prepositional object will receive a θ-role indirectly from the head that subcategorizes for a PP. In the second case, when the PP is in an adjunct position modifying some projection, XP, the composition of the lexical semantic properties of the XP will determine the θ-role assigned to the prepositional object. Alternatively, one might assume that a θ-role is base-generated on the prepositional object; this θ-role is then checked at LF, when interpretive rules apply. This latter treatment is somewhat analogous to the treatment of abstract Case assignment in Jaeggli (1982).

In both of the above cases, the prepositional object obeys the θ-Criterion, by virtue of bearing a θ-role. In neither case, however, is the preposition determining the θ-role on its object. Higginbotham (1983) argues that similar considerations apply to θ-roles carried by nominal complements. He observes that arguments of nouns, unlike those of verbs, are always optional. If we assume, as seems reasonable, that the θ-Criterion has the effect of making θ-role assignment obligatory, the optionality of nominal complements would appear to be problematic; either the apparently absent complements to N are realized as PRO (leading to the problems discussed above) or nouns freely violate the θ-Criterion. Let us assume, however, that the thematic properties of nouns are similar to the thematic properties of prepositions: nominal complements are not assigned a θ-role directly by the head N; a θ-role is generated on the nominal complement directly in the base (i.e. at D-Structure; see p. 10), subject to a checking process at LF. This checking process compares the θ-role on the nominal complement with the argument structure of the head noun and determines whether the complement is compatible with the argument structure of the head.[27] Alternatively, one might suppose that assignment of a thematic role by a noun or a preposition does not occur in the syntax, but, rather, takes place at LF. Any syntactic principles sensitive to thematic-role assignment (such as government across a maximal projection for purposes of Case assignment) would be blocked in the syntax, although LF principles would not distinguish between nouns and prepositions, on the one hand, and verbs and adjectives, on the other hand. At this point, we have no empirical basis for distinguishing between the two hypotheses, so, for the moment, we will treat them as notational variants.

2.7 Transparency and categories

The property that unites prepositions and nouns beyond the categorial feature [−V] is that neither category is capable of independent θ-role assignment. Their common property with respect to government may now follow not merely from their common categorial feature, but from properties of θ-role assignment. Our hypothesis, then, is that θ-theory, like Case theory, is sensitive to the grammatical category of elements; only items marked [+V] are capable of independent θ-role assignment:

(96) | N | V | Case assigner | θ-assigner |
|---|---|---|---|
| + | + | − | + |
| + | − | − | − |
| − | + | + | + |
| − | − | + | − |

In other words, Case theory specifies that only elements marked [−N] are capable of assigning Case directly and Thematic theory specifies that only elements marked [+V] are capable of assigning a θ-role directly.

It remains to define 'government across a maximal projection' in such a way as to exclude elements that do not directly θ-mark their complements:

(97) A maximal projection, XP, is transparent to government by an element Z if and only if Z assigns a θ-role to XP.

It follows from (97) that nouns and prepositions will not be able to govern into a complement phrase because they cannot directly θ-mark their complements (although a preposition may transmit a θ-role to its complement, given properties of the local syntactic environment). Formally, we can indicate thematic-role assignment in representations by means of superscripts. Following Kayne (class lectures, 1983), we will stipulate the following convention on θ-role assignment:

(98) If Z assigns a θ-role to XP, then co-superscript Z and XP.

The condition on transparency to government described in (97) may then be restated in terms of superscripts:

(99) XP^i is transparent to Z^j if and only if $i = j$.

Although nouns and prepositions may perfectly well govern a sister node, it follows from (98) and (99) that nouns will be incapable of governing into a maximal projection since such a maximal projection will always be transparent to them by virtue of θ-theory.

We have seen that nouns, unlike verbs and adjectives, do not directly θ-mark their complements. This incapacity has the consequence that maximal projections are always absolute barriers to government by nouns. We will now turn to the investigation of how the ability to govern across maximal projections relates to the structure of retroactive nominals.

2.8 PRO in NP

We have identified a cluster of properties associated with retroactive nominals. First, these nominals apparently contain an empty category with anaphoric properties, in that the empty category is sensitive to Specified Subject Condition effects. Second, retroactive nominals must be governed by a lexical element that falls into a restricted semantic class ('requirement verbals'). Finally, as the examples below illustrate, the head noun of a retroactive nominal has a restriction on its morphological form:

(100) a. *The baby could use some attention to.
       b. *These diplomats deserve some conversation with.
       c. *These ideas don't need any arguments about.
       d. *The status quo doesn't merit any revolution against.

None of the derived nominals in (100) involve -*ing* affixation whereas the examples of retroactive nominals given above all involve -*ing* nominalization. Non-*ing*-derived nominals are not absolutely barred from the object position of 'requirement' verbals as the examples in (101) show:

(101) a. The baby could use some attention.
       b. This scoundrel deserves a prompt conviction by the jury.
       c. John fully merits ostracization by the government.
       d. This body needs a rapid cremation by the mortuary.

The contrast between (100) and (101) indicates that only *-ing*-derived nominals allow preposition stranding within the NP. Compare the examples in (100) with those in (102):

(102)   a. The baby could use some attending to.
        b. These diplomats deserve some conversing with.
        c. These ideas don't need any arguing about.
        d. The status quo doesn't merit any revolting against.

The examples in (101) do share at least one property with other retroactive nominals; they show a Specified Subject Condition effect:

(103)   a. *This scoundrel deserves the jury's prompt conviction.
        b. *John fully merits the government's ostracization.
        c. *This body needs the mortuary's rapid cremation.

We can account for the contrast between (101) and (103) if we assume that there is an empty category in the object position of these nominals and that this empty category must be locally bound. Notice that the examples in (103) have syntactically well-formed representation which leads to a semantically anomalous interpretation; namely, the Genitive NP can be taken as the antecedent of the empty category in the object position of the nominal. Example (103b) would then have the representation in (104):

(104)   *$[_{N'}$ John$]_i$ merits $[_{N'}$ $[_{N'}$ the government's$]_i$ ostracization $[e]_i]$

The interpretation of (104) would be that John merits the government's being ostracized. This interpretation indicates that retroactive nominals have a passive interpretation.

I should note that this apparent SSC effect is not always present. For example, the nominal in the following seems less sensitive to SSC effects than the example in (104):

(105)   (?) The baby could use $[_{NP}$ the nurse's attention]

Roeper, furthermore, has brought examples of the following form to my attention (see Roeper 1986):

(106) a. John could use [$_{NP}$ the CIA's training]
b. The child needs [$_{NP}$ the court's supervision]
c. This bill merits [$_{NP}$ the Senate's approval]

Notice that the subject of the clause in each of the examples of (105) and (106) is interpreted as the logical object of the head noun of the object NP. These examples quite clearly cannot be accounted for under the assumption that the bracketed nominals in (105) and (106) contain a phonological unrealized anaphor since the anaphor would be free in the minimal domain which contains both it and a SUBJECT:

(107) John$_i$ could use [$_{NP}$ [$_{NP}$ the CIA's]$_j$ training t_i]

Similarly, we will lose an account of example (104) unless we assume that the object nominal contains a phonological null anaphor. Furthermore, examples such as those in (105) and (106) never involve a stranded preposition as we noted in connection with the examples in (100). It seems reasonable, then, to conclude that the examples under examination here and the examples in (105) and (106) do not form a unified class, given their separate behaviors with respect to the SSC. Roeper (1986) analyzes the examples in (105) and (106) as involving a type of binding that is not contingent on the overt syntactic realization of an argument position. We will see that this analysis works less well for examples which involve preposition stranding, as in (100). For the moment, however, we will leave aside discussion of these examples, focusing instead on clear examples of retroactive nominals.

Suppose, for the sake of discussion, that the structure of a retroactive nominal is as in (108):

(108) [$_{N'}$ [$_{N'}$ e]$_i$ a good talking to t_i]

The trace in the object position of the preposition is locally A-bound by a null element in the Specifier of the NP. Since the empty category is locally A-bound, it will be marked as a pure anaphor. Hence, the SSC effects and the locality condition, noted above, follow directly from the Binding theory and subjacency. Consider an example like:

(109) *[John's paper]$_i$ could use [$_{N'}$ [$_{N'}$ e]$_i$ some convincing (of) people [$_{\bar{S}}$ that [$_S$ they should read t_i]]]

The trace, t_i, must be bound in the minimal maximal category containing a governor and a SUBJECT. A trace in the governing domain of the head noun will be bound in its governing category. A trace in a relative clause or a clausal complement to the head noun will have as its governing category the embedded clause, not the superordinate NP; hence, such a trace will not be bound in its governing category and will violate condition A of the Binding theory. Furthermore, the movement of the null element to the Spec of the superordinate NP will violate subjacency.

Suppose that the derivation of (109) actually involved movement to Comp as in (110):

(110) *[John's paper]$_i$ could use [$_{N'}$ [$_{N'}$ e]$_i$ some convincing (of) people [$_{\bar{S}}$ t_i that [$_S$ they should read t_i']]]

That is, the element [e] moves from the object position of the embedded clause to Comp and then into the Spec of the object NP. Such a derivation is out, presumably for the same reason that (111) is ruled out:

(111) *[this paper]$_i$ seems [$_{\bar{S}}$ t_i that [$_S$ some people should read t_i']]

Example (111) is ruled out by the θ-Criterion under the assumption that an A-chain cannot be formed between the subject of the matrix clause and the trace in the object position of the embedded clause. This follows either if we adopt the proposal of Aoun (1985) that an S̄ breaks A-chains, or if we assume that an A-chain containing an Ā-position is impossible. In either event, the same principles which rule out (111) will also rule out (110).

The assumption that retroactive nominals involve NP-internal A-binding has other consequences. Recall that an overt subject seems impossible in these examples:

(112) *John$_i$ could use [$_{N'}$ [$_{N'}$ a competent psychiatrist's] talking to [e]$_i$]

For reasons that will be discussed below, the non-overt NP may not remain *in situ* as the object of a preposition; the non-overt NP must move to an A-position in the Spec of the NP. The subject position of the object NP in (112) is already filled, however. Hence the non-overt nominal has no landing site and must remain in place. Since this situation is, by hypothesis, impossible, we can account for the ungrammaticality of (112).

We are now confronted with the question of the status of the non-overt element in the Spec of NP. Since this element binds a nominal trace, we will assume that it is itself an NP.[28] This non-overt NP is, in turn, A-bound by the subject of the superordinate S. As argued above, the subject position of sentences containing retroactive nominals receives an independent θ-role (see the examples in (24)). Since the non-overt NP in the subject position of the retroactive nominal is A-bound by an NP bearing an independent θ-role, it must be interpreted as PRO.

If the non-overt nominal in the Spec of NP is, in fact, PRO, then we are faced with an apparent dilemma. The definition of government given in Aoun and Sportiche (1983) allows a head to govern throughout its maximal projection. This definition was intended, in part, to rule out a PRO in the Spec position of NP; it was argued that such a PRO should admit arbitrary interpretation which predicts that a pronoun bound by that PRO should receive an arbitrary interpretation:

(113)   [un livre sur sa vie] vient d'être publié.
         'A book on {his/*one's} life has just been published.'

Stowell (1983) observes, however, that some nominals in subject position may contain a pronoun with arbitrary interpretation:

(114)   a. [un livre sur sa vie] est toujours utile.
            'A book on one's life is always useful.'
         b. [hatred of oneself] is dangerous.

Following Horvath (1981), Stowell proposes that government contains a directional parameter. We may, therefore, assume the following definition of government:

(115)   *A* governs *B* if and only if
         (i)   *A* c-commands *B*;

(ii) if C is a maximal projection such that C dominates B and C does not dominate A, then C is transparent to A;

(iii) either A precedes B and the language is head-initial or B precedes A and the language is head-final

Since English is a head-initial language, the above definition has the consequence that elements occurring in the specifier of a head will not be governed by the head, since the head does not precede them.

Let us now reconsider the proposed structure of retroactive nominals:

(116) $[_{N'}$ PRO$_i$ a good looking at t_i]

Although the PRO is c-commanded by the head noun, *talking*, and is not separated from the head noun by a non-transparent maximal projection, the PRO precedes the head and is, therefore, not governed by it. If we assume the PRO theorem (Chomsky 1982), then the movement from object (of a preposition or of the noun itself) is forced. Consider the D-Structure associated with (116):

(117) $[_{N'}$ a good talking to PRO]

If the PRO remains *in situ*, it will occur in a governed position. Movement to the ungoverned Spec of NP position is, therefore, forced by definition of government and by the Binding theory. Since movement to the Spec of NP is forced under this analysis the SSC facts follow immediately, as argued above.[29]

2.9 Thematic properties and proper government

We observed in the previous section that, although any NP could occur in the retroactive construction when the trace is a right-sister of the head, only -*ing* nominals allowed preposition stranding. Nothing in our analysis so far predicts this curious asymmetry between -*ing* nominals and other types of derived nominals; nevertheless, there is a strong contrast in grammaticality between (118a) and (118b):

(118) a. *The baby needs some attention to.
b. The baby needs some attending to.

A contrast as strong as that found in (118a) and (118b) demands an explanation: we would like to capture the fact that preposition stranding is 'unusual' for PPs inside many derived nominals, but that *ing* nominals exceptionally allow preposition stranding.

It has often been noted by a number of theorists (van Riemsdijk 1978; Hornstein and Weinberg 1981; Stowell 1981; Jaeggli 1982; Kayne 1984, to name but a few) that preposition stranding is a marked property of English; it is commonplace for preposition stranding to be impossible in the majority of the world's languages. There have been a number of attempts to capture the ability of English to strand prepositions while properly reflecting the fact that this is a marked property of grammar. Suppose, following Chomsky (1981; see also Aoun *et al.* 1987), that empty categories must be properly governed by some head and that English, unlike most languages, allows prepositions to act as proper governors. Example (118a) indicates, however, that such an approach to preposition stranding will be of little use to us in dealing with the problem at hand. The trace in the object position of the PP will not only be locally A-bound by the PRO in the Spec of the NP, but it will be properly governed by the preposition, since, under this view, English admits prepositions into the class of proper governors. Alternatively, one might suppose that English admits a marked rule of reanalysis which permits prepositions to 'absorb' with a governing verb; the prepositional object would then be governed (properly) by the verb which governed the PP at D-Structure (see Hornstein and Weinberg 1981 for an account in terms of Case theory).

(119) $V \rightarrow V^*$ (where V c-commands all elements in V^*)

This rule will reanalyze (120a) as (120b):

(120) a. [$_S$ John [$_{VP}$ [$_V$ talked] [$_{PP}$ to Harry] [$_{PP}$ about Fred]]]
b. [$_S$ John [$_{VP}$ [$_{V^*}$ talked to Harry about] Fred]]

The NP *Fred* in (120b) is governed by a complex verb, *talked to Harry about*. If government by a verb is sufficient to license a trace, English should allow preposition stranding insofar as the environment of the reanalysis rule is satisfied.

In general, NPs do not satisfy the environment of the reanalysis rule, since reanalysis is defined only for verbs. This result seems correct since, as observed above (p. 44), NPs lack pseudo-passive constructions:

(121) a. *the diplomats' conversation with t by John ...
b. *the legislation's arguments about t by the congress ...
c. *the problem's thought about t by John ...

Since the prepositions in the above examples will not reanalyze with the head noun, the trace left by 'move alpha' will be governed by a preposition, which cannot be a proper governor.

Recall that the retroactive nominal construction is lexically governed, that is, a verbal of the appropriate semantic class must govern the retroactive nominal in order to trigger the NP-movement of PRO within the nominal. Furthermore, the head noun must be an -*ing* nominal in order to allow preposition stranding. One could complicate the reanalysis rule by directly stipulating that reanalysis applies in the following environment:

(122) V   ...   N   P → V*
       [+F]   [+M]
       where V governs N

The feature [+F] is a lexical feature denoting the semantic class of verbs that allow retroactive nominals as complements, and the feature [+M] is a morphological feature which selects -*ing* nominals. A verb of the semantic class may trigger reanalysis with an NP of a particular morphological class. This rule would convert the bracketing in (123a) to the bracketing in (123b):

(123) a. [$_S$ this problem [$_{VP}$ [$_V$ deserves] [$_{NP}$ thinking [$_{PP}$ about PRO]]]]
b. [$_S$ this problem [$_{VP}$ [$_{V^*}$ deserves thinking about] PRO]]

The rule in (122) states that a verb of a particular semantic class may form a complex predicate with a noun of a particular morphological class (-*ing* nominals) and a preposition. As a result of this complex predicate formation, the preposition may be stranded. Surely, this simply restates the explanatory problem at hand. The rule stipulates that only -*ing* nominals may undergo reanalysis, leaving it open that the world may have turned out differently. In essence, the rule is an element of a class of rules which, as an accident of history, English has selected. It could have happened that the morphological class could have been nouns ending in -*tion*, or plurals, or any other morphological class. The problem is that no rule can count as its own explanation.

Implicit, here, is the claim that it is no mere accident that only -*ing* nominals allow for preposition stranding in the retroactive construction. The insight underlying reanalysis account of preposition stranding is that verbs are crucially implicated in the reanalysis process. Taking the lead from this insight, we might assume that -*ing* nominals in the retroactive form share some crucial property or set of properties in common with verbs. Other types of nominals, by virtue of their morphological form, simply lack this distinguishing property.

The idea that -*ing* nominals are somehow 'verb-like' has been around for some time. Ross (1973), for example, uses -*ing* nominals and gerunds to argue that grammatical categories form a continuum with -*ing* nominals lying closer to the verb-end of the scale than other morphological types of nominals. Jackendoff (1977), based on observations of Schachter (1976), discusses the following class of constructions:

(124) a. There is [no enjoying this world without you]
b. [this telling tales out of school] has got to stop

The examples in (124) are of particular interest in the present context. The bracketed phrases in (124) are introduced by the determiners *no* and *this* and the phrases would appear to be headed by the -*ing* nominals *enjoying* and *telling*. Both nominals are followed by bare NPs, *this world* in (124a) and *tales* in (124b). How do these NPs receive Case if they are both governed by nouns, which as a theorem of Case theory, cannot assign abstract Case? The conclusion would seem to be that the -*ing* nominals in (124) retain sufficient 'verb-like' properties to assign abstract Case. We hypothesize, then, that the same mechanism which allows -*ing* nominals to assign Case in (124) also underlies their ability to license preposition stranding in retroactive nominal constructions.

For the sake of discussion, let us assume a form of the ECP which requires that an empty category be governed by a co-indexed element. Co-indexation will result in one of the following two ways, provided that we included co-superscripting as a special case of co-indexation:[30]

(125) An element, A, is co-indexed with an element, B, only if either:
    (i) A assigns a θ-role to B; or
    (ii) A binds B.

The requirement that empty categories must be governed by a co-indexed element has the result that, all else being equal, nouns and prepositions will not count as proper governors for their complements because, as argued above, they are normally incapable of directly assigning a θ-role to their complements.

Consider the case of a prepositional phrase that is a complement to a verb, as in:

(126)   [$_S$ John [$_{VP}$[$_V$ talked] [$_{PP}$ to Bill]]]

The verb *talk* will assign a θ-role to its complement, *to Bill*. By convention, the verb and the preposition phrase will be co-superscripted under θ-role assignment:

(127)   [$_S$ John [$_{VP}$[$_V$ talked]^k [$_{PP}$ to Bill]^k]]

The θ-role assigned to the prepositional phrase will, under standard assumptions, percolate to the head of that category, the preposition *to*. Let us suppose that English exceptionally allows co-indexation under θ-role transmission by the preposition; that is, the θ-role assigned to the PP may be transmitted by the head to its complement and, exceptionally, the head will be co-indexed with the complement. Given this mechanism, English exceptionally allows prepositions which head a subcategorized prepositional phrase to be co-superscripted with their complements:

(128) [$_S$ John [$_{VP}$[$_V$ talked]^k [$_{PP}$ to^j Bill^j]^k]]

Notice that the object of the preposition is co-superscripted with the head in (128). Thus, the process of θ-role assignment ultimately conditions the distribution of empty categories.

As Hornstein and Weinberg (1981) observe, following Chomsky (1965), adjunct PPs may not be stranded:

(129) a. *What time did John arrive at?
b. *Which inning did the Yankees lose the ball game in?

The facts in (129) follow from our analysis; since these PPs are not assigned a θ-role by the verb, the head preposition cannot transmit a θ-role to its complement and the head and its complement will not be co-superscripted. Notice that we predict that there will be considerable idiolectal differences as to which prepositional phrases are genuinely subcategorized for by a verb. This is as we would expect, given individual differences in linguistic experience. I will assume that this process subsumes reanalysis, at least insofar as preposition stranding is concerned.

We have now isolated some of the ingredients of a complete analysis of retroactive nominalization. First, the retroactive nominal must be governed by an element that is a member of a particular semantic class of verbals, 'evaluatives'. To capture this fact, let us assume that these verbals have some common element in their argument structure (i.e. the set of thematic roles assigned by a particular element). This common element may be a thematic role or a subcategorization feature.

Second, we have seen that *-ing* nominals take on 'verb-like' properties when they are governed by an evaluative. Their properties include the ability to license preposition stranding. We are now in a position to account for these phenomena more clearly.

The first point we must address concerns Thematic theory. It has generally been assumed that assignment of a θ-role is a unified process (see Chomsky 1986 for a discussion of the relation between θ-marking and government):

(130) X assigns a θ-role to Y just in case X is in a configuration of government with Y.

Let us refer to the core case of θ-role assignment as 'θ-marking' (replacing *assigns a θ-role* in (130) with *θ-marks*). The canonical example of θ-marking is the case of a verb and its complements. We will assume, then, that θ-marking induces the co-superscripting process, discussed above, which underlies the transparency of a category (see, the definitions in (98) and (99)). My basic claim is that θ-role assignment is not a unified process in that nouns and prepositions do not θ-mark their complements.

On the face of it, this claim would appear to violate the θ-Criterion, since we have, as yet, provided no account of how some elements receive a thematic role. How, for example, could a nominal complement satisfy the requirement that arguments must bear a θ-role?

Higginbotham (1985) delineates a number of ways in which a head may assign θ-roles. I have already noted that most familiar case, namely θ-marking. Higginbotham notes that, quite generally, common nouns have a θ-role which they may assign. Consider a case like:

(131)   John is a doctor.

which asserts that John is one of the things that count as doctors, just as (132) asserts that John is a thing that walks:

(132)   John is walking.

It is reasonable to assume that *doctor* in (131) assigns a θ-role to *John* just as the VP *walking* assigns a θ-role to its subject. That is, *doctor* is represented in the lexicon as:

(133)   doctor, $[+N, -V]$, $\langle \theta_1 \rangle$

where the material enclosed in angled brackets indicates the thematic role(s) assigned by the lexical item. Notice that *doctor* is represented as a one-place predicate in (133).

In order to convert the one-place predicate into a term which could act as an argument to another predicate, it is necessary to assign a range to the open thematic position. Higginbotham argues that this can be done by binding the open thematic position with the appropriate determiner, like *some, the, every*, etc., as in:

(134)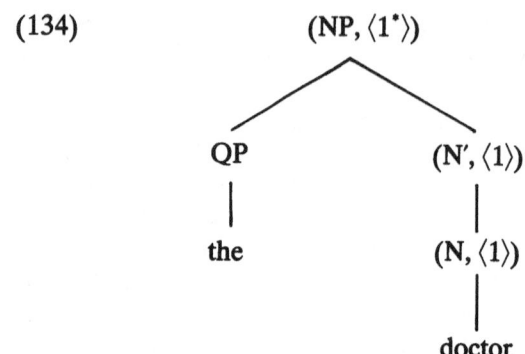

The phrase marker in (134) indicates that the one-place predicate *doctor* has been converted to a term via the binding of its open thematic position by the determiner *the*; the fact that the θ-role has been assigned is indicated by assigned a '*' to that position in the representation of the thematic roles of the head. Note that the above represents yet another form of θ-role assignment. Let us refer to this form of θ-role assignment as 'θ-binding'.

I will propose that the process of θ-binding may be generalized from the case of a determiner to arguments quite generally. While this is not in keeping with Higginbotham's theory, the basic idea is that here is an asymmetry between the way verbs associate thematic roles with their arguments and the way nouns associate thematic roles with their arguments. This generalization serves to illuminate a variety of phenomena.

Consider, for example, the following contrast:

(135) a. John is a doctor.
b. John is the doctor.

Example, (135a) asserts that John has the property of being a doctor, while example (135b) asserts that John is the same individual as some particular doctor. Example (135a) illustrates 'predicational *be*', while (135b) illustrates 'equational *be*' (see also the discussion in Safir (1985)).

The account of (135b) follows immediately from θ-binding. The definite article has converted the one-place predicate *doctor* to a referring expression by virtue of assigning a range to the open thematic position on *doctor*. *John* is inherently a referring expression. Example (135b), then, deals with a relation between two referring expressions, asserting that the two expressions denote the same thing, namely John.

Following Heim (1982), we will assume that the indefinite article, *a*, has no inherent range. If this is so, then there is no sense in which the indefinite article can supply the range to the open thematic position on *doctor*. Thus, the representation of *a doctor* would be:

(136)

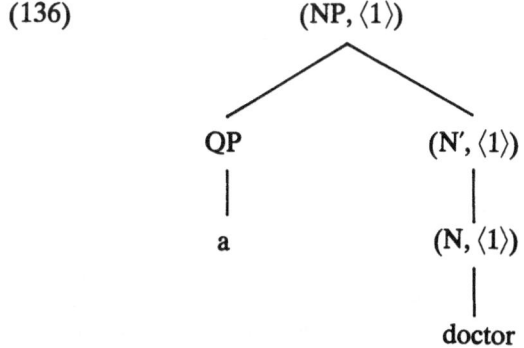

which indicates that the open θ-role on *doctor* has not been associated with an argument. If so, then *John* may bind the open θ-role on *a doctor* in (135a). Indeed, this binding is obligatory under the θ-Criterion. Hence, example (135a) takes *John* as being an argument of *doctor* while (135b) does not:

(137) a.

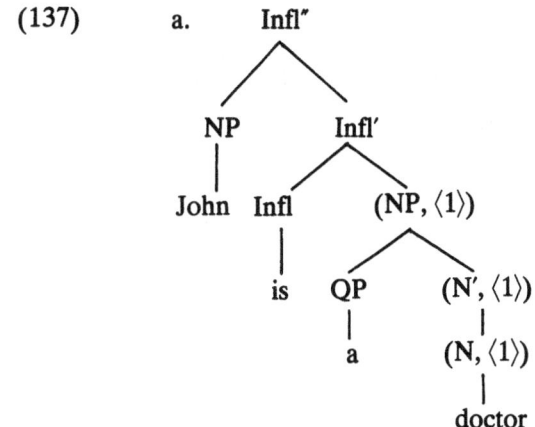

b.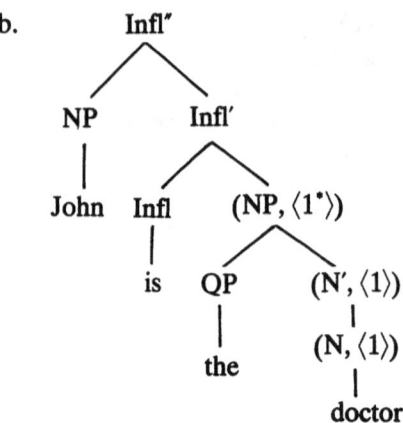

We conclude that an argument may acquire a θ-role by means of θ-binding and, as a related point, the assignment of θ-roles is not a homogeneous system, since it involves at least θ-marking and θ-binding.[31] It is, therefore, a logical possibility that categories behave differently according to the mechanism of θ-role assignment that they select. That is, complements of verbs are associated with a thematic role under θ-marking by the verb, while complements to nouns are associated with a θ-role under θ-binding. There is, further, no reason to suppose that θ-marking and θ-binding have identical syntactic consequences. θ-marking induces transparency of a category, while θ-binding does not. In summary:

(138)   a. Verbs θ-mark their complements.
       b. Nominal complements receive a θ-role in a systematically different way from verbal complements (possibly θ-binding).

(139)   If X θ-marks YP then X and YP are co-superscripted.

(140) YP is transparent to Z if YP are co-superscripted with Z.

(141)   Preposition stranding presupposes that the PP is co-superscripted with the head of the phrase in which it occurs.

2.10 Affixation and retroactive nominals

The conclusion from the discussion so far can only be that retroactive nominals θ-mark their complements in a manner analogous to the way verbs θ-mark their complements, since these nominals license preposition stranding. Retroactive nominals class with verbs rather than nouns in their mechanism of θ-role assignment. We might conclude that retroactive nominals are, in fact, verbs but for the fact that they select specifiers (like *some, any, a lot of*) which are restricted to the specifier position of NP. The ideal D-Structure representation would be:[32]

(142)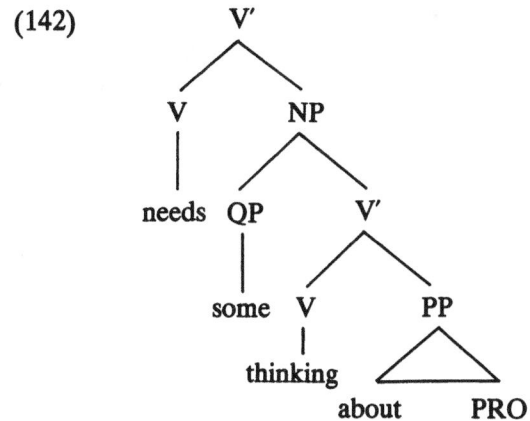

The problem here is that (142) is a violation of the X̄ schema, which requires that every phrase be headed. The object NP in (142) lacks a head.

Jackendoff (1977) in his work on X̄ theory notes a number of constructions, including gerunds, where the requirements which the X̄ schema places on phrase markers are too severe. He proposes that the X̄ schema be loosened to include configurations defined by the following (where 'af' = 'affix'):

(143) *Deverbalizing Rule Schema*

$$X^i \rightarrow af - V^i$$

The Deverbalizing Schema licenses structures of the following form (relative linear ordering of the elements in the phrase markers is irrelevant):

On a certain class of nominals

(144)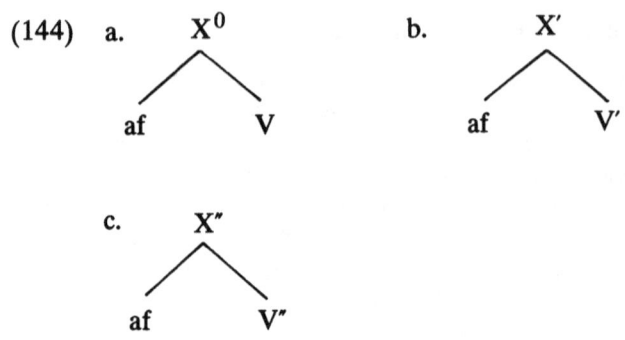

The structure in (144a), for instance, would correspond to derived nominals like *destruction* (see Selkirk (1982), Scalise (1984), and Di Sciullo and Williams (1987) for some recent discussions of affixation):

(145)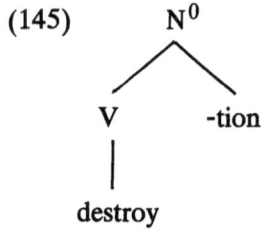

Jackendoff proposes that (144c) corresponds to gerunds. The structure in (144b) would correspond to examples like those in (124):

(146) This telling tales (must stop)
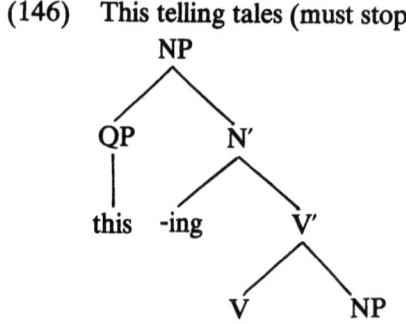

Notice that *tell* in (146) may assign abstract Case to its object. The V' is then made into an N' by the -*ing* affix.

I will refer to affixes which occur in structures of type (144a) as '0-affixes', those which occur in structures of type (144b) as '1-af-fixes', and affixes which occur in structures of type (144c) as '2-af-fixes'. Thus, the nominalizations in (147) involve '0-*ing*', the nominalization in (146) involves '1-*ing*', and gerunds, if we accept Jackendoff's analysis, involve '2-*ing*'.

(147)   a. the eating of the apple
            b. the binding of the anaphor
            c. John's paddling of the canoe

The 0-*ing* affix would deprive the verb of its ability to assign Case or θ-mark its complements and the phrase it heads would take specifiers associated with NPs. The 1-*ing* affix would allow the verb to assign Case and θ-mark its complements, but would prevent the verb from taking auxiliaries like *have, be,* or modals. Furthermore, a phrase headed by the verb plus 1-*ing* affix could take a determiner as its specifier. Finally, the 2-*ing* affix would create a phrase whose internal structure is indistinguishable from a VP. The head could assign Case and θ-mark its complements and could take some auxiliaries.

Retroactive nominals clearly fall into the 1-*ing* class:

(148)

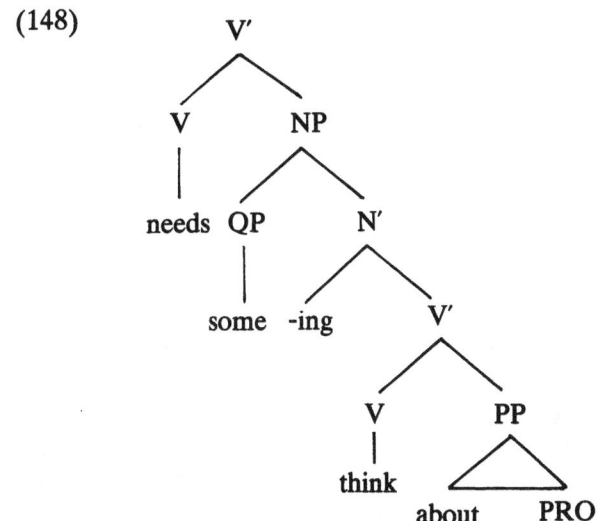

The class of evaluative predicates, then, subcategorizes for NPs headed by an N' of the 1-*ing* morphological class:

(149)　need, [−N, +V], ⟨1, 2⟩, [___ NP]
　　　　　　　　　　　　　　　　　　　[1-*ing*]

Given that the governing evaluative verbal subcategorizes for a nominal of the 1-*ing* class, the head of this nominal has the characteristics of a V'. In particular, the head of this V' is now free to θ-mark its complement. As a result, the complement which receives the θ-role under θ-marking will be co-superscripted with the head, as in (150):

(150)　[$_S$ John [$_{VP}$ [$_V$ needs]^k [$_{NP}$ a good [$_{N'}$ -ing [$_{V'}$ look^j [$_{PP}$ at PRO]^j]^k]]]]

Since the head of the PP complement of the object nominal now bears a fixed θ-role, it is able to assign that θ-role to its complement under the marked process of direct θ-transmission (see the discussion of preposition stranding, p. 6); hence, the preposition *to* and its NP complement, the PRO, will be co-superscripted as in (151):

(151)　[$_S$ John [$_{VP}$ [$_V$ needs]^k [$_{NP}$ a good [$_{N'}$ -ing [$_{V'}$ look^j [$_{PP}$ at^i PRO^i]^j]^k]]]]

'Move alpha' may now freely apply to the PRO, moving it into the Spec of NP; since the head of the prepositional phrase and the trace left by this movement are co-superscripted, the version of the ECP formulated above will be satisfied:

(152)　[$_S$ John [$_{VP}$ [$_V$ needs]^k [$_{NP}$ PRO$_1$ a good [$_{N'}$ -ing [$_{V'}$ look^j [$_{PP}$ at^i t_1^i]^j]^k]]]]

In (152) the empty category t_1 is governed by the preposition *to*. In addition, because of a conspiracy between the properties of the affix 1-*ing*, which converts a V' to an N', and the marked ability of prepositions to transmit θ-roles directly in English, the trace is governed by the empty category in the way that is relevant to the ECP. Finally, the trace is A-bound in its governing category by the

PRO in the Spec of NP. Since the trace obeys both condition A of the Binding theory and the ECP, the grammar will allow the representation in (152).

The D-Structure in (150) should be contrasted with the following D-Structure:

(153) [$_S$[$_{NP}$ some thinking [$_{PP}$ about PRO]] is necessary]

An -*ing* nominal occupies the subject position in (153). An NP in this position does not satisfy the subcategorization requirements of the verb (not being governed by it), so there is no reason to suppose that 1-*ing* affixation is licensed in the above position. Note that Case theory, for example, does not force such affixation as it does in examples like (124) where a post-head nominal must be assigned Case. Since θ-marking by the head 'noun' to its complements presupposes this affixation, the -*ing* nominal in (153) will not θ-mark the complement PP and the head will not be co-superscripted with its complement, which must be associated with a θ-binding. Preposition stranding, however, presupposes that the PP has been θ-marked. As a result, the preposition and its complement will not be co-superscripted. Extraction of the prepositional complement, as in (154), will therefore violate the ECP:

(154) [$_S$[$_{NP}$ PRO$_1$ some thinking [$_{PP}$ about t_1]] is necessary]

Movement of the PRO to the Spec of NP will trigger a violation of the ECP; the PRO, however, may not remain *in situ*, since it will be governed by the preposition. There is no well-formed derivation associated with example (153), since all the possible representations violate either the Binding theory or the ECP. Again, the conspiracy between properties of the morphology, θ-role assignment, and the requirement that empty categories be governed by a co-indexed element guarantees that the retroactive nominal construction will be isolated to the object position of verbals that assign subcategorize for nominals of the 1-*ing* class.

Consider the case of a derived nominal which is not formed by an affix of the 1-*ing* class; compare the D-Structure in (150) with:

(155) [$_S$[$_{NP}$ these people] [$_{VP}$[$_V$ merit] [$_{NP}$ some [$_{N'}$ [$_N$ convers-ation] [$_{PP}$ with PRO]]]]]

The verb *merit* in (155) need not have a 1-*ing* nominal as its complement. The head of the noun, *conversation*, is, however, a pure noun and, as such, uses canonically nominal means of associating a θ-role with its complements; *conversation* will not θ-mark its complement PP, which must be associated with a θ-role under θ-binding. From this step, the proof of the ungrammaticality of (155) is identical to that of example (153). The head of the PP, *with*, will not assign a θ-role to its complement; any resulting representation associated with this example will violate the ECP:

(156) $[_S[_{NP}$ these people$]$ $[_{VP}[_V$ merit$]$ $[_{NP}$ PRO$_1$ some $[_{N'}$ $[_N$ convers-ation$]$ $[_{PP}$ with $t_1]]]]]$

Finally, we can consider the case of extraction from a phrase which is not a complement of the head. Consider examples of the following form:

(157)   a. John falls asleep $[_{PP}$ during his matrix algebra class$]$
       b. Most farmers work $[_{PP}$ after a good rain$]$
       c. Most of the audience left $[_{PP}$ before John's film$]$

The PPs in the above examples are adjuncts which do not receive a θ-role from any head element in the sentence. As a result, it is impossible to extract the complement NPs, allowing the head preposition to be stranded:

(158)   a. *Which class$_i$ did John fall asleep $[_{PP}$ during $t_i]$
       b. *What kind of rain$_i$ do most farmers work $[_{PP}$ after $t_i]$
       c. *Which film$_i$ did most of the audience leave $[_{PP}$ before $t_i]$

The ungrammaticality of the examples in (158) follows immediately from our assumptions about the ECP and the nature of θ-role assignment: prepositions may directly assign a θ-role only insofar as they are transmitting a θ-role from a head. Since the PPs in (158) are not complements of a head, they are not in a position to transmit a θ-role. Hence, in each of the examples in (158) the head of the PP will not be co-superscripted with its complement. Since every empty category must be governed by an element which is co-indexed with it, none of the empty categories in (158) will pass the ECP.

Our analysis predicts that stranding of a preposition in retroactive nominals is possible only if the PP is assigned a θ-role by the head noun of the construction. A prepositional adjunct to the head noun should not allow stranding:

(159) a. *No class in matrix algebra deserves any falling asleep during.
b. *Most of the farmers agree that a good rain merits a lot of working after.
c. *Even though it was poorly made, John's film did not deserve any leaving before by the audience.

The examples in (159) are out for essentially the same reasons as examples (152) and (155). The PRO that is the D-Structure object of the prepositional adjunct will violate the ECP if it moves out of that adjunct and it will violate the Binding theory (by being in a governed position) if it remains *in situ*.

It is quite generally impossible to strand a preposition in retroactive nominal constructions unless the PP is directly θ-marked by the head; it is, therefore, impossible to strand a preposition that is inside a complement of the head noun:

(160) a. *Nixon deserves some rewriting of [a book [about *e*]]
(cf. 'Many books about Nixon deserve some rewriting.')
b. *John merits some talking to [friends [of *e*]]
(cf. 'Friends of John merit some talking to.')
c. *This foundation needs some rethinking of [gifts [to *e*]]
(cf. 'Gifts to this foundation need some rethinking.')

In each of the examples in (160), the PP containing the stranded preposition has not been θ-marked. Once again, any representation will ultimately involve a violation of the ECP (if movement occurs) or a violation of the Binding theory (if the PRO object of a preposition remains *in situ*). Either way, there is no mechanism that will save the representations.

2.11 Affixation and external thematic roles

The account of retroactive nominals that I have presented so far crucially relies on properties of the *-ing* affix. The lexical class of requirement predicates which govern retroactive nominals select the 1-*ing* affix which attaches to a V' to form an N'. There is, then, a systematic relation between (161a) and (161b):

(161) a. [$_{NP}$ this [$_{N'}$ -ing [$_{V'}$ tell [$_{NP}$ tales]]]]
b. [$_{NP}$ PRO$_i$ [$_{N'}$ -ing [$_{V'}$ argue [$_{PP}$ about t_i]]]]

Ken Safir (p.c.) has observed that the analysis of retroactive nominals in terms of affixation must address the problem of external θ-role assignment. If, as I have conjectured, retroactive nominals contain an internal V', then why doesn't the V' assign an external θ-role? If the V' assigned such a θ-role, then the NP-movement critical to formation of retroactive nominals would be blocked by the θ-Criterion.

The problem is that the PRO would receive a θ-role either directly from the verb or by means of indirect θ-role assignment by a preposition. If the Spec of NP received the external θ-role of the V', then the PRO would receive a second θ-role when it moved to the Spec of NP. The resulting A-chain would contain two θ-positions, which is impossible according to the θ-Criterion.

The solution to this problem is to claim that the 1-*ing* affix blocks assignment of an external θ-role. This absorption process is analogous to passive morphology (Fabb 1984; Jaeggli 1986; Baker 1988). The 1-*ing* affix would bear the external θ-role and, furthermore, could transmit this θ-role to a *by* phrase. As we have seen, retroactive nominals can take an external argument, just in case that argument is in a *by* phrase (see the examples in (22)):

(162) a. This problem$_i$ merits [some thinking about e_i [by the whole group]]
b. *This problem$_i$ merits [[the whole group]'s thinking about e_i]

The interaction between the morphology and θ-theory would ensure that the external argument could not appear in the Spec of NP.

I will note, in passing, that the treatment of the *-ing* affix as analogous to passive morphology gains some support from the history of English. Visser (1973) notes that, until the nineteenth century, the following was a well-formed passive in some dialects of English:

(163) The houses are building.

While this form of the passive has a number of semantic constraints, I hypothesize that the retroactive nominal is an historic remnant of this form of the passive.

If the analogy between retroactive nominals and passives is on the right track, then the verb which heads the V' should be unable to assign Accusative Case to its complement. This observation follows from the assumption that retroactive nominals fall into the class of constructions which obey Burzio's Generalization (see Burzio 1986). Burzio notes that, quite generally, if a verb does not assign an external θ-role, then it cannot assign Accusative Case. If Burzio's Generalization is correct, then we would not expect to find constructions like (164):

(164) [$_{NP}$ any [$_{N'}$ -ing [$_{V'}$ recite this poem] (by the children)]]

The NP *this poem* could not receive Case from the verb *recite* since the verb cannot assign an external θ-role. The representation in (164) would, then, violate the Case filter. Notice that the 'pseudo-passive' cases I have considered throughout the above discussion could be assimilated to this analysis if the Case-assigning properties of the subcategorized preposition were dictated by the governing verb. Since this assumption seems independently necessary in the account of pseudo-passives in general, I will assume that the same account holds in the special case of retroactive nominals. I should note that examples like (161a) cannot be fully assimilated to 1-*ing* affixation; I will leave a full account of this construction open, although the affix involved might be a case of 2-*ing* affix.

We have so far derived the following facts about retroactive nominals from the assumption that such nominals involve special morphology: first, the external argument cannot appear in the Spec of NP but must appear in a *by* phrase, given that the -*ing* affix receives the external θ-role; second, the NP complement of the

75

verb cannot receive Case if it remains *in situ*. The final step in the account is to assume, as seems reasonable, given the facts, that the requirement predicates which license retroactive nominals are control predicates; that is, the class with verbs like *try* with respect to control properties.

This analysis predicts that the examples in (165) will be ungrammatical:

(165) a. *I need [the poem's reciting (by the class)]
 b. *I need [(the class's) reciting the poem]

Example (165) violates the control properties of *need*; the explanation of this example would be analogous to the explanation of (166):

(166) *I tried [(for) the class to recite the poem]

The matrix subject has no argument to control in either (165a) or (166); the lexical requirements of *need* in (165a) and *try* in (166) would be violated; if control is a lexical property, then both examples violate the Extended Projection Principle.

Example (165b) minimally violates the Case filter, since *the poem* does not receive abstract Case from *recite*. If the external argument, *the class*, is present, then the example also violates the control properties of *need* and the θ-Criterion, since the *-ing* affix blocks assignment of the external θ-role to the Spec of NP.

The *prima facie* bizarre fact that predicates of requirement subcategorize for a 'passive' nominal follows directly from core principles on this analysis. The Case filter, θ-Criterion, and Extended Projection Principle interact with properties of the *-ing* affix and the predicate of requirement to force passivization of the internal argument of the retroactive nominal.[33]

2.12 A note on 'worth'

Throughout the discussion of retroactive nominals, I have systematically avoided examples involving *worth*. At first, it would appear that *worth* falls solidly into the class of verbals that license retroactive nominals:

(167) a. This problem is worth working on.
b. Picasso's later paintings are worth looking at.
c. John's arguments aren't worth any worrying about.

As pointed out by Safir (1984a), *worth* shows some systematic differences from the other class of verbals. First, the complement to *worth* does not show Specified Subject Condition effects:

(168) a. This problem is worth Bill's working on.
b. Picasso's later paintings are worth your students' looking at.
c. John's arguments aren't worth his wife's worrying about.

Second, the movement inside the complement to *worth* may be unbounded:

(169) a. This problem is worth [persuading some students [PRO to work on t_i]]
b. Picasso's later paintings$_i$ are worth [forcing [some students to look at t_i]]
c. John's arguments$_i$ aren't worth [convincing [anyone to worry about t_i]]

Third, the subject position of S may be a $\bar{\theta}$-position, since pleonastic *it* may occur there:

(170) a. It is worth working on this problem.
b. It is worth looking at Picasso's later paintings.
c. It isn't worth worrying about John's arguments.

These 'worth' sentences are strikingly similar to tough movement (for further arguments, see Safir 1984) and dissimilar to retroactive nominals, which have none of the above properties. Strikingly, however, if we disambiguate the complement of *worth* as to whether it is a true 1-*ing* nominal or a gerund, we begin to get a number of contrasts. This disambiguation can be carried out quite easily by prefixing a determiner to the complement of *worth*. Thus, if the complement to *worth* is unambiguously a 1-*ing* nominal, the properties of retroactive nominals return:

(171) a. This problem is worth some working on.
b. Picasso's later paintings are worth a lot of looking at.
c. John's arguments aren't worth any worrying about.

(172) a. *This problem is worth the working on.
b. *Picasso's later paintings are worth the looking at.
c. *John's arguments aren't worth the worrying about.

(173) a. *This problem$_i$ is worth [some persuading of some students [PRO to work on t_i]]
b. *Picasso's later paintings are worth [some forcing of [the students to look at t_i]]
c. *John's arguments$_i$ aren't worth [any convincing of [anyone to worry about t_i]]

(174) a. *It is worth some working on this problem.
b. *It is worth a little looking at Picasso's later paintings.
c. *It isn't worth any worrying about John's arguments.

Briefly, we can encapsulate the properties of *worth* as follows: unlike the other evaluative verbals that license retroactive nominals, *worth* allows a true gerund as its complement; the other verbals require an NP. If a gerund occurs as the complement of *worth*, a non-overt operator may undergo wh-movement inside the complement. This movement is analogous to tough movement. If a true 1-*ing* nominal occurs as the complement to *worth*, then the construction is another instance of retroactive nominals. This analysis makes an interesting prediction. Recall that retroactive nominals do not felicitously license parasitic gaps, which parasitic gaps may occur in tough-movement constructions. We should, then get a contrast depending on whether the complement to *worth* is a gerund or an -*ing* nominal:

(175) a. This problem$_i$ is worth working on t_i without losing any sleep over e_i
b. *?This problem$_i$ is worth some working on t_i without losing any sleep over e_i

The contrast between (175a) and (175b) indicates that *worth* does, in fact, subcategorize either for an NP or for a gerund and, further, that movement of a non-overt operator to an A-position, in a way which is analogous to tough movement, is possible in gerunds.

2.13 Summary

I began this chapter by considering what properties the empty category found in retroactive nominals must have. Although the empty category has anaphoric properties, treating it as a pure anaphor raised a number of problems for the theory of empty categories, since it appeared to be A-bound in its governing category by an element with an independent θ-role. This indicates that the empty category in question must be a PRO. This PRO, however, appeared to be in a governed position, a situation which is impossible in a theory which incorporates the PRO theorem. A systematic investigation of the other possible empty categories showed that none of them could completely account for the facts. A null pronominal in that position would violate condition B of the Binding theory and, furthermore, could not meet the requirement that pro be locally identified. An NP-trace would violate the θ-Criterion, since it would form a chain with its binder. The assumption that the empty category was a variable could not account for the SSC effects, the boundedness of the movement, or the relative unacceptability of parasitic gaps in this construction.

I was therefore led to the assumption that the construction involved NP movement of a PRO, leaving behind an NP-trace (notice that this analysis forces us to the conclusion that retroactive nominals involve two empty categories – an NP-trace and a PRO). This assumption immediately accounted for the bounded nature of the movement and the SSC effects since (1) NP-movement leaves behind a trace which is subject to condition A of the Binding theory; and (2) the PRO must be the subject of NP at S-Structure, thus accounting for the fact that an overt structural subject is impossible. If PRO is in the Spec of NP, then I must, tentatively, adopt the proposal that government is directional; this assumption allows the subject position of NP to be ungoverned.

A final empirical problem was to account for the complex of preposition-stranding facts found in retroactive nominals. Only *-ing* nominals allowed this preposition stranding and, furthermore, only a preposition that headed a PP complement to the head noun could be stranded; a prepositional adjunct to the NP remained an island to extraction. I accounted for these facts by assuming that the ECP requires a form of antecedent government (see Chomsky 1986). That is, an empty category is properly governed with respect to the ECP only if it is either governed by its antecedent or if it is governed by a lexical head which assigns the position occupied by the empty category a θ-role. Since 1-*ing* nominals θ-mark their complements, the ECP would be exceptionally satisfied in the retroactive nominal construction. Evaluative predicates like *need* and *could use* allow 1-*ing* nominals as their complements; the preposition-stranding facts follow immediately, given these assumptions. This response to the analytic problem posed by retroactive nominals requires an intimate connection between the theory of movement, thematic theory, and the morphology. Finally, I derived many of the properties of retroactive nominals from the assumption that 1-*ing* shares many properties with passive morphology. I will, henceforth, assume that thematic relations play a central role in governing the distribution of empty categories. The next chapter will be devoted to exploring the nature of the relationship between thematic theory and the distribution of empty categories.

Chapter three

Thematic domains and bounding*

In Chapter 2 I investigated the properties of retroactive nominals. I attributed the preposition-stranding facts, exemplified in (1), to the effects of the Empty Category Principle:

(1) a. This problem$_i$ needs some thinking about t_i
 b. *This problem$_i$ needs some thought about t_i

The empty category inside the NP in (1a) is properly governed either because it can be governed by its antecedent, a PRO in the Spec of the object NP, or by the preposition *about*. Lexical properties of the predicate governing the entire NP and properties of certain *-ing* nominals allow the *-ing* nominal to directly θ-mark the prepositional phrase. This renders the PP transparent to government from without. Subcategorization features, morphological features and θ-marking conspire to license preposition stranding.

The noun, *thought*, in (1b) may never θ-mark its PP complement (relying instead on θ-binding or some other mechanism distinct from direct θ-marking) due to the morphology involved in the derivation of this nominal from its associated verbal stem. The preposition, as a result, cannot transmit a thematic role to its object. The empty category in (1b) is, therefore, not governed by a direct thematic-role assigner. Furthermore, since *thought* does not directly assign a θ-role to its complement, the PP is opaque to government from without; hence, the empty category cannot be governed by its antecedent. In either event, the structure violates the Empty Category Principle.

In this chapter I will reject the hypothesis that the alternation in

(1) is attributable to the Empty Category Principle. Instead, I will propose that the alternation in (1) follows from a principle of Bounding theory which defines 'transparent domains' in terms of direct θ-role assignment. A constituent may move freely inside a transparent domain, subject, of course, to other grammatical constraints; a constituent may not be extracted out of a non-transparent domain, however. θ-theory, then plays a crucial role in Bounding theory. In section 3.1 I will develop the basic machinery used throughout the analysis; in section 3.2 I will turn to a range of empirical data and their analysis in terms of thematic domains.

The approach advocated here bears some resemblance to the 'barriers' framework of Chomsky (1986) which uses direct θ-marking to define the core notion of government. Direct θ-marking is crucial to both the Empty Category Principle and Bounding theory, if Chomsky is correct. In section 3.3 I will compare the approach developed in this chapter with the barriers framework. I will argue that the barriers framework must be supplemented with the notion of thematic domain developed here. Finally, in the last section of the chapter, I will consider some extensions of the framework presented in 3.1.

3.1 Thematic domains

In this section I will develop the intuition that the boundedness of syntactic movement depends on thematic relations between heads and constituents; in other words, movement within a subtree is sensitive to θ-role assignment. We have grounds for assuming that movement out of a phrase is legitimate only under conditions of θ-marking. Recall that in Chapter 2 I argued, following work by Kayne (1984), that a maximal projection is transparent to government from without only under conditions of direct θ-marking. We might suppose that a maximal projection is transparent to government (hereafter, 'government-transparency') under exactly the same conditions that it is transparent to extraction (hereafter, 'extraction-transparency'). There are two hypotheses: either extraction-transparency follows from the theory of government or extraction-transparency and government-transparency follow from the same underlying mechanism, namely Thematic theory. I will here assume the latter hypothesis; that is, Thematic theory provides the basis for both types of transparency.

Recall that in Chapter 2 I had defined government-transparency as follows:

(2) *Government-transparency*
 a. If X θ-marks YP then X and YP are co-superscripted.
 b. YP is transparent to Z if YP is co-superscripted with Z.

I will assume that 'θ-marks' in (2a) is essentially the marking relation that holds between a verb or adjective and its subcategorized complement and I will refer to this relation as 'direct θ-marking' following Chomsky (1986). Nouns and prepositions, following the discussion in Chapter 2, do not directly θ-mark their complements but use other mechanisms to associate θ-roles with their complements; by (2a) nouns and prepositions will not be co-superscripted with their complements except via some marked process. Following suggestions by Stowell (1981), it is possible that the index of the phrase receiving a θ-role is copied into the θ-grid of the head that assigns the θ-role to the phrase. We might subsume co-superscripting under this mechanism. For expository purposes, I will stay with the superscripting notation.

Suppose, for the moment, that θ-marking is the sole mechanism by which a phrase may come to bear a superscript. Define *transparency* as follows:

(3) *Transparency*
 An element A is transparent if:
 (i) A is not a maximal projection; or
 (ii) A bears a superscript; or
 (iii) A is an element of $\{VP, S (=Infl'')\}$

The notion of transparency could be incorporated into the definition of *Government* more or less directly:

(4) *Government*
 A governs B iff A c-commands B, and if C dominates B and C does not dominate A, then C is transparent.

From transparency, it follows that non-maximal projections and θ-marked maximal projections are always transparent. Clause (iii) of *Transparency* is a stipulation to which I shall return below (see

Thematic domains and bounding

p. 12). It follows, from this stipulation that VP is always transparent. Furthermore, the object of a verb is transparent, since the object is directly θ-marked by the verb. Movement is restricted in the following way:

(5) *Extraction-transparency*
An element, Y, may be extracted from Z only if Z is transparent.

Extraction-transparency states that if an element Y is contained in Z at some level of representation, it may be extracted from Z just in case Z is transparent (as defined in (3)); that is, Z is not a maximal projection or Z is a θ-marked phrase or Z is a VP or an S.

Consider, first, extraction from a direct-object position (for the moment, I will put aside Auxiliary Inversion):

(6) $[_{C''}$ who$_i$ $[_{Infl''}$ John $[_{Infl'}$ Infl $[_{VP}$ see $t_i]]]]$

where C" is the maximal projection of Comp (= S̃) and Infl is taken as the head of S (see Chomsky 1986 for a discussion of the extension of X̄ theory to the non-lexical categories Comp and Infl). I will assume, following Chomsky (1986) that 'movement to Comp' is actually movement to the Specifier of Comp. The VP will be extraction-transparent with respect to extraction of the direct object by virtue of the stipulation in (3iii). Hence, we may extract the object out of VP. In order to move the direct object to Comp, however, it must be the case that Infl" is extraction-transparent. Again, by virtue of the stipulation in clause (iii) of (3), Infl" is extraction-transparent. The only other nodes which dominate the gap and do not dominate its antecedent are non-maximal projections which are, by definition, always transparent. Hence, all the nodes separating the locus of extraction from the landing site in (6) are extraction-transparent and (6) is well-formed.

Consider successive-cyclic movement, as in:

(7) $[_{C''}$ who$_i$ $[_{Infl''}$ Mary $[_{Infl'}$ Infl $[_{VP}$ think $[_{C''}$ t_i $[_{Infl''}$ John $[_{Infl'}$ Infl $[_{VP}$ saw $t_i']]]]]]]]$

As was shown with regards to (6), extraction of the direct object of the embedded clause may go at least as far as the Comp of the embedded clause. The embedded C" is θ-marked by the verb, *think*. By clause (ii) of transparency, the embedded C" is transparent and, hence, extraction-transparent. It follows that an element in Comp may be extracted out of the C" which immediately dominates it just in case the C" is θ-marked. The matrix VP, headed by *think*, is transparent by virtue of clause (iii) of transparency. Therefore, extraction may take a phrase from the embedded Comp to a position external to the matrix VP. By reasoning parallel to that involved with (6), the matrix Infl" is transparent and, hence, extraction-transparent. All the other nodes separating the embedded Comp from the matrix Comp are not maximal projections and are therefore transparent. Given that the matrix Infl" is also transparent, a phrase may be extracted from the embedded Comp to the matrix Comp. The assumptions about extraction defined in (3) and (5) allow successive-cyclic movement just so long as the embedded C" is θ-marked. θ-marking of a C" will occur just in case the C" is a subcategorized complement.

Let us turn to extraction of a subpart of direct object as in (8):

(8) $[_{C''}$ of whom$_i$ $[_{Infl''}$ Mary $[_{Infl'}$ Infl $[_{VP}$ take $[_{NP}$ pictures t_i]]]]]

The direct object, headed by *pictures*, is θ-marked by the verb *take*. By clause (ii) of definition (3), the direct object NP is transparent, and by (5), extraction-transparent. Here the reasoning is exactly the same as seen above: the VP is extraction-transparent by clause (iii) of (3); Infl" is extraction-transparent for the same reason. All other nodes separating the gap from its antecedent are non-maximal and, as a result, extraction-transparent. Hence, a subpart of a direct object may be moved to Comp. I will spare the reader a proof of the fact that a subpart of a direct object may be moved successive-cyclically since it, again, parallels the reasoning behind the discussion of (7).

We turn now to consider the extraction of an object of a subcategorized preposition as in:

(9)   a.   Who$_i$ did John give the books to t_i
     b. $[_{C''}$ who$_i$ $[_{Infl''}$ John $[_{Infl'}$ Infl $[_{VP}$ give the books $[_{PP}$ to t_i]]]]]]

The prepositional phrase, headed by *to*, is θ-marked by the verb *give*. By clause (ii) of the definition of transparency, the prepositional phrase is transparent and, hence, extraction-transparent. As a result, the object of the preposition may be extracted out of the prepositional phrase. From here on, the proof is essentially identical to those given above — each maximal projection dominating the extraction site is extraction-transparent and all non-maximal projections dominating the extraction site are extraction-transparent. So movement to Comp is possible from the object position of a subcategorized preposition. Since movement to Comp is possible from this position, we would expect that successive-cyclic movement is also possible:

(10)   [$_{C'}$ who$_i$ did [$_{Infl'}$ Mary say [$_{C'}$ that [$_{Infl'}$ John thought [$_{C'}$ that [$_{Infl'}$ Bill gave the books [$_{PP}$ to t_i]]]]]]]]

As (10) shows, the facts fall as predicted.

In addition, the framework predicts that extraction of a subpart of such a phrase is not good:

(11)   a. *Who$_i$ did John give pencils to [friends of t_i]
       b. *Of whom$_i$ did John give pencils to [friends t_i]
       c. *Who$_i$ did John talk about [relatives of t_i]
       d. *Of whom$_i$ did John talk about [relatives t_i]

I have assumed that the head noun in these constructions does not directly θ-mark its complement; the marking properties of nouns differs qualitatively from that of verbs. The complement to the head noun does not satisfy clause (ii) of transparency and must not be extraction-transparent. Furthermore, the preposition does not θ-mark this NP; the thematic role assigned to the NP is transmitted by the preposition from the verb which subcategorizes for the PP. We assume that such θ-transmission does not invoke superscripting of the NP. Hence, the NP also fails clause (ii) of transparency. It must be the case, then, that the NP is not extraction-transparent. If this is true, however, then no phrase may be extracted from this opaque domain, by virtue of the definition of extraction-transparency. The framework, therefore, accounts for the examples in (11). Note that it does not account for the differences between the examples; nothing in the analysis explains why (11b) is worse than (11a), although a genuine contrast seems to exist. It may be possible to derive the contrast from the recoverability of deletion (see Chomsky 1965, among others). The empty categories in (11a) and (11c) have no governing element that will signal their presence; the head noun itself does not θ-mark this position. In (11b) and (11d), on the other hand, the Case-maker *of* is stranded. This fact is, we might suppose, sufficient to signal the presence of an empty category; its presence may upgrade the acceptability of the examples.

Consider, next, extraction of a subject. The extraction of a subject of a matrix Infl″ is shown in (12):

(12)   [$_{C''}$ who$_i$ [$_{Infl''}$ t_i saw John]]

Infl″ is transparent by clause (iii) of transparency and, therefore, is extraction-transparent. We may extract a subject out of Infl″ at least as far as the Spec of the Comp which governs the Infl″. Example (12) thus obeys our constraint that extraction occur only from an extraction-transparent domain.

Successive-cyclic extraction of a subject is also possible, for reasons discussed in connection with (8):

(13)   [$_{C''}$ who$_i$ does [$_{Infl''}$ Mary think [$_{C''}$ t_i [$_{Infl''}$ t_i' saw John]]]]

We have already seen, with respect to (12), that extraction is possible from the subject position of the embedded clause to the Spec position of the embedded C″. The proof that movement may proceed from the embedded clause to the Spec of the superordinate Comp should be fairly familiar: the embedded C″ is θ-marked by the verb *think*; by clause (ii) of transparency, this θ-marking results in superscripting of the C″, rendering it extraction-transparent. The matrix VP is, of course, extraction-transparent with respect to extraction from the embedded C″ by clause (iii) of transparency. Infl″ is extraction-transparent for the same reason that VP is. All other nodes separating the trace from its antecedent are non-maximal and, hence, transparent. We conclude that extraction from the embedded Comp may go at least as far as the superordinate Comp. But, then, successive-cyclic movement of an element originating in a subject position is also possible, as desired.

Extraction of a subpart of the subject position of tensed Infl″

will be ill-formed, according to extraction-transparency:

(14)   a. *$[_{C'}$ who$_i$ $[_{Infl'}$ $[_{NP}$ stories about t_i] $[_{Infl'}$ Infl $[_{VP}$ upset Mary]]]]

       b. *$[_{C'}$ [about whom]$_i$ $[_{Infl'}$ $[_{NP}$ stories t_i] $[_{Infl'}$ Infl $[_{VP}$ upset Mary]]]]

In (14a) the PP complement to the noun *stories* is not directly θ-marked, by the arguments developed in Chapter 2. Hence, this PP is not transparent and no element may be extracted from the PP. Furthermore, the subject NP itself is not directly θ-marked and so is not transparent. Hence, nothing can be extracted from inside the subject NP. Notice that the extraction crosses two non-transparent domains in (14a) and only one such domain in (14b). In either event, extraction from a subpart of the subject of a tensed clause should be impossible, given that the notion of extraction-transparency is contingent on θ-marking.

3.2 Subjects and adjuncts

In the preceding section, I informally defined the notion of transparency and extraction-transparency; a number of standard examples of extraction in English were then shown to be consistent with this approach. In this section, I will extend the empirical coverage a bit by considering a number of examples normally attributed to the ECP, Subjacency or various island conditions. I will discuss several different constructions and show that they follow without further stipulation from the transparency approach.

The Subject Condition

The Subject Condition prohibits the extraction of a subpart of a subject (see Kayne 1984; Pesetsky 1982b). We have already seen some Subject-Condition violations in (14) involving the subject of a tensed Infl. The exact scope of the Subject Condition is not *a priori* evident, of course, but I will attempt to delimit its range of application as well as consider some alternative treatments that have been proposed in the literature.

Consider, first, the small clauses[1] in (15):

(15)   a. John considers [*Bill* a fool]

b. John saw [*Mary* leave]
c. John heard [*the men* in the room]

As explained in note 1, I will follow Stowell (1983) in the assumption that the bracketed phrases in (15) form a constituent. The leftmost NP (italicized) in each of the examples acts as the subject of that constituent. This assumption accounts for the fact that the subject of a small clause obeys the Subject Condition (or Left-Branch Condition, as it is construed in Kayne 1984):

(16) a. *Of whom does John consider [[friends t] fools]
b. *Of whom did John see [[friends t] leave]
c. *Of whom did John hear [[relatives t] in the room]

Notice that the examples in (16) follow from our account of thematic-role assignment and bounding in the preceding section. The head noun may not θ-mark its object; hence, the head noun will not be co-superscripted with its complement; nor will the head noun contain the index of its complement in its thematic grid.

The predicate (the rightmost constituent in each of the examples of (15)) is the head of the bracketed phrases and, furthermore, assigns a θ-role to the subject under predication. Given these assumptions, it follows that the verb may not θ-mark the subject of a small clause since the subject would then bear two thematic roles. (Note that the verb θ-marks the entire small clause, however.) As noted in the previous section, the entire small clause is transparent. The framework predicts that the entire subject of the small clause may be extracted, provided that the trace left behind is properly governed:

(17) a. Who$_i$ does John consider [t_i a fool]
b. *Mary$_i$ was seen [t_i leave]²
c. What$_i$ did John hear [t_i in the room]

(18) a. Bill$_i$ is considered [t_i a fool]
b. *Mary was seen [t_i leave]²
c. The men$_i$ were heard [t_i in the room]

The verb directly θ-marks the small clause which is, as a result, transparent. Since the small clause is transparent, an element may be extracted out of it; the explanation of (17) and (18) then parallels the explanation for extraction of a subpart of an object (see example (8) above).

The behavior of the subpart of a subject of a small clause with respect to extraction is quite different, as we have seen:

(19) *[$_{C''}$ which man$_i$ does [$_{Infl'}$ John consider [$_{AdjP}$ [$_{NP}$ relatives of t_i] idiotic]]]

The head of the subject of the small clause will not directly θ-mark either its subject or a complement. Thus the subject of the small clause fails clause (ii) of the definition of transparency and is not extraction-transparent. Extraction-transparency will rule out extraction of an element out of the subject position of a small clause. Extraction-transparency predicts that the behavior of a subject of a small clause is parallel to that of the subject of a tensed Infl.

Notice that the account of extraction that has been developed in this chapter does not rely on elements of tree geometry. It focuses, rather, on thematic relations between elements; we may treat the precise details of tree structure as purely epiphenomenal, although thematic relations are represented by means of a tree. The exact position of a phrase in a tree has no direct effect on extraction of a subpart of that phrase. In particular, the framework developed here predicts that a postposed subject should be as much an island for extraction as when the subject occurs in preverbal position. Our account is distinct from the 'connectedness' approach of Kayne (1984) which relies on direction of branching to derive the effects of the Subject Condition. The connectedness approach classes subjects of tensed clauses with subjects of small clauses by virtue of the fact that both occupy a left branch. Since extraction of a subpart of a left branch is impossible according to the connectedness framework, extraction of a subpart of small-clause and tensed-clause subjects should also be impossible.

Consider, now, the class of Exceptional Case-Marking structures (Chomsky 1981):

(20) a. John believes [$_{Infl'}$ *Bill* to be the biggest fool in the class]
      b. John considers [$_{Infl'}$ *Mary* to be the most talented student]

c. The men proved [$_{Infl'}$ *John* to be incapable of building an acceptable set of shelves]

Each of the italicized NPs in the examples in (20) is associated with a θ-role internally to the embedded Infl". Notice that the matrix verb places no selectional restrictions upon that position, as can be seen in (21); pleonastic *it* and the reserved element *there* may occur in the position of the italicized NP:

(21) a. John believes [$_{Infl'}$ *it* to be raining]
b. The men proved [$_{Infl'}$ *there* to be severe malnutrition problems among the lower economic classes]

I will assume, following Chomsky (1981), that the position in question is the subject position of an embedded clause. This position has no way of receiving Case within the embedded clause since the subject may receive Nominative Case from a tensed Infl and the clauses in question are infinitivals. The subject must receive Case from an element which is external to the embedded clause. The embedded subjects in this class of structures receive Accusative Case from the verb of the superordinate clause; see the analysis of Exceptional Case Marking in Chomsky (1981). Thus *Bill* in (20a) will receive Accusative Case from the verb *believes*, though *believe* does not θ-mark *Bill*.

If the superordinate verb assigns Case to the embedded subject then it must be true that the verb governs this position, since Case assignment transpires under government. This result is perfectly consistent with our assumptions about transparency, since the superordinate verb directly θ-marks the embedded clause; the clause boundary is, therefore, transparent to government by the verb. Exceptional Case-Marking structures, like small-clause structures, represent instances wherein a verb may govern, but not θ-mark, a particular position.

Given that the verb directly θ-marks the complement clause in Exceptional Case-Marking structures, it should be possible to extract a subpart of the complement:

(22) a. [$_{C'}$ who$_i$ does [$_{Infl'}$ John believe [$_{Infl'}$ t_i to be the biggest fool in the class]]]

b. [$_{C'}$ who$_i$ does [$_{Infl'}$ John consider [$_{Infl'}$ t_i to be the most talented student]]]

c. [$_{C'}$ who$_i$ did [$_{Infl'}$ the men prove [$_{Infl'}$ t_i to be incapable of building an acceptable set of shelves]]]

(23) a. Bill$_i$ is believed [$_{Infl'}$ t_i to be the biggest fool in the class]

b. Mary is considered [$_{Infl'}$ t_i to be the most talented student]

c. John was proven [$_{Infl'}$ t_i to be incapable of building an acceptable set of shelves]

The examples in (22) and (23) show that both wh-movement and NP-movement are possible from the embedded subject-position of an Exceptional Case-Marking structure. Like the subject of a small clause, the embedded subject of an Exceptional Case-Marking structure falls under the Subject Condition:

(24) a. [$_{C'}$ who$_i$ does [$_{Infl'}$ John believe [$_{Infl'}$ [a friend of t_i] to be the biggest fool in the class]]]

b. [$_{C'}$ who$_i$ does [$_{Infl'}$ John consider [$_{Infl'}$ [relatives of t_i] to be the most talented students]]]

c. [$_{C'}$ who$_i$ did [$_{Infl'}$ the men prove [$_{Infl'}$ [students of t_i] to be incapable of building an acceptable set of shelves]]]

The embedded subjects of Exceptional Case-Marking structures are also islands to extraction, like the subjects of small clauses.

The facts in (24) are entirely expected from the definition of transparency. Since the subject is not directly θ-marked by either the Exceptional Case-Marking verb or by the predicate of the embedded clause, it is not transparent. No subpart of the subject may be extracted. The transparency approach, then, groups together the subjects of tensed clauses, infinitive clauses, and small clauses as islands to extraction.

A similar account holds for Raising-structures, as in:

(25) a. Bill$_i$ seems [$_{Infl'}$ t_i to be the biggest fool in the class]

b. Mary$_i$ appears [$_{Infl'}$ t_i to be the most talented student]

c. John$_i$ is certain [$_{Infl'}$ t_i to be incapable of building an acceptable set of shelves]

The superordinate verb or adjective in each of the examples in (25) may not θ-mark the embedded subject-position since that position is associated with a θ-role inside the embedded clause. Furthermore, the raising predicate may not assign a θ-role to the raised subject since such θ-role assignment would violate the θ-Criterion, which forbids a single argument from receiving two thematic roles; the raised subject receives its θ-role by virtue of forming a chain with the trace in the embedded subject-position.

As with Exceptional Case-Marking structures, this analysis receives support from the fact that pleonastic *it* appears when Raising fails to apply:

(26) a. It seems [$_{Infl'}$ Bill is the biggest fool in the class]

b. It appears that [$_{Infl'}$ Mary is the most talented student]

c. It is certain that [$_{Infl'}$ John is incapable of building an acceptable set of shelves]

As the examples in (26) show, extraction is possible in Raising structures. The raising verb or adjective directly θ-marks the embedded clause which is, therefore, transparent. The embedded subject-position may be moved to the matrix subject-position, since this movement stays within a transparent domain.

The subject of complement to the raising predicates is an island to extraction, as was the case with the subjects of small clauses and the subjects of Exceptional Case-Marking structures:

(27) a. *[$_{C''}$ who$_i$ does [$_{Infl'}$ it seem [$_{C''}$ that [$_{Infl'}$ [$_{NP}$ friends of t_i] will be late]]]]

b. *[$_{C''}$ who$_i$ is [$_{Infl'}$ it likely [$_{C''}$ that [$_{Infl'}$ [$_{NP}$ relatives of t_i] will be in town]]]]

c. *[$_{C'}$ who$_i$ does [$_{Infl'}$ it appear [$_{C'}$ that [$_{Infl'}$ [$_{NP}$ pictures of t_i] will be on sale]]]]

Thus, while it is possible to extract the entire subject of a raising complement, it is impossible to extract a subpart of the subject. The account of examples in (27) is exactly parallel to the account of extraction from the subject position of a tensed clause (see the discussion of (14), above), as should be evident by inspection of the examples.

So far, I have argued that the account of transparency informally developed in section 3.1 can account for many Subject-Condition effects without further stipulation. In all of the cases we have discussed, the subject is not directly θ-marked and, therefore, is not transparent. Because an element may not be extracted from a non-transparent constituent, all of the examples in (28) are ruled out:

(28) a. *Who$_i$ did [friends of t_i] surprise John
b. *Who$_i$ does John believe [[relatives of t_i] to be incompetent]
c. *Who$_i$ does John consider [stories about t_i] offensive

The account, here, does not appeal to subjacency (Chomsky 1973, 1981, 1986), nor does it appeal to special facts about tree geometry (Kayne 1984). Instead, thematic relations are taken as defining domains within which movement may take place. I will now turn to cases of extraction from an adjunct. I will argue that extraction from an adjunct classes with extraction from a subject under the transparency account.

Adjunct-Island effects

The Adjunct-Island Condition forbids the extraction of a subpart of a modifier. Extraction from an adjunct, as in (29) and (30), is often handled either by Subjacency or by a combination of Subjacency and a filter that rules out traces marked with Oblique Case when an adjunct preposition is stranded (as in Hornstein and Weinberg 1981):

(29) a. *Which inning$_i$ did the Yankees lose the ball game during t_i
b. *Which critical paper$_i$ did you write a review of Walter's new novel [without consulting t_i]

(30) *Where$_i$ did John get lost [walking t_i]

The bracketed phrases in (29b) and (30) are not subcategorized complements of any head. It follows, then, that these phrases will not receive θ-roles. Since adjuncts are not complements of a head and bear no marking relation with the head, they will never count as transparent domains. In the above examples the wh-element had to cross the maximal projection of the adjunct, in order to land in the Spec of the matrix Comp; hence, each of the examples will count as violations of extraction-transparency.

Similar effects hold for sentential adjuncts which act as predicates of the event denoted by the superordinate clause. Although these adjuncts may predicate something of some subject or, possibly, act in the creation of complex predicates, they do not receive a thematic role from any element. Consider the examples in (31):

(31) a. John eats his dessert [faster than he eats his vegetables]
b. Bill carried the table [without any help]
c. John twisted Bill's arm [to get him to confess to the crime]

Extraction from the bracketed phrases is ungrammatical:

(32) a. *What$_i$ does John eat his dessert [faster than he eats t_i]
b. *What$_i$ did Bill carry the table [without t_i]
c. *What$_i$ did John twist Bill's arm [to get him to confess to t_i]

Under the framework of assumptions developed here, it is clear that the above elements are not assigned a thematic role by direct θ-marking. Hence, the bracketed phrases cannot be transparent and no element may be extracted out of them.[3]

Thematic domains and bounding

Nominalizations

I have, so far, been developing the case for a thematic approach to the problem of defining locality for extraction. A phrase that is not directly θ-marked by a verb or adjective is not sufficiently transparent to permit extraction, although the entire phrase may be extracted provided the extraction stays within a transparent domain. For example, the complement of an adjunct prepositional phrase may not be extracted, although the entire prepositional phrase may be moved:

(33) a. *Which class$_i$ does John tend to fall asleep during t_i
b. [during which class]$_j$ does John tend to fall asleep t_j

According to the assumptions made in Chapter 2, nouns and prepositions do not directly θ-mark their complements. Hence, these complements should not be transparent to extraction. We have already seen that the complement to a subcategorized preposition is not transparent to extraction (the examples in (11), repeated here):

(34) a. *Who$_i$ did John give pencils to [friends of t_i]
b. *Of whom$_i$ did John give pencils to [friends t_i]
c. *Who$_i$ did John talk about [relatives of t_i]
d. *Of whom$_i$ did John talk about [relatives t_i]

Since the preposition merely serves to transmit a θ-role from the verb, it is not a direct θ-marker and does not induce co-superscripting. As a result, its complement is not transparent to extraction and the examples in (34) are ruled out.

In general, nominal complements and modifiers should class with prepositional complements, subjects, and adjuncts with respect to transparency. This prediction fails in certain, relatively well-defined, instances, as we will see. Let us first review the case of NP-movement within an NP and then turn to wh-movement.

As was observed in Chapter 2, pseudo-passives do not occur in (non-retroactive) NPs:

(35) a. *[$_{N''}$ the boat's$_i$ [$_{N'}$ decision [$_{PP}$ on t_i]]]
b. *[$_{N''}$ the men's$_i$ [$_{N'}$ conversation [$_{PP}$ with t_i]]]

c. *[$_{N''}$ the issue's$_i$ [$_{N'}$ arguments [$_{PP}$ over t_i]]]
d. *[$_{N''}$ the problem's$_i$ [$_{N'}$ thought [$_{PP}$ about t_i]]]

In these examples, the complement prepositional phrase does not receive a θ-role under direct θ-marking. The phrase is, then, not a transparent domain and no phrase may be extracted out of the PP. Notice that prenominal Genitive NPs will also fail to receive a θ-role under direct θ-marking and, so, should also be non-transparent. This predicts that extraposition out of the prenominal Genitive should be ill-formed, although postposing the entire Genitive NP may be possible:[4]

(36) a. [$_{N''}$ [$_{N'}$ a friend of John]'s book]
b. *[$_{N''}$ [$_{N'}$ a friend t_i]'s book [of John]$_i$]
c. [a book [of a friend of John]'s]

Since the prenominal Genitive cannot acquire a superscript under θ-marking, no subpart of the prenominal Genitive may be extraposed via movement.

Compare the above cases with the case of retroactive nominals discussed at length in the second chapter. Recall that the structure of a well-formed example of these nominals will be as in (37a), while an ill-formed example is shown in (37b):

(37) a. ... needs [$_{N''}$ PRO$_i$ some [$_{N'}$ working [$_{PP}$ on t_i]]] ...
b. *... needs [$_{N''}$ PRO$_i$ some [$_{N'}$ discussion [$_{PP}$ about t_i]]] ...

Both of the traces in (37a) and (37b) could be properly governed, since prepositions act as lexical governors; hence, I will assume that the ungrammaticality of (37b) does not follow from a violation of the ECP. Consider (37a) with respect to the version of transparency outlined above. The verb that governs the nominal, *need*, subcategorizes for a noun phrase of the proper morphological class (1-*ing*). Since *working* may be an instance of this class, the lexical requirements of *need* are satisfied. Members of the 1-*ing* class are indistinguishable from verbs at the single-bar level, and so *working* may directly θ-mark the prepositional phrase headed by *on*. Since the status of a maximal projection as a transparent domain is determined by θ-marking relations, the PP will be transparent in (37a). Hence, the derivation of (37a) is well-formed, as it violates neither transparency nor the ECP.

The head noun, *discussion*, in (37b) is not a 1-*ing* nominal. Hence, the noun will not θ-mark its complement PP. If this is so, then let us suppose that the PP does not stand in a proper marking-relation with any element. Now, the PP will count as non-transparent with respect to extraction of its object. The complement PP is, therefore, an island to extraction and (37b) is ruled out. The asymmetry between retroactive nominals and other types of nominals follows easily from the notion of transparency developed here.

I have so far restricted the discussion to NP-movement inside an NP. As the above examples show, such movement is highly restricted; in general, it appears that only complements governed by the head noun may move inside the NP. I will now turn to wh-movement of nominal complements. These cases correspond to cases of the complex-NP constraint of Ross (1967):

(38) a. *Who$_i$ did John see [$_{NP}$ the man [$_{C''}$ who$_j$ [$_{Infl'}$ t_j likes t_i]]]
   b. ?Who$_i$ does John believe [$_{NP}$ the rumor [$_{C''}$ that [$_{Infl'}$ Mary knows t_i]]]

Example (38a) illustrates movement out of a relative-clause modifier of a noun. In such a case, the relative clause is not a subcategorized complement and is not θ-marked by the noun. There is, then, no possibility that the relative clause will bear a superscript, and so it must be non-transparent to extraction. Since (38a) involves extraction out of a relative clause, it will be ruled ungrammatical.

Example (38b) contains a complement to the noun. Since we have been assuming that nouns do not directly θ-mark their complements, the account of (38b) is analogous to the account of (38a). Notice, however, that (38b) is somewhat more acceptable than (38a); I will provide an account of the contrast between (38a) and (38b) in a moment.

A more difficult case is illustrated in (39), which involves extraction from an object NP (see Bach 1977; Bach and Horn 1976; Chomsky 1977):

(39) a. Who$_i$ did you take [$_{NP}$ a picture of t_i]
 b. Who$_i$ did you hear [$_{NP}$ stories about t_i]
 c. Which theorem$_i$ did you read [$_{NP}$ a proof of t_i]

In example (39b), for instance, a preposition inside the object NP has been stranded. Unless some other process applies to the representation of (39b), this should be impossible, since the prepositional phrase is not assigned a θ-role, and so is not transparent. Hence, the prepositional phrase should be an island for extraction (compare these cases with the account of (35)).

One possibility is to assume that the cases in (39) follow from a marked process of restructuring (see Chomsky 1977 for one such proposal). For example, one might propose the following:

(40) If A directly assigns a θ-role to B, then A and the head of B may form a complex predicate, [$_A$ $A+B$], where the arguments of B are inherited as arguments of $A+B$.

The rule in (40) may be sensitive to various properties of A and B. I will put aside such questions, leaving them as a problem for future research.

As a result of (40), the verb *hear* can form a complex predicate with *stories* in (39b):

(41) Who$_i$ did you [$_V$ hear + stories] [$_{PP}$ about t_i]

The restructuring process in (41) results in a configuration where the PP headed by *about* is governed and directly θ-marked by a verb. Therefore, the PP is co-superscripted with the complex verb, [hear + stories].

The account of restructuring, given above, does not alter the account of examples like those in (34) if (40) cannot apply to its own output. The verb would have to restructure with both the subcategorized preposition and the complement of the preposition in (42):

(42) *Who did you give pencils to friend of t

The restructuring account may provide the key to the contrast between (38a) and (38b). Recall that extraction out of the sentential complement of an object noun was virtually well-formed. If the object noun can assimilate with the verb, making its sentential complement a complement of the new complex verb, then extraction out of the sentential complement should be well-formed. If the NP were to be embedded inside a PP, however, extraction should become worse:

(43) a. Bill had never heard about [the rumor that John loves Mary]
b. *Who$_i$ had Bill never heard about [the rumor that John loves t_i]

The clausal complement to *rumor* is not directly θ-marked by the head noun and cannot become a complement of a complex verb since the head of the PP, *about*, is the only argument directly θ-marked by the verb *hear*. Since *about* intervenes between *hear* and *rumor*, and since restructuring cannot apply twice, the derivation of (43b) is ruled out by transparency. Notice that a relative clause on an object NP will never enter into a direct θ-marking relation even if the object restructures with the verb. Since the relative clause is a modifier, it does not satisfy the lexical requirements of either the noun or the verb. Since (40) does not create new arguments, the relative clause will not be directly θ-marked by the complex verb. The account of (38a), then, remains unchanged.

Finally, pseudo-passivization inside NP is unaffected by (40), since restructuring is triggered by a direct θ-marker and nouns are not in this class. Note that a verb external to the NP could restructure with the head noun to form a complex verb, but then the passivized NP could not move to a position between the D-Structure verb and the head noun since the latter form a complex word (Lapointe 1980).

I should note that this account predicts that there should be a language which allows preposition stranding but, unlike English, does not allow preposition stranding with the complement of an object noun. Such a language would lack the restructuring process described in (40). I know of no such cases, so I will leave (40) as a tentative suggestion.

Summary

In this section I have considered cases of violations of the Subject Condition and the Adjunct-Island Condition as well as examples involving extraction from nominal complements. In all cases, the transparency condition described in section 3.1 made the correct cut. Extraction from subjects, adjuncts, and nominal complements involved extraction out of a non-transparent domain and were ruled out.

The account of these conditions made no appeal to either the Empty Category Principle or Subjacency. The character of transparency, however, seems to classify it as a bounding condition like Subjacency. Furthermore, since the relevant cases of the Complex-NP Constraint followed from transparency, we might suppose that NP is not, in general, a bounding node for Subjacency (see the discussion of Subjacency, below). Finally, transparency yielded an account of the nature of retroactive nominals that does not rely on the Empty Category Principle.

It remains for me to clarify the formulation of transparency and to determine what level or levels of representation make use of the notion of transparency. I will pursue this problem in sections 3.3–3.4. In the next section I will compare the informal notion of transparency with the formulation of government proposed in Chomsky (1986), the 'barriers' framework. I will argue that the barriers account must be supplemented by the notion of transparency formulated here.

3.3 Barriers and transparency

Chomsky (1986) attempts to unify the principles underlying the Empty Category Principle and Subjacency. He argues that both the theory of proper government and the theory of bounding can be unified by the notion of government. In essence, Chomsky's definition of government relies on lexical-marking relations (including direct θ-marking) to provide a core government configuration. Government itself is then defined recursively with respect to the core case.

Since the notion of 'barrier', which plays a central role in Chomsky's system, is contingent on θ-marking, the barriers framework shares some assumptions with the transparency framework developed here. I will argue, however, that the barriers framework must adopt the notion of transparency as discussed in the previous sections if it is to account for the same range of data. The two systems, in fact, are not incompatible, although some redundancies will exist if transparency is incorporated in the barriers framework. In the next subsections, I will review the barriers system and then compare its predictions with the predictions made by transparency.

The Barriers *system*

Exclusion, L-marking, and government

Chomsky (1986) assumes that the core case of government is exemplified by the relation that holds between a head and a subcategorized complement:

(44)

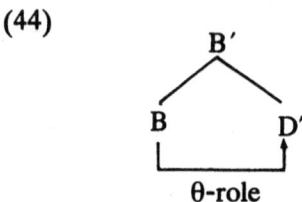

When a head B assigns a θ-role to its complement, D'', the two must occur as sisters in a strict sense; that is B and D'' must be immediately dominated by the same node (B'). Chomsky defines this relationship as 'direct θ-marking' and takes it as the core case of government:

(45)   θ-*government*
A θ-governs B if and only if A is a zero-level category that (directly) θ-marks B, and A, B are sisters.

Thus, a verb θ-governs its object and a noun θ-governs its complement.

If a head θ-governs its complement and the head is of a lexical category (a noun, verb, preposition, or adjective), then the head is said to 'L-mark' its complement:

(46)   L-*marking*
Where A is a lexical category, A L-marks B if and only if B agrees with the head of D that is θ-governed by A.

Since a phrase agrees with its own head, any item that is θ-governed by a lexical head will be L-marked by that head. In general, nouns, verbs, adjectives, and prepositions L-mark their complements, while Infl and Comp do not L-mark their complements, since they are not lexical.

The basic insight is that phrases which are not L-marked constitute barriers to government. That is, an element cannot govern into a phrase which is not L-marked. Furthermore, the notion of barrier is a relation that holds between a governor, a potential barrier, and a governed element; phrases which are not L-marked can transmit their barrierhood to nodes which dominate them. Thus, an Infl″ may not constitute a barrier by itself, but it can turn the C″ which dominates it into a barrier.

In order to capture these relationships, *barrier* is defined recursively with respect to phrases which are not L-marked ('blocking categories'):

(47) *Blocking category (BC)*
 A is a BC for B if and only if A is not L-marked and A dominates B.

(48) *Barrier*
 A is a barrier for B if and only if (a) or (b):
 (a) dominates D, D is a BC for B;
 (b) A is a BC for B, $A \neq $ Infl″.

In order to see how the above definitions work, let us consider two examples: Exceptional Case-Marking; and the distribution of PRO. Suppose, first, that A governs B just so long as no barriers separate them. An instance of Exceptional Case Marking is shown in (49a) and two possible representations are shown in (49b) and (49c):

(49) a. John believes Bill to be late.
 b. John [$_{VP}$ believes [$_{Infl″}$ Bill to be late]]
 c. John [$_{VP}$ believes [$_{C″}$ [$_{Infl″}$ Bill to be late]]]

The verb directly θ-marks the Infl″ in (49b) but not in (49c). In (49b), then, the Infl″ is θ-governed and L-marked by the verb. As a result, no barriers separate *believes* from *Bill* in (49b), so the verb can assign Case to *Bill*. In (49c), however, *believe* cannot L-mark the Infl″. The head of C″, Comp, is not lexical, and so cannot be an L-marker. As a result, the Infl″ is not L-marked and counts as a blocking category. Since C″ dominates the Infl″, it inherits barrierhood from Infl" by clause (a) of (48). So C" constitutes a barrier to government of *Bill* by the verb. Hence, the verb cannot assign Case to *Bill* and (49c) is thrown out by the Case filter.

Consider, now, a control case as in (50):

(50) a. John tried to be on time.
b. John [$_{VP}$ tried [$_{Infl'}$ PRO to be on time]]
c. John [$_{VP}$ tried [$_{C'}$ [$_{Infl'}$ PRO to be on time]]]

The structure in (50b) is exactly analogous to (49b). No barriers separate the verb from PRO, so the verb governs PRO. Since PRO cannot be governed, (50b) is ruled out. Example (50c) is analogous to example (49c). C" inherits barrierhood from Infl" since Infl" is not L-marked. Thus, C" is a barrier to government of PRO by *try*.

Before stating the formal definition of government, it is necessary to point out some properties of the transformational rule, 'move alpha'. The transformation may either substitute the moved element for an empty position or 'chomsky-adjoin' the moved element to another phrase. Chomsky-adjunction creates structures of the form shown in (51), where B" has been chomsky-adjoined to D":

(51)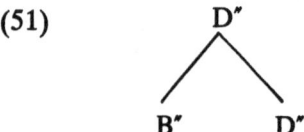

Chomsky assumes that B" may be adjoined to D" just in case D" is not assigned a θ-role. For our purposes, an element may chomsky-adjoin to an adjunct, VP, or Infl', but not to a subcategorized phrase or a subject. We will refer to the two copies of D" in (51) as 'segments' of D".

Following the work of May (1985), Chomsky adopts the convention that, if no segment of the maximal projection dominates A, then the maximal projection is said to 'exclude' A.

(52) *Exclusion*
A excludes B if no segment of A dominates B.

Thematic domains and bounding

Returning to the tree in (51), D'' does not exclude B'', although not every segment of D'' dominates B''.

Government can now be defined as in (54):

(53) *M-command*
A m-commands B if and only if A does not dominate B, and every maximal projection dominating A dominates B.

(54) *Government*
A governs B if and only if A m-commands B and there is no D, D a barrier for B such that D excludes A.

In the next subsection, we will briefly show how the above definition relates to the Empty Category Principle and to Subjacency. We will then be in a position to compare the predictions made by the barriers system with those made by transparency.

The ECP and Subjacency

The ECP requires that a trace be properly governed by some element. Proper government is a special case of government:

(55) *Proper government*
A properly governs B if and only if A θ-governs B or A antecedent-governs B.

Antecedent-government is the special case of government where the antecedent of an empty category is in a position to govern the empty category. θ-government is as defined in (45), above. By this definition, Infl cannot be a proper governor for an empty category in subject position since it cannot be a θ-governor (Infl is not lexical) and it is not the antecedent for the empty category (at least in English). It follows that an empty category in subject position must be antecedent-governed.

Consider the representation in (56):

(56) I wonder [$_{C''}$ who$_i$ [$_{C'}$ Comp [$_{Infl''}$ t_i [$_{Infl'}$ Infl [$_{VP}$ saw John]]]]]

The embedded clause in (56) contains a trace in subject position; the antecedent of the trace is in the Spec of Comp. Notice that *who* is separated from the trace by Infl″ which is not L-marked. By clause (b) of the definition of barrier (48), however, Infl" is not a barrier unless it inherits barrierhood from another barrier. Hence, the embedded Infl" is not a barrier to government from the Spec of Comp. As a result, *who* can govern the trace in subject position. Since *who* is the antecedent of the trace, the trace is properly governed, according to definition (55).

Recall that a trace in object position will always be θ-governed, and properly governed, by a head. As a result, the ECP should admit traces in the object position of nouns, verbs, prepositions, and adjectives, since all of these categories are lexical.

Following Lasnik and Saito (1984), Chomsky assumes that traces are marked according to whether or not they are properly governed. This marking assigns the features [+gamma] to properly governed traces and [−gamma] to traces which are not properly governed. Empty categories in argument positions are gamma-marked at S-Structure and empty categories in non-argument positions (Spec of Comp, adjuncts, and chomsky-adjoined positions) are gamma-marked at the level of LF. The marking applies indelibly so that a [−gamma] empty category cannot become [+gamma] by having its antecedent move to a position which governs it; equally, a [+gamma] empty category cannot be re-marked [−gamma] by having its antecedent deleted.

The form of the grammar with respect to gamma-marking and the ECP is shown in (57). Notice that Chomsky assumes, again following Lasnik and Saito (1984), that non-obligatory elements may be deleted at LF. Thus, traces which are not antecedent governors and which are not required by the θ-Criterion or the Extended Projection Principle may be deleted. Furthermore, *that* complementizers may also be deleted:

(57)   D-Structure
          |
        S-Structure ← gamma-marking of A-positions

         PF   LF ← gamma-marking of
                       non-A-positions and new
                       traces in A-positions;
                       optional deletion of
                       non-obligatory elements.
                       The ECP.

The ECP can be simply stated as in (58):

(58) *The Empty Category Principle*
 • [e]
  [−gamma]

To illustrate the effects of the ECP, consider the representation in (59) (irrelevant details omitted):

(59) *[$_{C''}$ how$_i$ [$_{C'}$ did [$_{Infl''}$ John [$_{VP}$ wonder [$_{C''}$ what$_j$ [$_{Infl''}$ Bill [$_{VP}$ fixed t_j] t_i]]]]]]

The above involves extraction of an adjunct (*how*) from a wh-island. The trace of *what* occupies the object position of the verb *fix*, so it is θ-governed. Since θ-governed positions are properly governed, the trace of *what*, t_j, is marked [+gamma] at S-Structure. Consider the trace of *how*, t_i. This trace is in a non-argument position, so it is not θ-governed. In order to pass the ECP, it must be antecedent-governed at LF. Its antecedent, however, is in the Comp of the matrix clause. Since the embedded Infl″ is not L-marked (its governor, Comp, is not lexical), the embedded Infl″ is a blocking category with respect to material in the matrix clause. The embedded C″ is a barrier, since it dominates the blocking category, Infl″. Since at least one barrier separates *how* from its trace, *how* cannot antecedent-govern the trace. As a result, the trace is marked [−gamma] at LF and violates the ECP.

Compare the ungrammaticality of (59), with the more acceptable (60):

(60) *[$_{C''}$ what$_j$ [$_{C'}$ did [$_{Infl''}$ John [$_{VP}$ wonder [$_{C''}$ how$_i$ [$_{Infl''}$ Bill [$_{VP}$ fixed t_j] t_i]]]]]]

In (60) *how* antecedent-governs its trace, since Infl″ is not a barrier, although it is a blocking category (clause (b) of the definition of barrier (48)). Hence, t_i is marked [+gamma] at LF and passes the ECP. Furthermore, the trace of *what* is θ-governed by *fix*, and so is marked [+gamma] at S-Structure. Thus, the empty categories in (60) uniformly pass the ECP. The acceptability of (60) is down-graded, however, since it violates the Subjacency Condition.

The Subjacency Condition can be stated as a relation between two positions: the landing site of a moved element and the position that the element moved from. Supposing, following Chomsky (1981, 1986) that 'move alpha' establishes a chain of positions, then Subjacency can be stated as a condition on adjacent links of the chain:

(61) *The Subjacency Condition*
If (a_i, a_{i+1}) is a link of a chain, then a_{i+1} is 1-subjacent to a_i.

(62) *Subjacency*
B is n-subjacent to A if and only if there are fewer than $n+1$ barriers for B that exclude A.

In order to derive the classical subjacency effects for English (see Chomsky 1973), it is necessary to assume that a tensed Infl″ always counts as an inherent barrier for the Subjacency Condition, although it does not count as an inherent barrier for the other conditions. With this in mind, let us return to (60). Recall that the empty categories in (60) uniformly obeyed the ECP. The embedded object, however, had been moved a long distance to the Spec of the Comp in the matrix clause:

(60) *[$_{C″}$ what$_j$ [$_{C′}$ did [$_{Infl″}$ John [$_{VP}$ wonder [$_{C″}$ how$_i$ [$_{Infl″}$ Bill [$_{VP}$ fixed t_j] t_i]]]]]]

The embedded Infl″ counts as an inherent barrier for Subjacency with respect to the trace of *what*. The C″ which dominates Infl″ inherits barrierhood from the embedded Infl″. There are, then, at least two barriers between the trace of *what* and the next link in the chain. Example (60) violates the Subjacency Condition, since there is a chain which has adjacent links that are not 1-subjacent to each other.

The Minimality Condition and the ECP

I will conclude this brief review of the barriers framework with a discussion of the Minimality Condition, which will become important when we compare barriers with transparency. Consider example (63):

(63)   *[$_{C''}$ who$_i$ do [$_{Infl''}$ you [$_{VP}$ wonder [$_{C''}$ t_i [$_{C'}$ if [$_{Infl''}$ t_i saw John]]]]]]

Example (63) is quite ungrammatical, although nothing so far predicts this. The trace in the embedded subject-position is antecedent-governed by the trace in the Spec of the embedded Comp, since Infl", although it is not L-marked, cannot count as a barrier. The subject trace will therefore be marked [+gamma] at S-Structure; the status of the trace in the Spec of Comp is of little concern since it may be deleted at LF – it has already done its job of antecedent-governing the subject trace at S-Structure.

Intuitively, the presence of the lexical complementizer *if* should cause a violation of the ECP. Chomsky (1986) proposes that *A* can be prevented from governing *B* if a potential governor of *B* intervenes between *A* and *B*:

(64)   *Minimality*

A is a barrier for *B* if *A* is the immediate projection of *D*, a zero-level category distinct from *B*.

In essence, a single-bar projection can be a barrier to government. Chomsky, then, allows single-bar projections to be pruned from a representation if either the head has no features (a null complementizer, for instance) or the single-bar level dominates exactly the same material that the maximal projection dominates.

Returning to (63), the presence of the complementizer *if* means that the head of Comp has features. The presence of the trace in the Spec of Comp means that C" does not dominate the same material that C' dominates. Hence, C' cannot be eliminated. But now C' is a barrier to government according to (64). As a result, the trace in Comp cannot antecedent-govern the trace in subject position and the latter is marked [−gamma] at S-Structure. At LF, the ECP will filter out the representation.

A final note on minimality; the Minimality Condition does not count in establishing whether or not adjacent links in a chain are 1-subjacent. Minimality applies in establishing proper government and Case-marking, however.

Summary

In the preceding subsections, I have attempted to provide a

condensed review of the barriers framework of Chomsky (1986). The framework, however, is extremely subtle and the reader is encouraged to examine Chomsky's monograph (Chomsky 1986) for a more detailed exposition.

The L-marking relation lies at the heart of the barriers system and provides the foundation for the definition of government which is crucial both to the ECP and to the Subjacency Condition. Since L-marking relations rely on direct θ-marking, it would appear that my notion of transparency is extremely similar to L-marking. I will argue in the next subsection that, in fact, transparency must co-exist with the ECP and the Subjacency Condition, even if the latter two are defined in terms of L-marking. This result indicates that transparency is a condition in its own right and not a special case of either Subjacency or the ECP.

A comparison of barriers and transparency

The transparency framework outlined in section 3.1 allows extraction from a phrase just in case that phrase bears a superscript, where superscripts are assigned under direct θ-marking. Transparency groups together subjects, adjuncts, and unrestructured nominal complements as islands to extraction, as I showed in section 3.2. I will now show that the barriers framework does not make these predictions; subjects of certain types of predicates, adjuncts, and nominal complements are not islands to extraction. If the barriers framework is to be maintained, then some notion of transparency similar to that outlined in section 3.1 must be adopted.

Subjects

Consider the examples in (65):

(65) a. *Who$_i$ does John believe [$_{\text{Infl}'}$ [$_{\text{NP}}$ stories about t_i] to be true]

      b. *Which president$_i$ does John consider [$_{\text{AdjP}}$ [$_{\text{NP}}$ rumors about t_i] vicious]

The subjects of Exceptional Case-Marking clauses and small clauses, although governed by a verb, are not directly θ-marked by the verb. Hence, such subjects are not transparent and no element may be extracted out of them.

Notice, however, that the verb does L-mark the Infl" in (65a) and the AdjP in (65b). Since the subject of a clause or small clause agrees with the head (Chomsky 1986), both subjects in (65) are L-marked. As a result, neither of the subjects count as blocking categories and no barriers are created. Hence, the chains in both examples obey the Subjacency Condition. The empty categories, furthermore, obey the ECP, since both are θ-governed by the preposition *about*.

In general, the barriers framework predicts that Subject-Condition effects hold only for the subjects of tensed clauses. While I agree that the violations in (65) are not as bad as extraction from within the subject of a tensed clause, they are not fully acceptable. This indicates that the transparency effect exists in addition to the Subjacency Condition; the cumulative effect of violations of both transparency and subjacency will down-grade Subject-Condition effects in tensed clauses. In small clauses and infinitivals, only transparency will be violated.

Adjuncts

Consider the examples in (66):

(66) a. *Who$_i$ did John leave the party because t_i insulted him

b. *Why$_i$ did John leave the party [because Bill insulted him t_i]

Both examples violate the Adjunct-Island Condition; the subject of an adjunct has been extracted in (66a) and the adverbial modifier of an adjunct has been extracted in (66b).

Consider a derivation of (66a) within the barriers framework. I will assume that *because* is in the head of the Comp of the adjunct clause. The D-Structure of (66a) is shown in (67):

(67) $[_{C''} [_{Infl''}$ John $[_{Infl'}$ Infl $[_{VP}$ leave the party]] $[_{C''} [_{C'} [_C$ because] $[_{Infl''}$ who insulted him]]]]]

If *who* is moved to the Spec of the adjunct Comp, then a minimality violation will result and the ECP will rule out the derivation.

Notice, however, that nothing forces *who* to move to the Spec of Comp. Since the adjunct clause does not receive a θ-role, *who* may chomsky-adjoin to the adjunct C″, by the convention regarding chomsky-adjunction. If this happens, then C″ dominates the same material that C′ dominates and C′ may be pruned, again by conventions regarding the presence of intermediate projections.

The above gives the following intermediate representation:

(68) $[_{C''} [_{Infl''} \text{John} [_{Infl'} \text{Infl} [_{VP} \text{leave the party}]] [_{C''} \text{who}_i [_{C'} [_C \text{because}] [_{Infl'} t_i \text{ insulted him}]]]]]$

Since C″ is not an immediate projection of Comp, the minimality condition will not apply to the relation between the position occupied by *who* in (68) and the trace in subject position. A further application of 'move alpha' will move *who* to the matrix Comp, giving (69) as an S-Structure:

(69) $[_{C''} \text{who}_i [_{Infl''} \text{John} [_{Infl'} \text{Infl} [_{VP} \text{leave the party}]] [_{C''} t_i [_{C''} [_C \text{because}] [_{Infl'} t_i \text{ insulted him}]]]]]$

Consider the relationship between the trace adjoined to C″ and the trace in subject position in (69). Infl″ dominates that latter trace and is not L-marked. By clause (b) of the definition of barrier, however, nfl″ is not a barrier. The C″, since it is an adjunct, is not L-marked either and, furthermore, it inherits barrierhood from Infl″. The C″ does not exclude the intermediate trace, however. Hence, the C″ does not count as a barrier either. If this is so, then no barriers intervene between the trace in subject position and the intermediate trace. As a result, the trace in subject position is antecedent-governed at S-Structure and is marked [+gamma]. Since the intermediate trace would not be gamma-marked until LF (it is not in an argument position) and since it may freely delete, its status is irrelevant. This argument can equally be applied to the derivation of (66b).

The above argument shows that (66a) is not a violation of the ECP. Careful inspection should also reveal that the chain of *who* obeys the Subjacency Condition at S-Structure. I conclude that, in absence of any auxiliary principles,[5] the barriers framework cannot account for violations of the Adjunct-Island Condition of the form exemplified by (66a).

Notice that transparency will rule out such examples. All we require is that the segment of the phrase dominating the moved element bear a superscript assigned under direct θ-marking. Since no segment of an adjunct will ever bear such a superscript, transparency will derive the Adjunct-Island Condition.

Nominals

Let us return to the case of pseudo-passives within NP:

(70) a. *$[_{NP}$ the boat's$_i$ $[_{N'}$ decision $[_{PP}$ on $t_i]]]$
 b. *$[_{NP}$ this bed's$_i$ $[_{N'}$ sleeping $[_{PP}$ in $t_i]]]$

Suppose that the head preposition θ-marks its complement. Then the empty categories in (70) are θ-governed and pass the ECP. Suppose, furthermore, that the head noun θ-marks its complement. Then the PP is L-marked and does not constitute a barrier. NP movement, then, crosses no barriers and the Subjacency Condition is obeyed. On the other hand, suppose that the head noun does not θ-mark the PP, as was argued in Chapter 2. Then movement will cross one barrier, which still obeys the Subjacency Condition.

Notice, then, that we cannot distinguish between the retroactive nominals in (71) using only the ECP and the Subjacency Condition:

(71) a. This idea bears some thinking about.
 b. *This idea bears some thought about.

It is possible to maintain that (71b) is an ECP violation under the assumption that neither nouns nor prepositions are θ-markers. In that case, the empty category is not θ-governed by the preposition. Furthermore, the empty category cannot be antecedent-governed since its PP is not L-marked and would constitute a barrier. Antecedent-government would still be possible in (71a), since *thinking* retains the θ-marking characteristics of a verb and would L-mark the PP, if the analysis of affixation from Chapter 2 is adopted.

Consider the violation of the Complex-NP Constraint discussed above with regard to example (43):

113

Thematic domains and bounding

(72) Who$_i$ had Bill never heard about [the rumor that John loves t_i]

If *about* L-marks its complement and *rumor* L-marks the embedded clause, the extraction of *who* from the embedded clause will cross no barriers. As a result, the Subjacency Condition is not violated and (72) should be well-formed.

As we have seen, the assumptions from Chapter 2 regarding the thematic properties of nouns and prepositions and transparency rules (72) out. If the analysis of restructuring presented in section 3.2 is on the right track, then we can also distinguish the ungrammatical (72) from the more acceptable (73):

(73) Who$_i$ did John hear a rumor that Bill likes t_i

The transparency condition again makes the proper cut with respect to nominal complements. This gives more support to the hypothesis that transparency plays a role as an independent principle of grammar.

Summary

In this section, I have presented the barriers framework of Chomsky (1986) and contrasted the framework with transparency. Transparency successfully rules out violations of the Subject Condition and the Adjunct-Island Condition that are not ruled out by either the ECP or the Subjacency Condition. Since both the ECP and Subjacency appear to be independently motivated, it is fair to conclude that transparency exists as an independent part of core grammar, which serves as a further constraint on the boundedness of movement. I will now move on to consider the formulation of transparency in more detail.

3.4 Extensions to transparency

The transparency framework seems to be making the right cut. Subjects, adjuncts, and certain other positions, like complements to nouns and prepositions, are islands to extraction. On the other hand, arguments which are θ-marked, like subcategorized complements of a verb, are transparent to extraction. In the preceding section, I argued that transparency could not be derived from the ECP and the Subjacency Condition. In the following subsections, I will consider the relationship between subjacency and transparency more carefully as well as exploring the relationship between transparency and levels of representation. Finally, I will explore some ways to simplify the definition of transparency presented in section 3.1.

Further effects of transparency

Subjacency and transparency

I have noted above that the effects of extraction-transparency closely parallel those of Subjacency. It is reasonable to ask whether we could simply replace Subjacency with the notion of extraction-transparency, since both conditions proscribe certain boundary conditions of syntactic movement and their effects seem almost identical.

The answer to the above question is clearly negative. Once a maximal projection is determined to be transparent, extraction may apply freely. A set of nested transparent domains is transparent and the assumptions developed above say nothing about extracting an element from the most deeply embedded domain out of the topmost domain in one step. In other words, the framework developed in this chapter does not place a condition on the maximal distance across which extraction may apply, given that all the nodes separating the landing site from the locus of extraction are transparent; but this is completely unlike Subjacency.

It is useful to consider a concrete example:

(74) $^*[_{C'}$ which book$_i$ do $[_{Infl'}$ you wonder $[_{C'}$ who$_j$ $[_{Infl'}$ t_j read $t_i]]]]$

Example (74) is a violation of Subjacency, since the wh-quantified NP, *which book*, must cross at least two barriers in one step. The example, however, does not extract out of a domain which is not transparent. This is simply because the wh-quantified NP is never extracted from a maximal projection that fails to meet the conditions laid down by the definition of transparency, as the reader may verify.

One could imagine ways of modifying transparency to capture

the effects of Subjacency. Some degree of caution, however, is in order. It is well known, for example, that Subjacency must be parameterized to account for the fact that in some languages Infl" is a bounding node, while C" counts as a bounding node in other languages (see, for example, Rizzi 1982; or Sportiche 1981; for a recent exposition, see Chomsky 1986). Given the assumptions of this chapter, such a variation must arise from parameters in thematic theory. The exact nature of such a parameter or set of parameters is unclear and would take much care to explore.

For present purposes, I will simply advocate that we maintain the version of Subjacency discussed in Chomsky (1986). Movement may not cross two barriers in a single step where Infl" and C" count as inherent barriers for Subjacency (see section 3.3). Languages select the inherent barriers for Subjacency from the set (C", Infl"). I will assume, finally, that Subjacency and transparency are both elements of the module of grammar concerned with boundary conditions.

Bridge verbs

I should note that transparency does allow for a simple treatment of cases that have classically been analyzed in terms of Subjacency. The standard account (e.g., Chomsky 1973) was that Infl", C", and NP formed the set of bounding nodes for English. The presence of C" in the set of bounding nodes was motivated by the effects of extraction from the complements of non-bridge verbs and by Subject-Condition effects, as in (75a) and (75b), respectively:

(75) a. *$[_{C''}$ who$_i$ did $[_{Infl''}$ John whisper $[_{C''}$ that $[_{Infl''}$ Mary saw t_i]]]]
b. *$[_{C''}$ who$_i$ $[_{Infl''}$ (did) $[_{C''}$ that $[_{Infl''}$ Mary saw t_i]] surprise John]]

I have argued that the Subject-Condition effect in (75b) follows from transparency, given that the C" in subject position is not θ-marked by a head. Thus, Subject-Condition effects do not motivate the presence of C" in the set of bounding nodes for English.

Consider non-bridge phenomena. The account given in Chomsky (1980) is that, while C" generally counts as a bounding node, bridge verbs have the lexical property of rendering their C" complements transparent to Subjacency. Notice that if bridge verbs could not do this, apparent long-distance dependencies would be impossible in English, since Comp-to-Comp movement necessarily crosses a C" and an Infl" in one step:

(76) [$_{C''}$ who$_i$ did [$_{Infl''}$ John say [$_{C''}$ t_i[$_{Infl''}$ Mary saw t_i']]]]

Non-bridge verbs, then, fail to render the C" which they govern transparent to Subjacency. Hence, extraction out of the complement of a non-bridge verb will always violate Subjacency. Notice that the ability to render a C" transparent to Subjacency is taken as a lexical property of certain verbs, the unmarked case is that of non-bridge verbs.

Given the present framework, we might take a different approach to the bridge/non-bridge distinction. Transparency is contingent on bearing a superscript which, itself, reflects the fact that the phrase has been directly θ-marked by a head. In general then, the C" complement to a verb will be θ-marked by the verb and, hence, transparent. We might suppose that non-bridge verbs have the marked property of not θ-marking their complement clauses; non-bridge verbs may, for example, have the thematic properties of nouns (no direct θ-marking). If so, then the complement to a non-bridge verb will never be transparent. Such a complement will not be government-transparent either, if government across a maximal projection is contingent on direct θ-marking. Consider the following set of facts:

(77) a. ?*John shouted [$_{C''}$ [$_{Infl''}$ Bill left]]
 b. ?*Mary whispered [$_{C''}$ [$_{Infl''}$ John was late]]
 c. ?*John wheezed [$_{C''}$ [$_{Infl''}$ Mary hit him]]

Apparently, the clausal complement of a non-bridge verb must be introduced by an overt complementizer; an empty head of Comp is not possible in this position. Following Stowell (1981), we might suppose that an empty Comp must be governed by a lexical head (see, also, the discussion of extraposition, pp. 119–22). If non-bridge verbs do not θ-mark their complements, then the facts in (77) follow immediately. The complement C" does not receive a superscript under θ-marking and is not government-transparent to the verb. The empty Comp cannot, then, be governed by the verb since the intervening C" is opaque to government from without. In

Thematic domains and bounding

general, then, the ability to govern the head of a phrase depends on direct θ-marking.

If this analysis is correct, then bridge verbs do not provide an argument that C″ is a bounding node for Subjacency. Given that neither Subject-Condition effects nor non-bridge verb phenomena provide arguments for C″ as a bounding node for Subjacency in English, we can simplify the set of bounding nodes at least to Infl″ and NP.

The class of bounding nodes

The status of NP as a bounding node for Subjacency is, itself, questionable given transparency. I have been assuming that nominal complements do not receive their θ-role in the same way that complements to verbs and adjectives receive theirs; the θ-marking relation between nouns and their complements does not induce superscripting. Since nominal complements are not superscripted, they will generally be unable to satisfy the definition of transparency and, as a result, will be opaque to extraction. We have already considered examples like the following:

(78) *$[_{C″}$ who$_i$ did $[_{Infl″}$ John hear $[_{PP}$ about $[_{NP}$ the rumor $[_{C″}$ that $[_{Infl″}$ Bill saw t_i]]]]]]]

My account of Complex-NP Constraint effects follows from the same underlying mechanisms that were used to account for the form of retroactive nominals, Subject-Condition effects, Adjunct-Island effects, and the failure of nouns to govern across maximal projections.

Notice that clausal complements to nouns are generally less acceptable if they are introduced by a null complementizer:

(79) a. ?*John believes $[_{NP}$ the claim $[_{C″}$ [e] $[_{Infl″}$ Bill was late]]]
 b. ?*Mary was surprised by $[_{NP}$ the fact $[_{C″}$ [e] $[_{Infl″}$ John quit his job]]]
 c. ?*John argued against $[_{NP}$ the idea $[_{C″}$ [e] $[_{Infl″}$ the deficit could be lowered]]]

The above examples follow given the assumption that null complementizers must be lexically governed in order to obey the ECP. Since the complement C″ is not transparent, the head noun cannot govern the null complementizer and the examples in (79) are ruled out.

We should contrast the behavior of complement clauses to nominal heads with the behavior of relative clauses. It is well known that relative clauses may, in certain environments, be introduced by a phonologically null complementizer:

(80) a. ... the man [$_{C''}$ [e] [$_{Infl''}$ John met e] ...
 b. ... the story [$_{C''}$ [e] [$_{Infl''}$ Bill told e] ...
 c. ... the meal [$_{C''}$ [e] [$_{Infl''}$ John prepared e]] ...

Notice that relative clauses are not complements to the head noun. Rather, they delimit the reference of the head noun. We might imagine that, given the contribution of the relative clause to the reference of the NP, the relative clause and the head noun bear the same index. If this is the case, then the head noun could exceptionally govern into the C″, acting as a proper governor for the null element in Comp.

If the above line of argumentation is correct, then the set of possible bounding nodes for Subjacency may be reduced to either Infl″ or C″, as argued in Chomsky (1986) in slightly different terms. The choice between the two is a matter of parametric variation. English would be a language where Infl″ is chosen as the bounding node and Italian would be a case where C″ is chosen as a bounding node. Many of the facts normally attributed to Subjacency follow from our account of transparency, which underlies both extraction from a domain and government across a maximal projection.

Some consequences of transparency

Extraposition

Extraposition structures have long been studied in generative grammar (see Guéron and May 1984, and references cited there). Consider the examples in (81) and (82):

(81) a. That John will borrow the keys is likely.
 b. That Bill stole the keys is certain.
 c. That Mary took the book is obvious.
(82) a. It is likely that John will borow the keys.

b. It is certain that Bill stole the keys.
c. It is obvious that Mary took the book.

It is quite well known that the sentential subjects in (81) are islands to extraction:

(83) a. *What$_i$ [$_{C''}$ that John will borrow t_i] is likely
b. *What$_i$ [$_{C''}$ that Bill stole t_i] is certain
c. *What$_i$ [$_{C''}$ that Mary took t_i] is obvious

If we assume that these sentential subjects originate in subject position at D-Structure and receive their thematic roles via transmission of a thematic role through Infl, then the facts in (83) are exactly what we would expect. The sentential C″ will not qualify as transparent and is, therefore, an island to extraction. The surface position of a subject makes no difference as to its status as an extraction-transparent domain (see p. 84); *prima facie*, we would expect that the extraposed sentences in (82) are islands to extraction. This is not the case:

(84) a. What$_i$ is it likely [$_{C''}$ that John will borrow t_i]
b. What$_i$ is it certain [$_{C''}$ that Bill stole t_i]
c. What$_i$ is it obvious [$_{C''}$ that Mary took t_i]

The asymmetry between (83) and (84) provides a *prima facie* strong argument in favor of Kaynes's (1984) connectedness framework. In this framework, extraction is contingent on the tree geometry; a subpart of a left-branch may not be extracted out of the left-branch. The embedded clauses in (83) are sentential subjects and, as such, form a left-branch; no element may be extracted out of the clause. Extraposition, however, places the embedded clause on a right-branch; since extraction out of a right-branch is always possible in English, it is possible to extract an element out of the extraposed clauses in (84). The contrast between extraposed and unextraposed clauses appears to be support for Kayne's analysis of left/right asymmetries.

In the discussion, above, I concluded that a non-root C″ could have an empty head only if the C″ were properly governed (see also Stowell 1981). The Comp, itself, is properly governed only if the C″ is transparent. Under this approach, we must claim that the extraposed C″ is transparent to government by the adjective in each of the above cases:

(85) a. *John will borrow the keys is likely.
b. *Bill stole the keys is certain.
c. *Mary took the book is obvious.

(86) a. It is likely John will borrow the keys.
b. It is certain Bill stole the keys.
c. It is obvious Mary took the book.

Transparency of a maximal projection to government by a head presupposes direct θ-marking of that maximal projection by the head. The facts in (85) and (86) indicate that the adjectives directly θ-mark the extraposed C″. But this conclusion conflicts with the assumption that the C″ in this structure originates in subject position at D-Structure.

Extraction out of an extraposed C″ in *it*-extraposition structures contrasts sharply with extraction out of phrases in other kinds of extraposition structures:

(87) a. A man with a glass eye arrived.
b. A man arrived with a glass eye.
c. There arrived a man with a glass eye.

(88) a. *What kind of glass eye$_i$ did a man with t_i arrive
b. *What kind of glass eye$_i$ did a man arrive with t_i
c. *What kind of glass eye$_i$ did there arrive a man with t_i

Given that the adjectives in examples like (82) directly θ-mark the C″, the D-Structure of, for example, (82a) must be:

(89) [$_{C″}$ [$_{Infl′}$ [*e*] Infl is [$_{AdjP}$ likely [$_{C″}$ that [$_{Infl′}$ John will borrow the keys]]]]]

Since a C″ does not require Case, the C″ complement of the adjective may remain *in situ* (see Safir 1985 on the assumption that C″ need not be assigned Case). In this case, since an empty expletive is impossible in English, presumably because an empty category needs to be lexically governed in order to obey the ECP, and Infl, the governor of the subject position is not a lexical governor, the expletive element, *it*, must be inserted in subject position:

(90) [$_{C''}$ [$_{Infl'}$ it is [$_{AdjP}$ likely [$_{C''}$ that [$_{Infl'}$ John will borrow the keys]]]]]

Since the matrix subject does not receive a thematic role, nothing prevents the complement C″ from moving into the subject position:

(91) [$_{C''}$ [$_{Infl'}$ [$_{C''}$ that [$_{Infl'}$ John will borrow the keys]$_i$ Infl is [$_{AdjP}$ likely t_i]]]]

Suppose that, as in (90), the sentential complement remains *in situ*. It is directly θ-marked by the head of the adjective phrase and is, therefore, transparent; hence, we would expect extraction out of the C″ to be possible. Suppose, on the other hand, that the sentential complement moves to subject position; then it will receive a θ-role by virtue of being linked with a trace. We can interpret this as meaning that it no longer receives a θ-role via θ-marking by the head of the phrase which contains it. If we take the relationship between an antecedent and a trace as an instance of θ-role transmission along a chain and not as direct θ-marking, it follows that a sentential subject in the cases above will not bear a superscript and, as a result, cannot count as extraction-transparent. In essence, we are claiming that the 'move alpha' operation does not preserve superscripts.[6]

Transparency and movement

It should be obvious that phrases do not count as transparent simply by virtue of being linked to a trace which receives a θ-role. Consider, for instance, cases of passivization. In the standard analysis of passives (see Jaeggli 1986; Keyser and Roeper 1984; Levin and Rappaport 1986 for some recent expositions), the ability to assign an external thematic role to the subject is blocked and the Case feature of the verb is absorbed (in accordance with Burzio's Generalization; Burzio 1986). These facts, along with the Extended Projection Principle, guarantee a D-Structure of the following form for a passive sentence:

(92) [$_{C''}$ [$_{Infl'}$ [$_{NP}$ e] be [$_{VP}$ broken [$_{NP}$ the vase]]]]

The passive participle *broken* will assign a thematic role directly to its object. Given the passive morphology, it is unable to assign Case to its object. In order to avoid the effects of the Case filter, the object must move to a position which receives Case. In order to satisfy the uniqueness condition on thematic roles that the θ-Criterion places on arguments, the position that the object moves to must be a $\bar{\theta}$-position. Since assignment of an external thematic role to the subject is impossible in passives, the object may move to subject position to receive Nominative Case from Infl:

(93) $[_{C'} [_{Infl'} [_{NP}$ the vase$]_i$ be $[_{VP}$ broken $t_i]]]$

If we interpret the relationship between the surface subject and the trace in object position as involving θ-role transmission and not direct θ-marking, then the surface subject will fail to be transparent; this is as desired, since extraction is impossible:

(94) a. *Who$_i$ were $[_{NP}$ stories about $t_i]_j$ told t_j
 b. *Who$_i$ were $[_{NP}$ pictures of $t_i]_j$ taken t_j
 c. *What$_i$ were $[_{NP}$ cartons of $t_i]_j$ loaded t_j into the truck

Passive sentences raise an interesting point. Suppose we have a D-Structure of the following form:

(95) $[_{C'} [_{Infl'} [_{NP} e]$ were $[_{VP}$ told $[_{NP}$ stories about who$]]]]$

The D-Structure object is directly θ-marked by the verb and, by definition, counts as transparent. It should be possible, then, to extract the wh-element inside the NP:

(96) $[_{C'}$ who$_i [_{Infl'} [_{NP} e]$ were $[_{VP}$ told $[_{NP}$ stories about $t_i]]]]$

From here, the derivation proceeds like that of a normal passive sentence. The object is moved to subject position in order to receive Case:

(97) $[_{C'}$ who$_i [_{Infl'} [_{NP}$ stories about $t_i]_j$ were $[_{VP}$ told $t_j]]]$

It would appear that we have a well-formed derivation of the ungrammatical examples in (94).

There is, however, no problem with ruling out the representation in (97), if transparency is taken as a constraint on representations. The logical object is the surface subject; the surface subject is not directly θ-marked by a lexical head, since its θ-role is transmitted by virtue of binding a trace in the object position. The surface subject of (97) may be interpreted as 'extraction-opaque' with respect to Infl". This problem may be reproduced by using not only passives, but also ergatives and middles as in (98) (see Keyser and Roeper 1984; Hale and Keyser 1987):

(98) a. Bureaucrats$_i$ bribe t_i easily
b. The frigate$_i$ sank t_i

In the examples in (98), an NP is directly θ-marked by the verb and then moves to the subject position for reasons of Case assignment. If transparency were taken as a constraint on rules, it should be possible to violate the Subject Condition (subsumed by transparency):

(99) a. *Which department$_i$ do [bureaucrats from t_i] bribe easily
b. *What country$_i$ did [a frigate from t_i] sink yesterday

The above examples demonstrate that transparency cannot be taken as a constraint on rules but, rather, must be interpreted as a constraint on representations, since the functioning of the rules in the class of derivations represented by (99) never violated a core principle. This fact gives us a further argument for distinguishing transparency from Subjacency. Subjacency is commonly viewed as a constraint on rules (see, for example, Lasnik and Saito 1984). Given the conceptual difference between constraints on rules and constraints on representations, the derivations of the S-Structures in (97) and (99) provide us with a good argument for keeping transparency distinct from Subjacency.

Simplifying the statement of transparency

Infl", VP, and selection

We are still faced with the question of why Infl" and VP are consistently transparent. Recall that clause (iii) of the definition of transparency in (3) merely stipulates that Infl" and VP are transparent, with the result that maximal projections of these categories are not islands to extraction. Consider, first, the relationship between Comp and Infl". It has been observed that the form of Comp affects the realization of Infl (see, for example, Stowell 1981). For example, a Comp headed by *for* obligatorily requires an infinitival Infl":

(100) a. It would be a mistake [$_{C''}$ for [$_{Infl''}$ John *to* refuse the offer]]
   b. *It would be a mistake [$_{C''}$ for [$_{Infl''}$ John refuses the offer]]

Similarly, a Comp headed by *that* requires a tensed Infl":

(101) a. It is strange [$_{C''}$ that [$_{Infl''}$ John would refuse the offer]]
   b. *It is strange [$_{C''}$ that [$_{Infl''}$ John to refuse the offer]]
   c. *It is dangerous [$_{C''}$ that [$_{Infl''}$ PRO to refuse the offer]]

Since tense is a property of Infl, we may assume that the form of Comp ultimately determines the form of Infl". The relationship between Comp and Infl appears to be a subcase of standard subcategorization relationships and is quite comparable to the relationship between a verb and its object. In both cases, the presence of the subcategorized element is obligatory, given the lexical properties of the head. As we saw in examples (100) and (101), the lexical properties of the complementizer are inviolable: the lexical properties of *that* are not satisfied by an infinitival nor are the lexical properties of *for* satisfied by a tensed clause.

I will assume, then, that the relationship between Comp and Infl is one of strict subcategorization and that the lexical properties of Comp must be satisfied in the syntax. The analogy between Comp/Infl and verb/object suggests that Infl" counts as transparent because of clause (ii) of the definition of transparency (3) which allows directly θ-marked categories to be transparent. *Prima facie*, the relationship between Comp and Infl" is not one of thematic-role assignment, since Infl" is not in any clear sense an argument of Comp in the way that an object, for example, is an argument of a verb. In brief, Comp and Infl bear a special relationship that seems comparable to θ-marking in some respects still to be made clear.

Similarly, VP bears a special relationship to Infl. The head of VP must satisfy requirements placed upon it by Infl. Thus a tensed Infl requires a VP headed by a verb that is morphologically marked as tensed:

(102) a. John [$_{Infl}$ [+tense]] {sees/saw} the accident
       b. *John [$_{Infl}$ [+tense]] {seeing/seen/see} the accident

If Infl contains a modal, the VP must be headed by a verb in the stem form:

(103) a. John [$_{Infl}$ {can/will/may}] leave tomorrow
       b. *John [$_{Infl}$ {can/will/may}] {leaves/left/leaving} tomorrow

In general, we have the following dependencies between auxiliary verbs and their complements (the notation is adapted from Baker 1981):

(104) a. be   ⟨ __ V ⟩
           [progressive]   ⟨ing⟩
       b. be   ⟨ __ V ⟩
           [passive]   ⟨en⟩
       c. have   ⟨ __ V ⟩
           [perfective]   ⟨en⟩
       d. modal   ⟨ __ V ⟩
                              ⟨stem⟩

We might assume an analysis under which Infl 'strictly subcategorizes' for features of the XP which follows it.

The Comp–Infl relation and the Infl–VP relation appear to be quite analogous to the relationship that holds between a verb and its object. As yet, however, we have not shown how this analogy can be derived from basic principles. Let us first consider the relationship between Infl and VP. Infl consists of an encoding of information regarding the tense (and possibly the aspect) of the sentence, as well as information regarding agreement with the subject. Following Higginbotham (1985, 1987) (based on work by

Davidson, reprinted in Davidson 1980), let us suppose that every verb includes a slot in its θ-grid which may be bound by an event operator. Consider an example like:

(105)   John walked rapidly.

The interpretation of example (105) entails the truth of the following:

(106)   John walked.

The problem here is to get *rapidly* to hold of John's walking while still preserving the entailment relation between (105) and (106). Davidson proposed that the adverb *rapidly* in (105) could be taken as predicated of the event of a walking by John. Simplifying somewhat, we could represent the interpretations of (105) as (where ∃ is the existential quantifier):

(107)   (∃e)[walked(John,e) & rapid(e)]

In a full representation of the Logical Form of (107), the adverb *rapidly* would be shown as a two-place operator which would entail that John's walking was rapid with respect to events of walking (in all probability, John's walking would not be rapid with respect to running or racing a car). Example (107) entails (108), as desired:

(108)   (∃e)walked(John,e)

The above analysis assumes that there is a thematic relation between verbs and an event operator. It is reasonable to assume that the event operator is intimately tied to Infl, since Infl is a repository for information regarding tense and aspect. In particular, we might assume that Infl and VP enter into a θ-marking relation.

More concretely, we might take the tense and aspect of Infl as being a one-place relation which takes the predicate as its argument. This would hold even in infinitivals where the interpretation of the event operator associated with an untensed Infl is dependent on the interpretation of the superordinate (see Stowell 1982):

(109) a. John will force Bill to get a job.
b. John forced Bill to get a job.

The action of the main clause in (109a) has not yet taken place and the infinitival complement is, correspondingly, interpreted as describing a possible future event. In example (109b) the action of the main clause is taken as a past event and the infinitival complement is, likewise, taken as a past event. We can account for this by assuming that the tense operator associated with an infinitival is anaphoric, dependent on the tense operator of the superordinate clause for its interpretation.

Summarizing, there is a relationship between information in Infl and a special 'event-slot' in the thematic grid of predicates. This relationship involves the discharge (following the terminology of Higginbotham 1985, 1987) of a slot in the verb's grid. If we assume that this relationship involves co-superscripting of Infl with VP, then it follows from clause (ii) of the definition of transparency (3) that VP is transparent and, therefore, not an island to extraction. Hence, we need not stipulate that V̂P is transparent; its transparency follows as a theorem from the definition of transparency and the relationship VP holds with tense and aspect information encoded in Infl.

Transparency and empty heads

This analysis does not completely eliminate the stipulation in clause (iii) of the definition of transparency (3). We still have the stipulation that Infl″ is always transparent. We can break the problem into three cases. First, there is the case where an untensed Infl″ is governed and θ-marked by a superordinate verbal (a verb or adjective):

(110) a. John$_i$ is likely [$_{Infl''}$ t_i to be late]
b. Mary believes [$_{Infl''}$ John to have taken the money]

The case represented in (110) falls under clause (ii) of the definition of transparency. That is, since C″ is absent, we may assume that the superordinate verbal directly governs and θ-marks the complement clause. But, then, the complement Infl″ is superscripted and, therefore, transparent and extraction-transparent.

The second case is that of a tensed Infl″ immediately contained in a C″. In the previous case, an untensed clause with no Comp position, the structure in question must be embedded. The case at hand, however, represents matrix clauses as well as embedded tensed clauses:

(111) a. $[_{C''}$ who$_i$ did $[_{Infl''}$ John see $t_i]]$
b. $[_{C''}$ who$_i$ did $[_{Infl''}$ Mary say $[_{C''}\ t_i [_{Infl''}$ John saw $t_i]]]]$

In Chapter 2, following Stowell (1983), I proposed that government is directional. This allowed for an ungoverned PRO to occur in the Spec position of NP, as seemed independently necessary by the form and interpretation of retroactive nominals. *Prima facie*, this analysis poses a problem for Nominative-Case assignment since the subject of Infl″ is always to the left of Infl and government in English is to the right. Stowell addresses this problem by allowing the tense information in Infl to raise to Comp and, thus, occur in a position to govern and assign Case to the subject of Infl″. Under this proposal, the structure in (112a) would map onto the structure in (112b), the movement being forced by Case theory:

(112) a. $[_{C''} [_{Infl''}$ John $[_{Infl''}$ [+tense]] walked]]
b. $[_{C''}$ [+tense]$_i [_{Infl''}$ John $[_{Infl}\ e_i]$ walked]]

The tense information in Comp would antecedent-govern the empty category in Infl and would be in a position to assign Case to the subject. Notice, furthermore, that the tense feature would have scope over the entire Infl″, which is sensible, given the analysis of the tense feature as an event operator.

We have two possible analyses of the transparency of Infl″ at this point. First, we could assume that movement of the tense feature to Comp preserves all indices, including superscripts. This analysis would be at odds with the assumption, discussed in connection with passives and middles, that 'move alpha' does not preserve superscripts. A second approach would be to take a maximal projection as transparent if the head of that projection is null. Assuming that the tense feature is the head of Infl″ and that the tense feature is raised to Comp to take scope over Infl″ would then entail that Infl″ is transparent because it is headed by a null element.

The apparent problem with this latter analysis is that nouns apparently cannot govern across a maximal projection even when the head of that maximal projection is null (see the discussion of null complementizers of sentential complements to nouns on pp. 98–100). We can remedy this by proposing that a maximal projection with a null head is transparent if it is governed by its antecedent. This derives the asymmetry between sentential complements to nouns and relative clauses:

(113) a. *the fact [$_{C''}$ [e] [$_{Infl''}$ John left]]
      b. the man$_i$ [$_{C''}$ [e]$_i$ [$_{Infl''}$ Bill saw t_i]]

In (113a) the clause is not co-indexed with the head and is therefore not transparent. In (113b) the relative clause and the head noun are co-indexed and, as a result, the relative clause is transparent to government.

The final case of transparency of Infl" is when an infinitival Infl is contained in a C":

(114) a. [$_{C''}$ which game$_i$ does [$_{Infl''}$ John want [$_{C''}$ t_i[$_{Infl''}$ PRO to play t_i]]]]
      b. [$_{C''}$ what$_i$ would [$_{Infl''}$ you prefer [$_{C''}$ t_i[$_{Infl''}$ PRO to do t_i]]]]

But this case collapses with the previous case. We are assuming that there is a tense operator associated with infinitivals that is anaphoric to the interpretation of the tense operator of the superordinate clause. If this is so, the [−tense] feature must still be assigned a scope, which we are taking as movement to Comp. Given that this tense operator is anaphoric, we might force movement to Comp under the Binding theory. That is, the subject of the infinitival clause could act to define the syntactic domain in which the tense operator must be associated with an antecedent. Given that [−tense] is anaphoric and that it has no possible antecedent as its clausemate, movement to Comp is forced. In this case, the local domain in which the [−tense] element would need an antecedent in the superordinate clause. The binding domain for an anaphor in Comp is the superordinate clause (see Aoun 1985, 1986):

(115) [John$_i$ wonders [$_{C''}$ [$_{NP}$ which pictures of himself$_i$]$_j$ [$_{Infl''}$ Mary will choose t_j]]]

This analysis captures the fact that the tense interpretation of infinitivals is contingent on the tense of the superordinate clause.

Given that movement of the [−tense] feature to Comp is forced by virtue of the fact that this element is an anaphor, the case of infinitivals immediately contained in a C″ collapses with the case of a tensed Infl″. That is, the infinitival is transparent because its head is null and it is antecedent-governed.

We have eliminated the stipulations in clause (iii) of the definition of transparency (3). The transparency of VP follows from assumptions regarding θ-marking (and thus follows as a special case of clause (ii)) and the transparency of Infl″ follows either from clause (ii) (for cases of C″ deletion) or from the fact that the head is null. I have tried, in this chapter, to build a case for the relationship between thematic theory and extraction asymmetries. My account of the Subject Condition, the Adjunct-Island Constraint, and other island phenomena has relied on the non-homogeneous nature of thematic-role assignment. While hierarchical structure is the syntactic expression of thematic relations, I have not relied on particulars of tree geometry in developing this account.

3.5 Summary

In this chapter I have attempted to place the problem posed by retroactive nominals (Chapter 2) into a wider context. In Chapter 2 I argued that these nominals allow NP-movement of a PRO from a complement position into Spec of NP. Furthermore, this movement is quite restricted; in particular, the PRO can be moved out of a complement to the head noun only if the noun is a 1-*ing* nominal and the governing verbal is of a restricted semantic class. I hypothesized that, in the unmarked case, nouns do not θ-mark their complements. The governing verbal involved in this class of constructions has the property of subcategorizing for a nominal of a special morphological class; this class of nominals is particularly verb-like and may θ-mark its complements. θ-marking by the head noun, in turn, makes the complement 'transparent' to extraction, thus allowing NP-movement of a governed PRO to the Spec position of NP.

In 3.1 and 3.2 I developed a bounding condition based on thematic-role assignment by a lexical element. This *boundary* condition (extraction-transparency) is defined analogously to transparency for government; extraction out of an XP is possible only if that XP counts as transparent. We found that this approach generalized across a variety of constructions, providing an analysis which unified the data concerning retroactive nominals with Subject-Condition effects, and so on. Unlike Subjacency, which is a condition on rules, this condition is stated as a condition on representations which applies, minimally, to S-Structure representations (section 3.4). Furthermore, transparency generalizes across extraction-transparency and transparency to government across a maximal projection. Both extraction-transparency and government-transparency rely on the same underlying mechanism.

In section 3.3 I compared transparency with the barriers framework of Chomsky (1986). While the two approaches have some similarity, I argued that the former approach could provide a more satisfying account of the Adjunct-Island Condition and made stronger predictions with respect to retroactive nominals.

The account of bounding and government developed here takes the relation of direct thematic-role assignment as the core relation which defines local movement. If this approach is correct, then argument structure (the thematic roles associated with a head) is a foundation for the core relation of government. On this view, the syntax is highly sensitive to thematic relations; the configuration of direct θ-role assignment can be viewed as a highly salient structure around which much of the syntax organizes itself. In the following chapter, I will turn to the relationship between argument structure and interpretation. The focus will be on a unified representation of control relationships in the grammar.

Chapter four

Control and non-overt operators

In this chapter I will develop the hypothesis that PRO is best treated as a phonologically unrealized (non-overt) operator; that is, the element PRO is best treated on analogy with wh-elements. I will examine cases of obligatory control (Faraci 1974; Chomsky 1981; Manzini 1983; Nishigauchi 1984), 'double' control as in some purposive clauses (Chomsky 1980), as well as control by an implicit argument, and so-called 'non-obligatory' (or 'arbitrary') control. As I will show, obligatory control is an S-Structure phenomenon which involves the identification of a non-overt operator under predication. Non-obligatory control is an LF phenomenon which involves the identification of a non-overt operator under Ā-binding.

The first section will summarize some recent approaches to the distribution and control of PRO. In addition, I will review some problems with current approaches to control, including the 'PRO gate' (Higginbotham 1980). In section 4.2 I will develop an approach to the distribution of non-overt operators using a generalized binding theory (Aoun 1985, 1986); I will assume that the reader is familiar with the Binding theory as discussed in Chomsky (1981, 1982). In the third section I will show that the distribution of non-overt operators is consistent with the distribution of PRO. In the remaining sections, I will discuss obligatory and non-obligatory control. I will argue that obligatory control involves the binding of a non-overt operator at S-Structure, while non-obligatory control involves binding at LF. Obligatory and non-obligatory control, then, differ only as to the level of representation at which binding occurs. Finally, I will show how a number of control phenomena (linked readings of PRO and interactions with certain adverbs) follow from the approach developed in this chapter.

The analysis of control will have a number of consequences. PRO as a pronominal anaphor does not exist (see Bouchard 1983; Sportiche 1983, among others); instead, we will treat PRO as an operator/variable pair. Next, the treatment of obligatory and non-obligatory control developed in this chapter crucially relies on the existence of distinct levels of syntactic representation with distinct properties; the analysis of control developed here will constitute an argument in favor of a theory with multiple levels of representation. Finally, the PRO gate will not constitute an exception to the analysis of weak cross-over phenomena, but will instead follow naturally from the properties of non-overt operators.

4.1 Approaches to control

Control theory is involved with the syntactic distribution and referential possibilities of a special element, PRO. In this section I will bring up a number of empirical issues that a theory of control must answer to. I will rely on a careful examination of the theory of control found in Manzini (1983; see also Nishigauchi 1984). I will also look at the problem of the PRO gate.

The distribution of PRO

In Chomsky (1981) PRO is taken as having the feature specification [+pronominal, +anaphor]. PRO, then, falls under conditions A and B of the Binding theory. Since no element could possibly satisfy both conditions A and B of the Binding theory – to do so would mean that such an element would be both free and bound in the same local domain – PRO cannot have a governing category. This is taken as implying that PRO must not be governed.[1] The only A-position which is not governed is the subject of a non-finite clause. Thus, PRO is restricted to occurring in the subject position of infinitivals and gerunds:

(1) a. John persuaded Bill [PRO to study counterpoint]
    b. [PRO to study counterpoint] would be a hardship beyond endurance
    c. [PRO studying counterpoint] is probably worthwhile

One goal of Control theory is to explain which NP PRO may corefer with, if any. Thus, in (1a) PRO is taken as coreferring with *Bill* but not *John*. In (1b) and (1c) PRO is taken as being 'arbitrary' in reference; that is, the PRO is taken as having a quantificational interpretation, somewhat along the lines of universal quantification.

Manzini (1983) outlines a number of the important properties of PRO that a Control theory must account for. First, when PRO occurs in a sentential complement, it must be coreferential with the subject or with the object of the superordinate clause:

(2)   a. John$_i$ asked Bill$_j$ [PRO$_j$ to paint himself$_j$]
     b. *John$_i$ asked Bill$_j$ [PRO$_i$ to paint himself$_i$]
     c. *John$_i$ asked Bill$_j$ [PRO$_{arb}$ to paint oneself]

(3)   a. John$_i$ promised Bill$_j$ [PRO$_i$ to paint himself$_i$]
     b. *John$_i$ promised Bill$_j$ [PRO$_j$ to paint himself$_j$]
     c. *John$_i$ promised Bill$_j$ [PRO$_{arb}$ to paint oneself]

The special index *arb* is taken as designating an arbitrary PRO. In (2a) the PRO obligatorily corefers with the object, *Bill*, and may not be taken either as coreferring with the subject, *John*, or as free in reference. In (3a) the PRO must be taken as coreferential with the subject, *John*, and any construal under which the PRO corefers with the object or is free is ungrammatical. Facts like those in (2) and (3) have led to the identification of the feature [+anaphor] with PRO since, intuitively, the PRO in these constructions refers only by virtue of being related with some other NP that either refers independently or is bound.

The exception to the generalization that PRO in a sentential complement is anaphoric appears to be certain verbs of saying, as in (4):

(4)   John {whispered, shouted, said, etc.} [PRO to behave oneself]

The verbs in these cases have some rather special properties. For example, many, but not all, of these verbs are non-bridge verbs. In other words, these verbs do not easily allow for extraction of a subpart of their complements (CP = the maximal projection of Comp; IP = the maximal projection of Infl):

Control and non-overt operators

(5) a. *Who$_i$ did John whisper [$_{CP}$ t_i [$_{IP}$ Mary saw t_i]]
 b. *What kind of poison$_i$ did Mary shout [$_{CP}$ t_i [$_{IP}$ Bill drank t_i]]

In a sense, these verbs do not denote a relation between entities and propositions (compare verbs of belief) but, rather, they set up a relation between entities and utterances. Thus, one can whisper, say, shout, etc. an order:

(6) a. John shouted to leave.
 b. Bill whispered to stand up straight.
 c. The general said to be quiet.

This is despite the fact that orders do not bear a truth-value. Since it is plausible that verbs of saying fall into a special class, it should come as no surprise that they have special control properties. We will not be too concerned with the control properties of this class of structures, although the analysis of the possibility of extracting from the complements of these verbs, presented in Chapter 3, may be relevant.

The contrasts above are generally interpreted as demonstrating that control of PRO involves some sort of lexical specification on the part of the verb that subcategorizes for the non-finite complement, although it seems reasonable to invoke some form of the Minimal-Distance Principle of Rosenbaum (1967). Thus, minimal-control contrasts like the following

(7) a. John$_i$ promised Bill$_j$ [PRO$_{\{i,*j\}}$ to leave]
 b. John$_i$ persuaded Bill$_j$ [PRO$_{\{j,*i\}}$ to leave]

may be accounted for by appealing to the differences in the lexical structure of *promise* and *persuade*; *promise* designates its external argument as the controller of PRO, while *persuade* designates its internal argument as the controller. Structurally, however, (7a) and (7b) are identical. Thus, obligatory control is not based on purely structural factors, unlike determining the range of possible antecedents for a particular anaphor. Elements of lexical semantics must be taken into account in determining the controller of PRO (see Nishigauchi 1984 for discussion).

Crucially, PRO is outside of the government domain of the

superordinate verb which determines its controller. This is an unusual property of obligatory control, since the verb must determine a property of PRO although the verb may never govern it; if the verb governed the PRO, then PRO would have a governing category in which it must be both free and bound.

The relationship of obligatory control which is by hypothesis specified by a verb is also sensitive to properties of Comp. In particular, a [+WH] Comp blocks obligatory control:

(8) a. John$_i$ asked [PRO$_i$ to shave himself$_i$]
 b. *John$_i$ asked [PRO$_{arb}$ to shave oneself]
 c. John$_i$ asked [$_{CP}$ how [$_{IP}$ PRO$_i$ to shave himself$_i$]]
 d. John$_i$ asked [$_{CP}$ how [$_{IP}$ PRO$_{arb}$ to shave oneself]]

The verb *ask*, in the usage exemplified in (8), specifies the subject as the controller of PRO, as shown in (8a) and (8b), where the presence of the impersonal reflexive element, *oneself*, results in ungrammaticality. When a wh-element occurs in Comp, as in (8c) and (8d), control is not obligatory, the PRO subject may be indexed with arb, and the impersonal reflexive is permitted. The verb of the superordinate clause cannot govern the PRO (on pain of violating the Binding theory) in any of the examples in (8); the theory of control must have some way of tying together properties of the CP containing the PRO with the lexical properties of the verb in the superordinate clause. When the Spec of Comp contains a [+WH] element, the lexical property of the superordinate verb which specifies the controller of the verb is over-ridden and the PRO is interpreted as not obligatorily controlled.

A further property of control that must be accounted for by a control theory is that control is generally optional when the clause containing a PRO subject occurs as a sentential subject:

(9) a. [PRO$_i$ to behave oneself in public] is desirable
 b. [PRO$_i$ to kill himself$_i$] would bother Bill
 c. Mary thinks that [PRO$_i$ to make a film about herself$_i$] would be profitable

It should be noted that judgements regarding control into a sentential subject seem to be fairly elastic. For many of the speakers I consulted, control appears to be obligatory in (9b) and strongly preferred in (9c). I will accept these judgements, although they run counter to judgements occasionally found in the literature.

To summarize, we have found three features of PRO that a control theory must account for:

(10)   a. A PRO subject of a subcategorized sentential complement must be controlled by an element in the superordinate clause.
   b. A head may specify the controller of PRO.
   c. A PRO subject of a sentential subject need not be controlled; its controller, furthermore, need not be in the immediately superordinate clause (see (9c)).

A Binding-theoretic analysis of PRO

Manzini (1983) derives the generalizations in (10) by treating controlled PRO as an anaphor. Since this anaphor occurs in an ungoverned position, it will not have a governing category and, *prima facie*, it has no minimal domain in which it must be bound. To resolve this, Manzini defines 'domain-governing category' (see note 1 for a discussion of 'accessible SUBJECT'):

(11) A is a *domain-governing category* for B iff
   a. A is a governing category for the c-domain of B; and
   b. A contains a SUBJECT accessible to B.
(12) A is the c-domain of B iff A is the minimal maximal category dominating B.

The definitions in (11) and (12) have a very uniform effect. The c-domain of PRO will be the IP that immediately dominates the PRO. The minimal category which contains the c-domain of PRO and a SUBJECT accessible to PRO will, in the case of subcategorized sentential complements, be the immediately superordinate clause. If the c-domain of PRO occurs in subject position (i.e., a non-finite sentential subject) then the superordinate clause will not contain a SUBJECT accessible to PRO. This is because the sentential subject and the Infl of the superordinate clause are obligatorily co-indexed; co-indexing the PRO with the Infl will result in the PRO's being co-indexed with the clause that immediately contains it (a violation of the *i-within-i* condition of Chomsky

1981). Hence, the domain-governing category of such a PRO will have to be higher than the superordinate clause (if there is anything higher).

To make this more concrete, consider an example like:

(13) John$_i$ Infl$_i$ tried [$_{IP}$ PRO to shave himself]

The c-domain of PRO is the IP that contains it – the embedded clause. We will assume that the Comp of the embedded clause is not present, since it is not independently required as, for example, a landing site. If this is so, then the embedded IP is governed by the matrix verb *try*, since the Comp dominating the embedded clause does not branch. the governing category for the c-domain of PRO will be the matrix IP, since the matrix IP is the minimal maximal category containing a governor for the embedded clause and a SUBJECT accessible to the embedded clause; in this case, the matrix Infl is the accessible SUBJECT for the embedded clause. The matrix Infl is also an accessible SUBJECT for the PRO inside the embedded clause. Hence, the matrix clause is the domain-governing category for PRO.

We can contrast example (13) with the following:

(14) John$_i$ Infl wondered [$_{CP}$ how [$_{IP}$ PRO to solve the problem]]

The c-domain of PRO is, again, the embedded clause. But this time Manzini assumes that the embedded clause is not governed, due to the presence of *how* in the Spec of the embedded Comp. If the embedded IP is not governed, then it cannot have a governing category. But if the c-domain of PRO has no governing category, then PRO lacks a domain-governing category. A similar result may be derived for sentential subjects, since the embedded clause is, under Manzini's assumptions, ungoverned due to the presence of Comp. Hence, a PRO in a sentential subject or in a CP with a phonologically overt Comp will lack a domain-governing category.

In general, then, if PRO has a domain-governing category, its domain-governing category will be the superordinate IP; otherwise, PRO will simply lack a domain-governing category. Recall that one of the features of PRO is that a PRO in the subject position of a subcategorized complement is controlled by an element in the superordinate clause. We can restate this as: a PRO which has a domain-governing category must be bound in that domain-governing category. Manzini states this as:

(15) An anaphor without a governing category is bound in its domain-governing category.

In the case of obligatorily controlled PRO, we have seen that it is always bound in its domain-governing category, the superordinate clause. In case the PRO lacks a domain-governing category – the cases of clauses with an element in Comp, subordinate non-finite clauses in subject position, and so on – the constraint on PRO being bound in its domain-governing category is trivially satisfied, since PRO lacks a domain-governing category to be bound in.

Manzini's account has a number of rather interesting ramifications. We will primarily be interested in successive-cyclic movement, which, in the sense in which this term is normally taken, is not possible. Consider the following set of sentences:

(16) a. John$_i$ decided [PRO$_i$ to shave himself$_i$]
   b. *John$_i$ decided [PRO$_{arb}$ to shave oneself]
   c. How$_i$ did John$_i$ decide [t_i [PRO$_i$ to shave himself$_i$ t_i]]
   d. *How$_i$ did John$_i$ decide [t_i[PRO$_{arb}$ to shave himself$_i$ t_i]]

The contrast between (16a) and (16b) shows that *decide* is an obligatory control verb since it is impossible to have an impersonal reflexive in the embedded clause. It must be the case, then, that the c-domain of PRO (the embedded IP) has the matrix IP as its governing category. This implies that the matrix verb, *decide*, governs the embedded IP. It was argued above that the matrix verb could do this only if CP does not branch. Hence, there can be no CP. Now consider (16c). If the wh-element moved to the intermediate Comp on its way to its ultimate landing site, then the embedded CP must branch; but then we would not expect obligatory control. Nevertheless, (16d) shows that control is still obligatory. Thus, for this version of Control theory to work, Comp-to-Comp movement must be impossible. Intermediate traces must, rather, be adjoined to IP (or, perhaps CP, depending on your theory of adjunction and government) so that the CP will not branch in obligatory control structures. In order to make this serviceable, we need a constraint like the following:

(17) An element in Comp may not undergo 'move alpha'; an element adjoined to S in the syntax must undergo 'move alpha'.

or some other constraint that will guarantee that intermediate traces are never in the Spec of Comp. One could, for example, eliminate CP altogether, and simply filter out multiple adjunctions to IP at S-Structure. This proposal would have a number of consequences (and problems) that would take us far afield, so we will put this approach aside. Notice that this proposal is at odds with the theory of adjunction developed in May (1985) and Chomsky (1986), who argue that no element may be adjoined to an argument. Since the embedded IP would be an argument of the verb *decide* in (16), nothing could adjoin to the IP.

Thus, under Manzini's theory of control, we must rework some commonly held assumptions about the nature of successive-cyclic movement, the role of Comp in the theory of grammar, and the theory of adjunction. Furthermore, we must add the notion of 'domain-governing category' to the Binding theory. This definition ensures that some superordinate category will be the governing category for PRO. Notice that, in the previous section, we saw a similar state of affairs with regard to non-overt operators. We will return to this parallelism in greater detail below (see pp. 147–61).

The PRO gate

Let us turn now to the question of the PRO gate, which we discussed briefly above (p. 133). Following Higginbotham (1980), I will assume that a pronoun could be interpreted as a bound variable only if it is locally A-bound by a variable (or locally A-bound by an element that is ultimately bound by a variable). Crucially, a pronoun could not be locally Ā-bound. This convention derived the weak cross-over effects as illustrated in:

(18) [his$_{\{i,*j\}}$ mother] loves every man$_j$

Control and non-overt operators

The quantified NP, *every man*, is adjoined to the matrix IP in the LF representation of (18):

(19) [$_{IP}$ [every man]$_j$ [$_{IP}$ [his$_{\{i,*j\}}$ mother] loves t_j]]

If the Genitive pronoun, *his*, bears the same index as the quantified NP, it will be locally Ā-bound at LF, in violation of our interpretive convention. Hence, the Genetive pronoun must be interpreted as disjoint from the quantified NP:

If we invert the surface order of the two NPs in (20), then the Genitive pronoun may be bound by the quantified NP:

(20) every man$_j$ is loved by [his$_{\{i,j\}}$ mother]

This is so because in the LF representation of (20), the Genitive pronoun will be locally A-bound by the variable left by QR (Quantifier Raising), rather than being locally Ā-bound by the quantified NP itself:

(21) [$_{IP}$ [every man]$_j$ [$_{IP}$ t_j is loved by [his$_{\{i,j\}}$ mother]]]

Since the Genitive pronoun is (optionally) locally A-bound by a variable, it may be interpreted as a bound pronoun.
Consider a sentences like:

(22) a. [PRO$_i$ kissing [his$_i$ mother]] bothers every boy$_i$
      b. [$_{IP}$ [every boy]$_i$ [$_{IP}$ [PRO$_i$ kissing [his$_i$ mother]] bothers t_i]]
      c. [$_{CP}$ who$_i$ does [$_{IP}$ [PRO$_i$ kissing [his$_i$ mother]] bother t_i]]

In all of the above sentences, the PRO may receive a 'bound-pronoun' interpretation. The examples in (22) are troubling. In a theory where PRO bears the features [+pronominal, +anaphor] its pronominal character should prevent its interpretation as a bound variable unless it is locally A-bound by a variable. In (22a) and its associated LF, (22b), the PRO is never locally A-bound by a variable; in the LF representation, in fact, the PRO is locally Ā-bound.

In (22c), the PRO is locally Ā-bound at S-Structure. It was facts like those in (22) that led Higginbotham (1980) to formulate the PRO gate, which stipulates that pronominals, except for PRO, are interpreted as bound variables only if locally A-bound by a variable; PRO may be locally Ā-bound despite its specification as a pronominal.

The examples in (22) have another implication. Chomsky (1982) proposes that the features of empty categories may be determined by their syntactic environment and, therefore, there is no reason to suppose that empty categories have any inherent features. He proposed a sort of algorithm, the functional determination of empty categories, which could assign features to empty categories on the basis of purely syntactic considerations. Thus, an empty category which occupies an A-position and is locally Ā-bound must be a variable and is assigned the features [−pronominal, −anaphor]; otherwise, the empty category is assigned the feature [+anaphor]. If the empty category is free or locally A-bound by an antecedent which bears an independent thematic role, it is assigned the feature [+pronominal], thus making it [+pronominal, +anaphor] or, in other words, PRO. The other possibility is that the empty category is bound by an antecedent in a θ̄-position. In this case, the empty category is assigned [−pronominal], making it a pure anaphor, or, in other words, NP-trace. Notice that this algorithm lacks a way of assigning features to an empty pronominal, pro. It is not difficult to find ways to incorporate pro into the above algorithm by, for example, stating that an empty category that is identified in the appropriate way is a pure pronominal.

This approach, despite its shortcomings, has a certain appeal. The functional determination of empty categories represents a codification of a very elegant theory of empty categories. There is a rather large hole in this approach to empty categories. Specifically, the PRO gate runs counter to the functional determination (as observed in Brody 1984; Safir 1985). Let us look more closely at an example:

(23) [$_{CP}$ who$_i$ does [$_{IP}$ [PRO$_i$ kissing [his$_i$ mother]] bother t_i]]

The empty category in the subject position of gerund occupies an

A-position and, furthermore, it is locally A-bound by *who*; hence, the functional determination would have us assign this empty category the features [−pronominal, −anaphor]. In other words, the functional determination of empty categories systematically mis-identifies PRO as a variable in certain structural environments. It should be noted that PRO is identified as a variable so far as the semantic interpretation is concerned; as we will see, however, it is not obvious that the syntax can accept this identification.

This mis-identification of PRO may not appear to be such a terrible thing. Consider, however, a theory in which variables and traces are subject to some form of the ECP. The PRO in (23) will violate whatever version of the ECP you care to select simply because the PRO occupies an ungoverned position and every version of the ECP presupposes some form of government of the empty category by some element.

There is a further problem with treating the PRO in (23) as a variable. Specifically, it is at least highly marked, if not impossible, for a single operator to locally bind two variables (see Koopman and Sportiche 1983). Until recently, a proposed case of an operator locally binding two variables was in parasitic-gap constructions. As we will see, however, the idea that a single operator bound the two variables in parasitic-gap structures was replaced by the proposal that the parasitic gap is locally Ā-bound by a non-overt operator. If this is correct, then constructions like (23) represent the only case where a single operator locally Ā-binds two variables. Furthermore, if we admit the possibility of a single operator locally binding two variables, then we must find an independent means of filtering out ungrammatical examples like:

(24) *Who$_i$ did John describe t_i without any pictures of t_i being on file

The defunct parasitic-gap analysis of Chomsky (1982) is now back, since an empty category may be generated inside the subject position of the adjunct clause only to be reanalyzed as a variable at S-Structure. Recall that we cannot use a 'connectedness'-style ECP (Kayne 1984) to rule out (24) without also ruling out (23).

It would appear, then, that we must assume that some, if not all, empty categories have inherent features. This assumption will prevent the problems we have seen with locally Ā-bound PRO, since PRO will have inherent features which it cannot change in the course of a derivation. While this approach will solve the technical problem of PRO being converted to a variable, it leaves unanswered a rather interesting problem. Let us first put the question in a general form, and then add some theoretical considerations. What is the relationship between a PRO in an A-position and an operator in an Ā-position? Why is it that a PRO may be treated as a variable with respect to binding and interpretation, but as a PRO with respect to the conditions which license other empty categories?

Koopman and Sportiche (1983) have proposed that, in general, there is a bi-uniqueness relationship between Ā-binders and bound elements in A-positions. They propose the Bijection Principle, which requires that operators locally bind one and only one variable. The most famous counterexample to this proposal, parasitic gaps, is a red herring, since in these constructions the overt wh-element locally binds only one variable, the true gap; the other element bound by the overt wh-element is a non-overt operator. Non-overt operators are distinct from true variables, since they occupy Ā-positions, while a variable, by definition, occupies an A-position.

We have already seen that pronouns may not be locally Ā-bound from the weak cross-over effects discussed above (p. 142). R-(Referential) expressions, like names, must be both A- and Ā-free. This leaves anaphors as elements that may, in some sense, be locally Ā-bound. It would appear to be a theorem of the Binding theory that A-anaphors could not be locally Ā-bound from condition A of the A-binding system. Even so-called 'psych verbs' do not allow this construction. Consider the sentences in (25):

(25) a. [stories about himself$_i$] annoy John$_i$
 b. [pictures of himself$_i$] please Bill$_i$
 c. [a reflection of himself$_i$ in the mirror] might startle Bill$_i$

In the above sentences, an anaphor inside a subject is co-indexed with, but apparently not c-commanded by, an NP in object position. Most speakers I have asked seem to dislike sentences like those in (26):

(26) a. *?Who$_i$ did [stories about himself$_i$] annoy t_i

  b. *?Which politician$_i$ do [pictures of himself$_i$] please t_i

  c. *?Which psychotic$_i$ did [a reflection of himself$_i$ in the mirror] startle t_i

(27) a. Who$_i$ t_i was annoyed by [stories about himself$_i$]

  b. Which politician$_i$ t_i was pleased by [pictures of himself$_i$]

  c. Which psychotic$_i$ t_i was startled by [a reflection of himself$_i$ in the mirror]

The examples in (27) are well-formed, since the anaphors are locally A-bound; the examples in (26) are out precisely because the anaphor is not locally A-bound. This fact seems to follow from the Bijection Principle, since an operator in each of the examples in (26) (unlike (27)) locally Ā-binds two argument-positions.

As things stand, however, locally Ā-bound PRO (as in the examples in (22)) is a true counterexample to the Bijection Principle, since an operator must at some level locally Ā-bind two argument-positions. As things stand, we must simply modify the Bijection Principle with the stipulation that an operator may locally Ā-bind PRO in addition to some other argument position. Such a stipulation would, of course, represent a genuine explanatory gap in the theory.

Notice, however, that such a theory contains a number of quite unexpected 'coincidences'. First, given that Manzini's theory of obligatory control is essentially correct, the domain-governing category of an obligatorily controlled PRO is the clause that is superordinate to the one containing the PRO. The analysis of non-overt operators given below (p. 147–61) requires that non-overt operators must be 'identified' (either bound or receive an index under predication) in the superordinate clause. Thus, PRO and non-overt operators seem to have the same properties with respect to the local domain in which they must be bound. Second, PRO may be locally Ā-bound in violation of the Bijection Principle; we have seen in the analysis of non-overt operators that they too may be locally Ā-bound by an operator that also locally binds an element in an argument position.

One way to derive these parallelisms between PRO and non-overt operators is to identify the two. Such an approach would collapse control phenomena with phenomena that currently fall under the analysis of parasitic gaps; in particular, control, parasitic gaps, purposive clauses, infinitival relatives, and tough movement would be treated as fundamentally the same sort of phenomena. In the following sections, I will explore this hypothesis.

4.2 A theory of non-overt operators

The distribution of non-overt operators

The hypothesis that some variables are bound by phonologically empty operators has been motivated by structures like the following:

(28) a. John$_i$ is easy [$_{CP}$ Op$_i$ [$_{IP}$ PRO to please t_i]]
b. John bought the book$_i$ [$_{CP}$ Op$_i$ [$_{IP}$ PRO to read t_i to the children]]
c. [the man$_i$ [$_{CP}$ Op$_i$ [$_{IP}$ PRO to see t_i]]] is John

Example (28a) illustrates a case of tough movement, example (28b) is a purpose clause, and example (28c) is an infinitival relative. As has been discussed in a variety of places (see, for example, Chomsky 1977; Bach 1982; Fiengo 1980; and Stowell 1985), these constructions show a number of properties that are similar to wh-movement. There appear, for example, to be wh-island effects:

(29) a. *John$_i$ is easy [$_{CP}$ Op$_i$ [$_{IP}$ PRO to tell Mary [$_{CP}$ how [$_{IP}$ PRO to please t_i]]]]
b. *John made up the story$_i$ [$_{CP}$ Op$_i$ [$_{IP}$ PRO to show Bill [$_{CP}$ how [$_{IP}$ PRO to trick the children with t_i]]]]
c. *[the man$_i$ [$_{CP}$ Op$_i$ [$_{IP}$ PRO to show Bill [$_{CP}$ where [$_{IP}$ PRO to see t_i]]]]] is John

The ungrammaticality of the examples in (29) does not follow from a strict boundedness condition between the overt element in an A-position and the variable itself: the variable may be very deeply embedded, as the examples in (30) show:

(30) a. John$_i$ is easy [$_{Cp}$ Op$_i$ [$_{IP}$ PRO to persuade Mary [$_{IP}$ PRO to please t_i]]]
b. John made up the story$_i$ [$_{CP}$ Op$_i$ for [$_{IP}$ Bill to trick the children with t_i]]
c. [the man$_i$ [$_{CP}$ Op$_i$ [$_{IP}$ PRO to tell Bill [$_{IP}$ PRO to see t_i]]]] is John

The variable is well-formed in positions from which wh-movement is well-formed, no matter how deeply embedded the extraction site is.

Furthermore, condition C of the Binding theory requires that variables must be free in the domain of their operator. Assuming that the empty categories in the examples of (28) and (30) are variables, notice that each one is coreferential with an element in an A-position. If there were no operator to locally Ā-bind these variables, the examples in (28) and (30) would be ungrammatical. The empty categories in (28) and (30) cannot be NP-trace, since they are not locally A-bound. They cannot be PRO since they occur in governed, Case-marked positions. The only remaining possibility is a syntactic variable.

There is some evidence, both empirical and theory-internal, for the existence of non-overt operators. It has recently been proposed, by Contreras (1984), that non-overt operators are crucially involved in parasitic-gap constructions. Parasitic-gap constructions are exemplified in (31):

(31) a. ?Which articles$_i$ did John file t_i without reading e_i
b. ?the man who$_i$ Mary called t_i an idiot as often as Jane called e_i a cretin

where t represents the true gap and e represents the parasitic gap.

Chomsky's (1982) analysis of parasitic gaps derives the following facts:

(32) a. A parasitic gap is licensed by a variable that does not c-command it.
b. A parasitic gap cannot be licensed by an element in an A-position even if that element is a wh-element *in situ*.

As pointed out in Kayne (1984), however, Chomsky's analysis predicts that a parasitic gap may be generated anywhere just so long as it is not c-commanded by the variable that licenses it. As Kayne and Contreras have shown, this is not correct; Kayne notes contrasts like the following:

(33)   a. ?the person that John described *t* without examining any pictures of *e*
       b. *the person that John described *t* without any pictures of *e* being on file
       c. ?the paper that we should destroy *t* before someone steals a copy of *e*
       d. *the paper that we should destroy *t* before a copy of *e* gets stolen by someone

Kayne derives the above contrasts by appeal to his reformulation of the ECP. Contreras, on the other hand, argues that the above facts follow if the parasitic gap arises through movement of a non-overt operator. In particular, example (33a) would have a D-Structure like:

(34)   [$_{NP}$ the person [$_{CP}$ that [$_{IP}$ John described *WH* without [$_{CP}$ [$_{IP}$ PRO examining any pictures of Op]]]]]

where *WH* stands for the relative operator, and *Op* stands for the non-overt operator. In the syntax, 'move alpha' would apply both to the relative operator, *WH*, and to the non-overt operator, *Op*:

(35)   [$_{NP}$ the person [$_{CP}$ that *WH*$_i$ [$_{IP}$ John described *t*$_i$ without [$_{CP}$ Op$_j$ [$_{IP}$ PRO examining any pictures of *t*$_j$]]]]]

Below, we will return to the question of how the non-overt operator assigns the same range as the 'overt' operator. For the moment, we will simply assume that some mechanism independently guarantees this identity.

If the non-overt operator approach is correct, then a number of otherwise fairly puzzling facts follow immediately. The contrast noted by Kayne (see the examples in (33) above) follow either from extraction-transparency developed in Chapter 3 or from

Control and non-overt operators

Chomsky's recent reformulation of Subjacency (Chomsky 1986). Subjacency derives facts like the following:

(36) a. *the woman who$_i$ John saw t_i without [$_{CP}$ Op$_i$ [$_{IP}$ PRO wondering [$_{IP}$ who$_j$ [$_{IP}$ t_i met e_i]]]]
b. *the paper which$_i$ John studied t_i after [$_{CP}$ Op$_i$ [$_{IP}$ Bill talked to him without [$_{CP}$ PRO reading e_i]]]
c. *the story which$_i$ John believed t_i without [$_{CP}$ Op$_i$ [$_{IP}$ PRO realizing [$_{NP}$ the fact that Bill made e_i up]]]

Example (36a) involves extraction of the non-overt operator out of a wh-island and is, therefore, ruled out by Subjacency. Example (36b) involves extraction of the non-overt operator out of an adjunct and is ruled out by transparency (see Chapter 3). Example (36c) involves extraction of the non-overt operator out of a complex NP and is, similarly, ruled out.

Given the existence of non-overt operators, consider the following representations:

(37) a. [$_{CP}$ Op$_i$ [$_{IP}$ John hit t_i]]
b. [$_{CP}$ Op$_i$ [$_{IP}$ Mary believes [$_{CP}$ t_i [$_{IP}$ t_i' saw Bill]]]]
c. [$_{CP}$ [$_{IP}$ Mary knows [$_{CP}$ Op$_i$ [$_{IP}$ t_i saw Bill]]]]

which would be associated with the following strings:

(38) a. *John hit.
b. *Mary believes saw Bill.
c. *Mary knows saw Bill.

While examples (37a) and (37b) could be eliminated by the ECP, granted the assumption that non-overt operators must be properly governed, example (37c) cannot be so eliminated since the non-overt operator is in a Comp, which is, presumably, properly governed by the verb *know*. Consider, for example, (39), which involves successive-cyclic movement:

(39) [$_{CP}$ who$_i$ [$_{IP}$ does Mary know [$_{CP}$ t_i [$_{IP}$ t_i' saw Bill]]]]

Example (39) illustrates the fact that *know* may properly govern into Comp. Stating the problem slightly differently, why is it that we do not get apparent violations of the Projection Principle like those illustrated in (38)?

The fault does not lie with the variables in the examples in (37). Each of the variables in (37) is properly governed and Ā-bound in its governing category; and the non-overt operator is, furthermore, extracted out of an extraction-transparent domain. We can safely assume that the ungrammaticality of the above examples does not follow from the violation of a core principle on the part of the variable. This leaves the non-overt operator as our culprit. Some principle, or set of principles, acts to constrain the distribution of non-overt operators.

In a recent paper (Aoun and Clark 1985), J. Aoun and I argued that non-overt operators have anaphoric properties. The assumption was that, in a sense, non-overt operators are truly empty in that they simply lack a range. This means that a non-overt operator has no inherent restrictions. Consider, for example, a wh-element like *who*. An overt wh-operator has lexical specifications; among these lexical specifications are features that give a clue as to the kind of elements of domain D this operator may range over.

(40) a. the rock who John threw ...
b. Who did John fill the tub with?
c. Who elapsed?

In example (40a) the relative clause is predicated of *the rock*. But the lexical features of *the rock* are in conflict with the features that specify the potential range of the relative operator *who*; hence, the example is odd. Under one reading, example (40b) presupposes that John filled the tub using some person; since people are not generally the sort of material one uses to fill a tub, this reading is again odd and the comitative reading is the only natural one. The address of (40b) is most easily captured by assuming that *who* may only range over the set of humans. The verb *elapse* in (40c) selects nouns that measure time as its subject; given that *who* is restricted to range over humans, the example is again odd.

The behavior of non-overt operators contrasts markedly from that of overt operators insofar as a non-overt operator may range over just about anything:

Control and non-overt operators

(41) a. We found a person$_i$ [$_{CP}$ Op$_i$ [$_{IP}$ PRO to hire t_i]]
  b. [an hour [$_{CP}$ Op$_i$ [$_{IP}$ PRO to waste t_i]]] would be a nice luxury
  c. John gave Mary a rock$_i$ [$_{CP}$ Op$_i$ [$_{IP}$ PRO to throw t_i at Bill]]
  d. We need some water$_i$ [$_{CP}$ Op$_i$ [$_{IP}$ PRO to fill this tub with t_i]]

As the above examples illustrate, non-overt operators may range over just about anything: people, units of time, rocks, water, etc. It is a plausible operating assumption that non-overt operators have no inherent range; they must, rather, pick up their range from some other element.[2]

A reasonable proposal is that non-overt operators must be identified; that is, non-overt operators must pick up their range from some other element. Furthermore, this identification procedure may apply at S-Structure, as the parasitic-gap examples show. Let us first consider parasitic-gap constructions.

A parasitic gap is licensed by a variable that (apparently) does not c-command it. Thus, an example like:

(42) Who$_i$ did John snap [$_{NP}$ photos of t_i] without warning e_i

is well-formed, although the licensing variable almost certainly does not c-command out of the NP which contains it. Further, a wh-element that remains *in situ* at S-Structure is never capable of licensing a parasitic gap:

(43) *Why did John snap [$_{NP}$ photos of who(m)$_i$] without warning e_i

The simplest hypothesis is that these two properties of parasitic-gap constructions are not unrelated; that is, the fact that a parasitic gap must be licensed by a variable which does not c-command it and the fact that wh-elements *in situ* cannot license parasitic gaps are really the same fact. Notice further that the operator which binds the licensing variable must c-command the parasitic gap:

(44) *[$_{NP}$ the book [that Mary filed t_i]] was reviewed (by John) without reading e_i

In (44) the relative operator may not c-command out of the relative clause and the parasitic gap is contained in an adjunct on the matrix IP; hence, the relative operator cannot c-command the non-overt operator. We assume, then, that the operator which binds the licensing variable must c-command the non-overt operator, although the licensing variable may not c-command the non-overt operator.

Given the above evidence, the hypothesis that the non-overt operator involved in parasitic-gap structures has anaphoric properties has explanatory force. First, the non-overt operator has no inherent range; rather, it must pick up a range from some other element. Second, the non-overt operator must be c-commanded by the element from which it receives its range. This second requirement looks very much like a standard binding relationship, so we will hypothesize that the non-overt operator must be bound. I will now turn to a brief summary of a generalized binding theory, the principles of which can be used to constrain the distribution of non-overt operators.

A generalized binding theory

In recent work, J. Aoun (1981, 1985, 1986) has explored the idea of extending the Binding theory to cover not only the possible co-indexing relationships that may hold between A-positions (as in the Binding theory of Chomsky 1981), but also the possible co-indexing relationships that may hold between A-positions and Ā-positions. Such a binding theory predicts the existence, for example, of Ā-anaphors in addition to the A-anaphors like reflexives (e.g. *herself*) and reciprocals (e.g. *each other*). In particular, one might imagine that the following possibilities obtain for antecedent/anaphor relations:

(45) | *Antecedent* | *Anaphor* |
| --- | --- |
| a. A-position | A-position |
| b. A-position | Ā-position |
| c. Ā-position | A-position |
| d. Ā-position | Ā-position |

Schema (45a) represents the case where the antecedent and the anaphor both occupy A-positions. This is, of course, the case covered by condition A of the standard Binding theory outlined above (p. 26–31).

Schema (45b), where the anaphor is in an Ā-position and the antecedent is in an A-position, represents a more interesting case. Let us suppose that condition A of the Binding theory is now formulated as:

(46) An X-anaphor must be X-bound in its governing category.

We turn now to (45c), which represents an element in an Ā-position which locally binds an anaphor in an A-position. This relationship is exemplified by wh-trace which must occur in an A-positions and must be bound by an element in an Ā-position. The standard Binding theory of Chomsky (1981) requires only that these elements not be locally bound by an element in an A-position. The Binding theory does not explicitly require that wh-trace be bound by an element in an Ā-position. The Ā-binding of variables must be guaranteed by a principle which lies outside the binding conditions *per se*. In general, it is assumed that unbound variables are ruled out, along with vacuous quantification, by the Bijection Principle (see Koopman and Sportiche 1981).

A generalized binding theory would treat the operator/variable relationship as falling under condition A. At the same time, variables appear to obey condition C:

(47) *Who$_i$ does he$_i$ think that Bill saw t_i

Example (47) is ungrammatical under the interpretation where the pronoun *he* is taken as bound by the wh-operator, *who*. This follows from condition C of the Binding theory, since the pronoun binds the wh-trace from an A-position.

At first glance, these principles would seem to be in conflict, since condition A requires that an element be bound in its governing category while condition C requires an element to be free. It is helpful to think of a generalized binding theory as defining two parallel systems of binding. One, the A-system, holds of relationships between A-positions only. The Ā-system adds Ā-positions to the set of possible relationships. Thus, it is possible to obey condition A of the Ā-system and condition C of the A-system at the same time. Such an element would be obligatorily bound from an Ā-position but could not be bound from an A-position. These are exactly the properties of wh-traces.

To give a brief illustration of the generalized binding theory, consider sentences like the following:

(48) a. [$_{CP}$ who$_i$ did [$_{IP}$ John say [$_{CP}$ t_i [$_{IP}$ t_i' saw Bill]]]]
 b. *[$_{CP}$ who$_i$ did [$_{IP}$ John say [$_{CP}$ t_i that [$_{IP}$ t_i' saw Bill]]]]

(49) a. [$_{CP}$ who$_i$ did [$_{IP}$ John say [$_{CP}$ t_i [$_{IP}$ Bill saw t_i']]]]
 b. [$_{CP}$ who$_i$ did [$_{IP}$ John say [$_{CP}$ t_i that [$_{IP}$ Bill saw t_i']]]]

An ECP account of the facts in (48) and (49) (see, for example, Chomsky 1986) would claim that the position occupied by t_i', in (48) is not a position which is properly governed by a lexical head. In order for a variable in these positions to be properly governed, then, they must be antecedent-governed from the Spec of Comp. But antecedent-government from the Spec of Comp is blocked by the Minimality Condition (Chomsky 1986) due to the presence of the complementizer *that* in (48b); hence, the trace would be neither lexically governed nor antecedent-governed and would violate the ECP. In the well-formed example, (48a), the complementizer is absent, so the trace in the Spec of Comp may antecedent-govern the trace in subject position. The examples in (49) show that a variable in object position would not violate the ECP, since this position is θ-governed by the verb.

In terms of a generalized binding theory, the question becomes one of what governing category a trace has, where a governing category is the smallest domain containing the trace and a SUBJECT (i.e. a nominal element) accessible to that trace. Variables in A-positions other than subject have no governing category since they never have an accessible SUBJECT. This follows from the fact that variables are subject both to condition A of the Ā-binding system and condition C of the A-binding system: a SUBJECT is accessible to a position only if that position may legally be bound by that SUBJECT; but a variable in object position which is co-indexed with the Infl of the clause will be A-bound, since the Infl is obligatorily co-indexed with the subject under agreement.

One consequence of this approach is that variables in object position need not be Ā-bound in a local domain. It is, therefore, possible to leave wh-elements in non-subject position *in situ*, since LF movement will not result in a violation of condition A of the Ā-system. Hence, the grammaticality of the examples in (49) follows immediately.

The contrast in (48) follows if subject traces acquire a governing category. Since the subject position may be co-indexed with Infl, the agreement element of Infl will act as an accessible SUBJECT for the trace. Hence, a subject trace must be Ā-bound in the CP which most immediately contains it. If the complementizer, *that*, blocks antecedent-government by the trace in the Spec of Comp in (48b), then the subject trace will be Ā-free in its governing category, which violates condition A of the Ā-system of binding. Since antecedent-government is not blocked by a complementizer in (48a), the trace in subject position is Ā-bound in its governing category, as required by the generalized binding theory.

The preceding discussion of the generalized binding theory is not intended to be comprehensive; the reader is encouraged to consult Aoun (1985, 1986) for a thorough discussion. The crucial notion for my present purposes is that of an Ā-anaphor which must be locally bound from a non-argument position. I will argue that non-overt operators fall into exactly this class of elements.

Non-overt operators as anaphors

We are operating under the assumption that the Binding theory really represents two systems of binding – the A-system and the Ā-system. A parasitic gap is not well-formed if the licensing variable c-commands it. This fact follows immediately if we assume that non-overt operators are pure Ā-anaphors. Given that non-overt operators are pure Ā-anaphors, they may not be locally A-bound. Consider examples like:

(50) a. *$[_{CP}$ which papers$_i$ $[_{IP}$ t_i were filed [without $[_{CP}$ Op$_i$ $[_{IP}$ PRO reading t_i]]]]]

b. *$[_{CP}$ who$_i$ $[_{IP}$ t_i left [without $[_{CP}$ Op$_i$ $[_{IP}$ John's seeing t_i]]]]]

In each of the examples in (50) there is a variable in the subject position of the matrix IP. This variable will c-command the non-overt operator in the Comp of the adjunct CP. Given these conditions, the variable in the subject position of the matrix IP will locally A-bind the non-overt operator. If this is correct, then the non-overt operator is not locally Ā-bound, which violates condition A of the Ā-system of binding.

Our assumption that non-overt operators are Ā-anaphors makes an additional prediction, if we assume that they are pure Ā-anaphors subject only to condition A of the Ā-system of binding. Let us consider, for a moment, the minimal domain in which such an anaphor must be bound:

(51) [$_{CP}$ who$_i$ [$_{IP}$ John Infl admire t_i [without [$_{CP}$ Op$_i$ [$_{IP}$ PRO ever having met t_i]]]]]

The non-overt operator is in the Comp of the adjunct clause, and so may not have the adjunct CP as its governing category. The question is whether or not the governing category of the non-overt operator is the superordinate CP. But we already have evidence that the governing category for anaphors in Comp is the superordinate CP; consider the contrast in (52):

(52) a. John$_i$ wondered [$_{CP}$ [$_{NP}$ which pictures of himself$_i$]$_j$ [$_{IP}$ Sue liked t_j]]
 b. *John$_i$ said [$_{CP}$ that [$_{IP}$ Mary wondered [$_{CP}$ [$_{NP}$ which pictures of himself$_i$]$_j$ [$_{IP}$ Sue liked t_j]]]]

Example (52a) shows that an anaphor in an embedded Comp may have an antecedent in the superordinate IP. Example (52b) shows that the anaphor in Comp may look no higher than the superordinate CP for its antecedent. Similarly, we have already seen that traces in Comp must be bound in the superordinate CP. We will assume, then, that the governing category for pure anaphors in the Spec of a Comp is the superordinate clause.

If this is correct, then we have a very strict locality condition on the distribution of non-overt operators. Consider examples like those in (53) (see Longobardi 1985):

(53) a. *[$_{CP}$ which famous professor$_i$ [$_{IP}$ did Mary persuade t_i [$_{CP}$ that [$_{IP}$ John invented the binding theory without [$_{CP}$ Op$_i$ [$_{IP}$ PRO consulting t_i]]]]]]
b. *[$_{NP}$ the girl [$_{CP}$ who$_i$ [$_{IP}$ I talked to t_i [$_{CP}$ without [$_{IP}$ PRO knowing [$_{CP}$ that [$_{IP}$ John was a very happy man before [$_{CP}$ Op$_i$ [$_{IP}$ he met t_i]]]]]]]]]]

In example (53a) the adjunct containing the non-overt operator is itself contained in an embedded clause; by our assumption, the governing category of the non-overt operator must be the embedded CP. The antecedent for the non-overt operator is in the matrix clause, however. The non-overt operator is free in its governing category and the example is ungrammatical. In (53b) the non-overt operator is contained in an adjunct (headed by *before*) that is itself contained in an adjunct (headed by *without*). The CP governed by *without* must be the governing category for the non-overt operator, under our operating assumption. The antecedent, however, is outside of the non-overt operator's governing category, which means, of course, that the non-overt operator is free in its governing category. As expected, the example is ungrammatical.

There are, however, a number of apparent counterexamples to the hypothesis that non-overt operators are Ā-anaphors:

(54) a. John$_i$ is easy [$_{CP}$ Op$_i$ [$_{IP}$ PRO to please t_i]]
b. The book$_i$ was bought [$_{CP}$ Op$_i$ [$_{IP}$ PRO to read t_i to the children]]
c. A shovel$_i$ is [$_{CP}$ Op$_i$ [$_{IP}$ PRO to dig with t_i]]

Example (54a) is a tough-movement construction, (54b) is a purposive, and (54c) has an infinitival clause in the predicate position of the matrix clause. In each of the examples, the subject of the matrix c-commands a non-overt operator. Under the assumption that the subject in each of the above sentences is co-indexed with the non-overt operator, we are apparently forced to admit that the non-overt operator in each of the above examples is A-bound, a state of affairs which, as argued above, is not allowed under the binding analysis of non-overt operators. One could, of course, argue that the structures in (54) all involve predication.

Non-overt operators have no implicit range; the only way a non-overt operator can assign a range to the variable which it binds is if it can pick up a range from some other element. In the case of parasitic gaps, the non-overt operator picks up a range from some operator which locally binds it. Let us suppose that the structures in (54) involve a form of predication. That is, in (54a) the CP complement to *easy* is predicated of the matrix subject, *John*; in (54b), the purpose clause, *to read to the children*, is predicated of the object, *the book*; and in (54c) *to dig with* is predicated of the subject, *a shovel*.

Following Williams (1980), let us assume that predication involves the copying of the index of the subject onto the predicate that applies to this subject. The co-indexation involved in predication must be distinct from that involved in binding. Specifically, the co-indexation involved in predication involves the identification of an open slot in the predicate's θ-grid (see the discussion of Higginbotham 1985 in Chapter 3), while the co-indexation involved in binding involves delimiting the range or reference of a noun phrase. Under this treatment, then, non-overt operators may correspond to an open argument in a predicate's θ-grid and this open argument must be identified by an element with referential content.

A standard assumption of $\bar{X}$ theory is that the features of a node are shared by all the projections of that node. In particular, an index assigned to a projection will be shared by all its projections, including the head. For example, the representations in (54) are structures of predication, so the index on the subject will be copied onto the predicate, as in (55):

(55) a. John$_i$ is easy [$_{CP}$ Op$_j$ [$_{IP}$ PRO to please t_j]]$_i$
b. The book$_i$ was bought [$_{CP}$ Op$_j$ [$_{IP}$ PRO to read t_j to the children]]$_i$
c. A shovel$_i$ is [$_{CP}$ Op$_j$ [$_{IP}$ PRO to dig with t_j]]$_i$

The index assigned to each of the CPs in (55) under predication will percolate down to the head of CP (Comp). The non-overt operator occupies the Spec of Comp which must agree with (i.e. bear the same index as) Comp (see Chomsky 1986 for some discussion). The non-overt operator (and the trace it binds) will be re-indexed to agree with Comp by this convention. The result is shown in (56):

(56) a. John$_i$ is easy [$_{CP}$ Op$_i$ [$_{IP}$ PRO to please t_i]]$_i$
b. The book$_i$ was bought [$_{CP}$ Op$_i$ [$_{IP}$ PRO to read t_i to the children]]$_i$
c. A shovel$_i$ is [$_{CP}$ Op$_i$ [$_{IP}$ PRO to dig with t_i]]$_i$

Since the non-overt operator now bears the same index as the subject of the CP that dominates it, the range of the non-overt operator is delimited by that of the subject of the predication. Notice that the 'range' of the subject is sometimes identical to the reference of a term, as in (56a), where the proper noun, *John*, refers to a unique individual.

Summarizing the analysis put forth in this section, we have assumed that non-overt operators lack any referential content and, so, must be treated as anaphoric. The following, then, acts as a constraint on their distribution:

(57) Non-overt operators must be identified.

'Identification' is intended to mean that the element bears an index. This identification requirement holds minimally of S-Structure representations, although identification may also take place at LF. Given that prediction is an S-Structure property, we would expect that much of the identification of non-overt operators is carried out at S-Structure. This derives that fact that parasitic gaps are licensed at S-Structure.

In general, elements in non-argument positions are prevented from freely receiving indices. The only way that an element in a non-argument position may receive an index is by virtue of being associated with an A-position under 'move alpha'. At S-Structure, the variable will receive an index and this index will be copied onto the operator by convention.

Our hypothesis is that R-expressions and pronominals freely receive an index at S-Structure, since they may refer independently. Anaphors receive an index by virtue of being related to an element which may refer independently. The output of indexation is, of course, subject to a generalized binding theory. Non-overt operators have no inherent range. The only way a non-overt operator and the variable which it binds can receive an index is by being associated with an element that independently receives an index. We have seen that there are two ways in which a non-overt operator may be associated with an element that bears an index. First, the non-overt operator may enter into a binding relation with the other element. In this case, the binder must occupy an Ā-position and the relationship between the non-overt operator and its binder is subject to condition A of the Ā-binding system. Second, the non-overt operator may occur in the head position of a predicate in a predication structure. In this case, the index on the subject will be copied onto the predicate and percolate down to the non-overt operator. Since the relationship between a predicate and its subject is local, this second manner in which a non-overt operator may be identified is quite restrictive.

4.3 Non-overt operators and control

The idea that the control of PRO has some connection with Ā-binding was, to my knowledge, first discussed in Epstein (1984) and Lebeaux (1984), both of whom noted the similarity between the interpretation of PRO_{arb} and a quantified argument. I will, following Epstein, assume that PRO_{arb} is universally quantified, although the actual interpretation is closer to that of a generic.

Epstein points out that a sentence like:

(58) It is fun $[_{CP}$ $[_{IP}$ PRO_{arb} to play baseball]]

seems to have an interpretation similar to:

(59) [for all x [it is fun [x to play baseball]]]

Epstein argues that the arbitrary PRO itself could not be treated as an operator, since that would allow a reading like the following:

(60) It is fun [for all x [x to play baseball]]

where *fun* has scope over the universal quantifier. He argues, instead, that there is a non-overt argument in (58) which acts as the controller of the 'arbitrary' PRO. Notice that *fun* may take an overt benefactive, which may be taken as an obligatory controller for the PRO:

(61) It is fun for $John_i$ $[_{CP}$ $[_{IP}$ PRO_i to play baseball]]

He identifies this non-overt argument with pro; thus, (58) has a structure parallel to:

(62)   [$_{CP}$ [$_{IP}$ it is fun pro$_i$ [$_{CP}$ PRO$_i$ to play baseball]]]

The pro in (62) is subject to quantifier raising and interpretation as a universal quantifier, thus yielding an LF where the universal quantifier has scope over the matrix predicate, *fun*, as desired:

(63)   [$_{CP}$ [$_{IP}$ pro$_i$ [$_{IP}$ it is fun t_i [$_{CP}$ [$_{IP}$ PRO$_i$ to play baseball]]]]]

Similarly, Lebeaux proposes that a non-overt operator that will Ā-bind the arbitrary PRO is inserted at LF. He points out that it is not always plausible to induce an 'implicit' argument (as in the above example):[3]

(64)   a. John likes stories about PRO bettering oneself.
       b. PRO to know him is PRO to love him.

The interpretation of the above examples does not seem to admit another non-overt argument. Lebeaux argues, then, that a non-overt operator must be inserted into the LF representations of the above sentences rather than originating in a phonetically null argument-position. Nevertheless, both Epstein and Lebeaux agree that arbitrary PRO behaves, ultimately, as though it were bound by some operator, possibly a universal quantifier, at LF.

The proposal to be developed in this section is somewhat different. In general, we will take PRO, whether it is obligatorily controlled or arbitrary, to be a special case of a non-overt operator which undergoes movement to a non-argument position. A number of analytical problems must be addressed. We must determine whether the movement of this putative non-overt operator takes place in the mapping from D-Structure to S-Structure or in the mapping from S-Structure to LF. Furthermore, we must find some evidence regarding the position that the non-overt operator moves to (i.e. it may be constrained to move only to Comp or it may be adjoined to some other category). Finally, there is an apparent correlation between PRO and the subject position of non-finite clauses; we must show that an analysis of PRO that identifies it with a non-overt operator can capture this perceived correlation. The best way to develop the analysis is to consider the various control structures case by case, and trace out the ramifications these structures have for our set of assumptions.

An operator analysis of PRO

I will begin with some cases of undisputed obligatory control as in:

(65) a. John$_i$ tried PRO$_i$ to leave
 b. Bill$_i$ wanted PRO$_i$ to kick himself$_i$
 c. Mary$_i$ promised PRO$_i$ to talk to Bill

Under the assumption that PRO is a non-overt operator, these examples would have the representations at some level:

(66) a. [$_{CP}$ [$_{IP}$ John$_i$ tried [$_Y$ Op$_x$ [$_{IP}$ t_x to leave]]]]
 b. [$_{CP}$ [$_{IP}$ Bill$_i$ wanted [$_Y$ Op$_x$ [$_{IP}$ t_x to kick himself$_x$]]]]
 c. [$_{CP}$ [$_{IP}$ Mary$_i$ promised [$_Y$ Op$_x$ [$_{IP}$ t_x to talk to Bill]]]]

We want to know what category 'Y' is in each of the above examples. If we identify 'Y' with CP, then the non-overt operator is in the Spec of Comp. Further, we must determine whether the above examples are S-Structure representations or representations at some other level, perhaps LF.

I will assume, following, for example, Chomsky (1977) and Stowell (1981), that a head that subcategorizes for a CP may subcategorize for certain features of the head of that CP. For example, *wonder* subcategorizes for a Comp marked [+WH]:

(67) a. John wondered [$_{CP}$ what$_j$ [$_{IP}$ he should sell t_j]]
 b. *John wondered [$_{CP}$ [$_{IP}$ he should sell his car]]

Example (67b) would be ruled out because the embedded Spec of Comp does not agree with Comp for the [+WH] feature. The requirement placed on the lower CP by *wonder* is not satisfied. Other verbs, like *hope*, subcategorize for a [−WH] CP:

(68) a. Bill hoped [$_{CP}$ (that) [$_{IP}$ John would buy a new corvette]]
  b. *Bill hoped [$_{CP}$ what$_i$ [$_{IP}$ John would buy t_i]]

Similarly, verbs may specify whether or not the Comp is related to a tensed Infl or a non-finite Infl:

(69) a. John knows [that he is too tall]
  b. *John knows [to be too tall]
(70) a. John tried [to enter the race]
  b. *John tried [that he would enter the race]

although some verbs place no such restriction on their complement and may take either a finite or non-finite complement:

(71) a. John thought [that Bill is a fool]
  b. John thought [Bill to be a fool]

Given that verbs may place restrictions on the content of the Comp of a CP complement, we could merely say that obligatory control verbs subcategorize for a CP that contains a non-overt operator; technically, this is analogous to the class of verbs (e.g., *wonder*) that subcategorize for a wh-element in the Comp of their sentential complements. Continuing the analogy with verbs like *wonder*, we can say that a Comp that contains a non-overt operator is marked with the feature [+N(on-overt) O(perator)], possibly related in some way to the feature [±WH], since the two are in complementary distribution. Thus, obligatory-control verbs subcategorize for a [+NO] Comp. We may instantiate 'Y' in the structures in (66) as CP and say that the non-overt operator is in the Spec of Comp:

(72) a. [$_{CP}$ [$_{IP}$ John$_i$ tried [$_{CP}$ Op$_x$ [$_{IP}$ t_x to leave]]]]
  b. [$_{CP}$ [$_{IP}$ Bill$_i$ wanted [$_{CP}$ Op$_x$ [$_{IP}$ t_x to kick himself$_x$]]]]
  c. [$_{CP}$ [$_{IP}$ Mary$_i$ promised [$_{CP}$ Op$_x$ [$_{IP}$ t_x to talk to Bill]]]]

We can easily eliminate the feature [±NO] by assuming that the class of control verbs are distinguished by the fact that they subcategorize for a Comp associated with an infinitival clause ([−that]) and the fact that these verbs are not Exceptional Case-Marking verbs ([−S-Deletion]). The apparent exceptions to these generalizations, *want* and *prefer*, are putative Exceptional Case-Marking verbs:

(73) a. I want [John to win the race]
      b. I prefer [it to rain once a year]
(74) a. I want [*e* to win the race]
      b. I prefer [*e* to do my own paper work]

Chomsky (1981) argues that, in fact, these verbs are not true Exceptional Case Markers but, rather, they allow for the deletion of the complementizer *for*. This analysis accounts for the fact that these verbs have no passive form corresponding to the passives found with Exceptional Case-Marking verbs (the contrast in (75) and (76)):

(75) a. *John$_i$ is wanted [t_i to win the race]
      b. *It$_i$ is preferred [t_i to rain once a year]
(76) a. John$_i$ is believed [t_i to be the winner]
      b. His move$_i$ was considered [t_i to be a tactical error]

Assuming the correctness of Chomsky's analysis, control verbs can be represented in the lexicon in the following way, where the Š-Deletion feature marks the properties of Exceptional Case-Marking verbs:

(77)
$$\begin{bmatrix} /\text{CONTROL VERB}/ \\ +[\underline{\quad} \quad S'\,] \\ [-\text{that}] \\ [-\text{Š-Deletion}] \\ \vdots \end{bmatrix}$$

These features ensure that no lexical NP may occupy the subject position of the clausal complement, since there will be no means of assigning Case to that NP; the infinitival nature of the complement clause prevents Nominative-Case assignment and, since the superordinate verb is not an Exceptional Case-Marking verb, Accusative-Case assignment is also blocked.

It follows that the subject of the infinitival complement clause must be an empty category – pro, NP-trace, or wh-trace. The null pronominal, pro, is blocked in this position due to the identification requirement on null pronominals; its presence is not locally recoverable from the morphology. The assumption that the empty category is an NP-trace entails that the empty category must be locally bound from an A-position; this A-binding will ultimately lead to a violation of the θ-Criterion, since the NP-trace would form an A-chain with its binder which is θ-marked (in traditional terms, the controller of PRO always heads a θ-marked A-chain, see Chomsky 1982). We are left with the hypothesis that the empty category in question is a variable and, hence, that it is locally Ā-bound by some operator. This is exactly the hypothesis we are entertaining here.

If the above analysis is on the right path, then the feature [±NO] does little work for us. The non-overt operator is forced by the theory of empty categories and Case theory; this operator must be identified under the conditions discussed above (p. 160). Since these conditions involve either predication or Ā-binding, we might expect conditions on these relations to be relevant to the form and distribution of control structures. I will continue to use the feature [+NO] to designate control structures where convenient, keeping in mind that we are not committed to the place of this feature in the theory of control.

Levels of representation

I will turn now to the question of the level of representation at which the non-overt operator is in the Spec of Comp. Lasnik and Saito (1984) have argued that restrictions placed on CP must be satisfied at S-Structure in English. Their argument is based on examples like those in (67). That is, we know that *wonder* requires a [+WH] Comp since it must have an interrogative complement. Consider the following contrast:

(78) a. John wondered [$_{CP}$ what$_i$ [$_{IP}$ Bill bought t_i]]
     b. *John wondered [$_{CP}$ [$_{IP}$ Bill bought what]]

The examples in (78) differ minimally in that wh-movement has applied to *what* in the syntax in (78a), while *what* has remained *in situ* in (78b). I assume, as is standard, that wh-movement must apply to wh-elements left *in situ* in the syntax in the mapping from S-Structure to LF. Thus, the LF representation of (78b) will be identical to that of (78a). Given that the two structures are indistinguishable at LF, it must be the case that they are differentiated at some level prior to LF. Assuming that the two structures have identical D-Structures, then it must be the case that the requirement that the sentential complement to *wonder* have a [+WH] Comp must be checked at S-Structure. Generalizing from this, we can say that such requirements are uniformly checked at S-Structure in English.[4] Under the assumption that obligatory control verbs subcategorize for a [+NO] Comp and the assumption that this restriction is checked at S-Structure, then the representations in (78) are S-Structure representations. If we drop the feature [±NO], then the identification requirement on non-overt operators may be appealed to; as we shall see, obligatory control involves predication which we will take to be an S-Structure phenomenon. If so, then the representations in (21) are, again, S-Structures.

Obligatory control and predication

In preceding sections, it was argued that non-overt operators must be identified (that is, receive an index) at S-Structure and that this identification took the form either of Ā-binding or of predication. In the latter case, the index of the subject of predication was copied onto the CP containing the non-overt operator. This index, in turn, percolated down to the head of CP under the standard conventions of X̄ theory; the non-overt operator, since it is in the Spec of Comp, receives the index under agreement with the head of CP. We have also seen that this identification is strictly local. The non-overt operator must find its identifier in the immediately superordinate clause.

Notice that the configurations in (67) collapse with the configurations which Williams (1980) identified as predication structures, although the theory of predication we are assuming is much closer to that of Chierchia (1985) – interested readers should consult the latter for details. Among these structures is:

Control and non-overt operators

(79) NP V X

where the NP is the subject of the predication and X is the predicate. This schema represents sentences like the following:

(80) a. [$_{NP}$ John] [$_V$ looks] [$_{AP}$ ill]
  b. [$_{NP}$ Bill] [$_V$ became] [$_{NP}$ a logical positivist]
  c. [$_{NP}$ Frank] [$_V$ grew] [$_{PP}$ into a sorry example of mankind]

It is a lexical property of verbs like *look*, *become*, and *grow* that their complement is predicated of the subject of IP. In order to satisfy this requirement, the complement must come to be co-indexed with the subject of IP:

(81) a. [$_{NP}$ John]$_i$ [$_V$ looks] [$_{AP}$ ill]$_i$
  b. [$_{NP}$ Bill]$_i$ [$_V$ became] [$_{NP}$ a logical positivist]$_i$
  c. [$_{NP}$ Frank]$_i$ [$_V$ grew] [$_{PP}$ into a sorry example of mankind]$_i$

Our proposal is that control verbs are another instantiation of this schema, where X is taken as equal to CP, somewhat along the lines of Williams (1980). It is a lexical property of these verbs that a sentential complement must be co-indexed with the subject of IP (or some other element specified by the verb).

To take a concrete example, consider:

(82) John tried to enter the race.

Example (82), under our analysis, will have the following D-Structure:

(83) [$_{CP}$ [$_{IP}$ John tried [$_{CP}$ [$_{IP}$ Op to enter the race]]]]

If *try* subcategorizes for a [+NO] Comp, the non-overt operator must move to the Spec of Comp in the syntax; otherwise the Spec of Comp will fail to agree with the head of Comp:

(84) [$_{CP}$ [$_{IP}$ John tried [$_{CP}$ Op$_x$ [$_{IP}$ t_x to enter the race]]]]

In addition, *try* specifies that its CP complement must be predicated of the subject of IP. Thus, the following S-Structure results from this indexation plus the normal constraints on percolation and agreement:

(85) $[_{CP} [_{IP} \text{John}_i \text{ tried } [_{CP} \text{Op}_i [_{IP} t_i \text{ to enter the race}]]_i]]$

Thus, the non-overt operator in (85) obeys our constraint that non-overt operators must be identified.

Dropping the assumption that the grammar includes the feature [±NO], we achieve the same result, given that the empty category in subject position must have some referential properties in order to bear a θ-role. The only available mechanism for receiving a range is to be associated with an operator. If the operator moves to the Spec of Comp, it will bear the index associated with that Comp. If the operator does not move to the Spec of Comp, it will be unidentified, resulting in a violation of the θ-Criterion. The identification of the non-overt operator through predication of the CP obeys the constraint on locality discussed above (p. 156); the non-overt operator is associated with an element in the super-ordinate clause. Under either set of assumptions regarding the feature [±NO], obligatory control is an S-Structure phenomenon.

Let us take another example of control. In particular, let us consider the case of 'psych' verbs:

(86)   a. [PRO$_i$ shaving himself$_i$] bothers John
       b. ??[PRO$_{arb}$ shaving oneself] bothers John

Psych verbs present a problem to theories which treat controlled PRO as an anaphor, since the controlled PRO is never c-commanded by its antecedent. Most generally, such theories have treated PRO in these cases as arbitrary; this is often interpreted as meaning that the PRO has pronominal properties. In other words, the PRO may freely range over individuals in domain D. Thus, accidental coreference is possible between the PRO inside the sentential subject and an object NP.

There is a shortcoming in this account, however. If PRO may accidentally corefer with any NP by virtue of ranging freely over elements in domain D, then we would expect that PRO could be taken as coreferential with any NP in the sentence. J. Aoun (personal communication) has pointed out that this is not the case:

Control and non-overt operators

(87) a. *[PRO$_i$ shaving himself$_i$] bothers [John$_i$'s mother]$_j$
 b. *[PRO$_i$ feeding themselves$_i$] worries [the man in charge of [the lions]$_i$]$_j$

While we will return to cases of non-obligatory control below, we can develop an account of controlled PRO in the above examples. Notice that psych verbs, like obligatory control verbs discussed above (p. 136), establish a relation between individuals and propositions. Like obligatory control verbs, we can say that psych verbs require a predication relation between the subject of IP and an object; in other words, psych verbs require co-indexing between subject and object.[5] Unlike obligatory control verbs, the embedded sentence is in subject position rather than object position; as a result, the verb does not govern, and so cannot place restrictions on, the embedded CP. The D-Structure of an example like (88a) would be (88b):

(88) a. To shave himself$_i$ would bother John$_i$.
 b. [$_{IP}$ [$_{CP}$ [$_{IP}$Op to shave himself]] would bother John]

In the syntax, the non-overt operator could optionally move to the Spec of Comp, as in:

(89) [$_{IP}$ [$_{CP}$ Op$_x$ [$_{IP}$ t_x to shave himself]] would bother John]

Obligatory indexation of the subject and object, along with the usual percolation, agreement, and re-indexation conventions, would yield:

(90) [$_{IP}$ [$_{CP}$ Op$_i$ [$_{IP}$ t_i to shave himself$_i$]]$_i$ would bother John$_i$]

In example (90) the non-overt operator in the Spec of the CP of the sentential subject ultimately receives an index under predication and is, as a result, identified as required by our account of the distribution of non-overt operators. Notice that we do not generate examples like those in (87), where the PRO is co-indexed with an NP that is not a sister to the verb. This is because the indexation specified by psych verbs must hold between the subject and some complement to the verb; given the usual assumptions about government and complementation, the verb could not specify that a non-complement be co-indexed with the subject of IP. Chierchia (1985) should be consulted for some discussion of the notion of predication that underlies this discussion.

Finally, notice that the sentential subject c-commands and is co-indexed with *John* in (90). At first blush, this appears to be a condition C violation. Since the sentential subject is predicated of *John*, however, I would argue that it lacks the referential properties to bind *John*; I will maintain the distinction between binding and predication, although both systems use the same notational device, co-indexation.

Obligatory control and adjuncts

Another environment where control of PRO seems to be obligatory is in certain adjuncts:

(91)   a. $John_i$ felt old after [PRO_i seeing $himself_i$ in the mirror]
       b. *$John_i$ felt old after [PRO_{arb} seeing oneself in the mirror]

The contrast in grammaticality between (91a) and (91b) demonstrates that PRO in these examples may not be taken to be arbitrary. The necessity for PRO to be controlled in examples such as these even over-rides the inherently [+human] interpretation that PRO normally receives:

(92)   a. It never snows after [PRO raining] in this part of the world
       b. *[PRO raining] would be a disaster now

Example (92b) is anomalous precisely because PRO_{arb} is normally taken as ranging over humans; thus, the restrictions placed on the subject position of weather verbs is violated in this example. Nevertheless, when the weather verb occurs in an adjunct, it may have a PRO subject as demonstrated in example (92a).

Notice, further, that by hypothesis the controller of a PRO in an adjunct may not be lexically specified. This is because an adjunct, by definition, does not satisfy lexical requirements; an adjunct may never be subcategorized for by a lexical head. Nevertheless, there are strong restrictions on the controller of an adjunct PRO:

(93) a. John$_i$ kissed Mary$_j$ after [PRO$_i$ seeing himself$_i$ in the mirror]
b. *John$_i$ kissed Mary$_j$ after [PRO$_j$ seeing herself$_j$ in the mirror]

The examples in (93) show that there is a strong tendency to take the subject of the matrix IP as the controller of PRO. If some other NP is to be taken as coreferential with the subject of the adjunct clause, an overt pronominal must be used:

(94) John$_i$ kissed Mary$_j$ after [she$_j$ saw herself$_j$ in the mirror]

The relationship between the PRO in an adjunct and the subject of a sentence is local, as can be seen by considering the readings of the following sentence:

(95) John$_i$ thought that Bill$_j$ died after PRO$_{\{i,j\}}$ seeing himself$_{\{i,j\}}$ in the mirror

If the PRO in the above sentence is taken as coreferential with *John*, then the entire adjunct clause must be taken as modifying the root IP. In other words, the interpretation should be that after John saw himself in the mirror, the thought that Bill died struck him (i.e. John). If, on the other hand, the PRO is taken as being controlled by *Bill*, then the adjunct must be taken as modifying the embedded IP. In this case, the interpretation should be that John thought that Bill died after Bill saw himself in the mirror. It is impossible, however, to get a 'crossed' interpretation. That is, if *John* is taken as the antecedent of PRO, then the adjunct clause cannot be interpreted as modifying the embedded clause. Thus, example (95) may not be interpreted as meaning that John thought that Bill's death occurred after John saw himself in the mirror. Similarly, if *Bill* is taken as the antecedent for the PRO, then the adjunct may not be interpreted as modifying the root IP. In other words, it cannot be the case that John's thinking that Bill had died occurs after Bill saw himself in the mirror. These facts support the contention (found in Williams 1980 and Chomsky and Lasnik

1977) that the controller of PRO must be in the clause immediately superordinate to the clause containing the PRO, just as in the cases of obligatory control examined above.

The derivation of the above cases should, by now, be apparent. The D-Structure of such a case will be like:

(96) [$_{CP}$ [$_{IP}$ John felt old [after [$_{CP}$ [$_{IP}$ Op seeing himself in the mirror]]]]]

'Move alpha' may apply in the syntax to the non-overt operator, yielding:

(97) [$_{CP}$ [$_{IP}$ John felt old [after [$_{CP}$ Op$_x$ [$_{IP}$ t_x seeing himself in the mirror]]]]]

The adjunct clause will enter into a predication relation with the matrix subject. The conventions regarding predication, percolation, agreement, and re-indexing apply, yielding the following:

(98) [$_{CP}$ [$_{IP}$ John$_i$ felt old [after [$_{CP}$ Op$_i$ [$_{IP}$ t_i seeing himself$_i$ in the mirror]]]]]

The non-overt operator in (98) is identified, under predication, with the matrix subject, as required. Since the predication process is restricted to the IP containing the subject of the predication, the 'crossed' interpretations, discussed above, will not be derived.

Compare (98), where the 'control' interpretation is forced, due to the interaction between the non-overt operator and predication, with (99), where the non-overt operator has been replaced by a pronoun:

(99) John thought Bill died after he saw himself in the mirror.

The interpretation of the pronoun is free to vary independently of whether the adjunct clause is taken as modifying the root or embedded IP.

Infinitival relatives

Next, I will turn to cases of infinitival relatives such as:

(100) [$_{NP}$ the right person [PRO to fix the sink]] could not be found

Restricting our attention to the subject NP in (100), the D-Structure is:

(101) [$_{NP}$ the right person$_j$ [$_{CP}$ [$_{IP}$ Op to fix the sink]]]

'Move alpha' may apply to the non-overt operator to give:

(102) [$_{NP}$ the right person$_j$ [$_{CP}$ Op$_i$ [$_{IP}$ t_i to fix the sink]]]

whereupon the CP may be predicated of the head of the NP causing the relative to become co-indexed with the head. The index on the relative will percolate down to head of CP and be copied onto the non-overt operator under agreement with the head, giving (103) as the S-Structure representation:

(103) [$_{NP}$ the right person$_j$ [$_{CP}$ Op$_j$ [$_{IP}$ t_j to fix the sink]$_j$]]

The non-overt operator is identified under predication at S-Structure, as required by our account.

Purposives

The account of control developed to this point collapses obligatory control with other cases of identifying non-overt operators. This idea, in fact, can be traced back to Chomsky (1980), where purposive clauses are treated as having the following S-Structure:

(104) a. John bought Bill a dog to play with
       b. John bought Bill a dog [$_{CP}$ PRO$_j$ [$_{IP}$ PRO$_i$ to play with t_j]]

The purposive clause in (104a) contains two PROs. One PRO is, of course, in the subject position of the non-finite clause, and the other occurs in Comp and Ā-binds the variable in the object of the preposition, *with*. Both of the PROs in (104) are then subject to a rule of control. Chomsky's theory of control consisted of the following principles:

(105) ... V ... [$_{CP}$ COMP ... PRO ...]
where V = [−F], and V and CP c-command one another.

(106) NP is a *controller* for V in [105] if
   a. NP is an indexed NP properly related to V;
   b. if V = [+S(ubject) C(ontrol)], then NP is the subject of V.

Some comments on (105) and (106) are perhaps in order. The feature [±F] is used to indicate whether or not a particular verb is a control verb; it is, in some ways, quite analogous to the feature [±NO] in this chapter. The notion 'properly related to V' is intended to include argument positions like subject, object, and indirect object. We could, thus, express the intended relation in terms of the thematic grid on the verb. Finally, the feature [±SC] stipulates that if a verb is [+SC], then its subject will control the PRO. This stipulation is necessary, since a minimal-distance principle is assumed to be involved with the rule of control in the unmarked case. Chomsky then gives a rule of control:

(107) In [105]
   a. if Comp ≠ null and has no controller, then PRO is assigned *arb*;
   b. PRO is assigned the index of the nearest controller.

Clause (a) in (107) is intended to account for examples like:

(108) John won't tell [$_{CP}$ how [$_{IP}$ PRO$_{arb}$ to solve the problem]]

where PRO is taken as ranging over the set of humans rather than as being controlled by *John*. We will return to these examples below. Clause (b) is the minimal-distance principle alluded to earlier in this paragraph. To see how this principle works, let us return to the application of control to the double-PRO cases:

(109) John$_1$ bought Bill$_2$ a dog$_3$ [$_{CP}$ PRO$_j$ [$_{IP}$ PRO$_i$ to play with t_j]]

The indexing and control algorithm goes from the top of the tree down, so we are first concerned with the PRO in Comp. Since *a dog* is properly related to the verb *buy*, it may count as a controller, Clause (107b) requires PRO to be assigned the index of the nearest possible controller. In this instance, the nearest possible controller is *a dog*:

(110) John$_1$ bought Bill$_2$ a dog$_3$ [$_{CP}$ PRO$_3$ [$_{IP}$ PRO$_i$ to play with t_3]]

The algorithm now applies to the next PRO, which is in the subject position of the purposive. *Prima facie*, the indexing algorithm appears to identify *a dog* as the controller of this PRO, since it is the nearest NP that can count as a controller. In current terms, co-indexing the PRO in the subject position of the purposive would induce a violation of condition C of the Binding theory, since the PRO would locally A-bind the variable in the object position of the preposition.[6] Since this indexing would violate a core principle, we may take it as given that *a dog* is not a possible controller for this PRO. This leaves *Bill* as the nearest possible controller for the PRO. The indexing algorithm thus predicts the following indexing:

(111) John$_1$ bought Bill$_2$ a dog$_3$ [$_{CP}$ PRO$_3$ [$_{IP}$ PRO$_2$ to play with t_3]]

It should be noted that the example just discussed is the 'dative-shifted' version of:

(112) John$_1$ bought a dog$_3$ for Bill$_2$ [$_{CP}$ PRO$_3$ [$_{IP}$ PRO$_2$ to play with t_3]]

The control properties of (112) are identical to those of (111) despite the difference in word order. This fact implies that some care must be taken in the definition of 'nearest controller' in (107). In brief, Chomsky defines 'nearest controller' to be the nearest NP such that mutual c-command holds between that NP and the CP containing the PRO.[7] Failing that, the nearest controller is defined to be the closest NP (presumably in terms of the string) that is c-commanded by the CP. Thus, the nearest NP for control of the PRO in Comp in (112) is *a dog*, despite the fact that, purely in terms of the ordering of the string of words, *Bill* appears to be the

Control and non-overt operators

nearest controller. This is because *Bill* is the object of the preposition *for* and so does not c-command the CP containing the PRO.

The above discussion of control in the 'On binding' framework of Chomsky (1980) is intended to give something of a historical precedent for the position taken in this chapter; namely, that control of a PRO is best treated as a special case of the analysis of non-overt operator constructions like purposive clauses. There are some important differences between the two treatments which bear noting. First, Chomsky assimilates the binding of non-overt operators to a special subsystem of grammar, Control theory. Here I am asssimilating Control theory, as far as possible, to a generalized system of binding. This latter approach itself has some precedent in recent work (see, for example, Bourchard 1983; Lebeaux 1984; Manzini 1983; and Sportiche 1983, to name but a few).

Second, there are some empirical problems with the approach taken in Chomsky (1980). For our purposes, it is sufficient to focus on one such problem. We have seen that Chomsky blocks control of PRO in only a very restricted set of environments; crucially, the subject position of a purposive was assumed not to be an environment for arbitrary PRO. This last assumption was necessary in order to induce the putatively obligatory nature of double control in these structures. Let us consider control into a purposive like the following:

(113) John$_1$ bought a dog$_2$ [$_{CP}$ PRO$_i$ [$_{IP}$ PRO$_j$ to play with t_i]]

As we have seen, the PRO in Comp in (113) will be controlled by the nearest controller, *a dog*. We must now determine the controller of the PRO in the subject position of the purposive; since *a dog* is already a controller, we are left with only one possible nearest controller, the subject of the matrix clause. After application of the control algorithm with respect to the subject position of the purposive, we predict the following indexing:

(114) John$_1$ bought a dog$_2$ [$_{CP}$ PRO$_2$ [$_{IP}$ PRO$_1$ to play with t_2]]

This indexing seems to accord with the naive interpretation of example (113). This example should be contrasted, however, with an example like:

(115) Armageddon Inc. makes {bombs/them} to drop on communists.

Example (115) will have the following S-Structure:

(116) Armageddon Inc.$_1$ makes bombs$_2$ [$_{CP}$ PRO$_2$ [$_{IP}$ PRO$_j$ to drop t_2 on communists]]

We have already exemplified how the PRO in Comp comes to be controlled by the object of the verb *make* under Chomsky's theory. At issue here is the problem of the control properties of the PRO in the subject position of the purposive clause. Under the 'On binding' assumptions, the PRO will be obligatorily controlled by the subject of the matrix IP, *Armageddon Inc.*, as shown in (117):

(117) Armageddon Inc.$_1$ makes bombs$_2$ [$_{CP}$ PRO$_2$ [$_{IP}$ PRO$_1$ to drop t_2 on communists]]

I am assuming that indices are eventually interpreted by a function that maps indices onto elements of domain D and that this function is constrained to preserve identity of indices; if two indices are identical in the syntax then they must be mapped onto the same element of domain D by the interpretive function. This assumption about the link between syntactic indices and the interpretation of reference implies that (117) is interpreted as true under some interpretation if and only if the same individual that makes bombs also drops the bombs on communists. Surely, example (117) implies nothing of the sort; the sentence in (117) is consistent with a state of affairs where Armageddon Inc. makes bombs and someone else drops these bombs on communists.

To press the point somewhat further, consider the following examples:

(118) a. John bought these books to read to the children.
b. The school board bought these books to read to the children.

In the absence of any prior context, many speakers are inclined to say that in order for (118a) to be true, John must both buy the books and read them to the children; in other words, *John* is apparently taken as the controller of the PRO in the subject position of the purposive clause in (118a). Example (118b) differs from (118a) only in the NP that occupies the subject position of the matrix clause; we may assume that there is no syntactically relevant structural difference between (118a) and (118b), since the two are identical up to the choice of lexical items for the subject NP. Nevertheless, speakers I have consulted have consistently allowed an interpretation where the school board buys the books and some other party reads them to the children. Thus, identifying the PRO subject of a purposive with a position of obligatory control runs the risk of destroying any connection at all between the syntactic notion of 'identity of indices' and the semantic notion of 'identity of reference' (but see the discussion of 'arbitrary' control on p. 161).

Some comment is in order on the tendency to take the subject of IP as controlling the subject of the purposive clause. A complete discussion of this proclivity will, of necessity, foreshadow some of the analysis that will be developed below, so comments here will be of a somewhat tentative nature. Taking the examples at hand, notice that the verb *buy* allows the appearance of a benefactive argument; this benefactive may appear as the object of the preposition *for*, or it may appear immediately after the verb in 'dative-shift' constructions:

(119) a. John bought Bill these books to read to the children.
b. The school board bought these books for the teachers to read to the children.

This benefactive argument need not be realized in the syntax, as the examples in (118) illustrate. Notice that realization of this argument by an empty category is not possible in English under the assumption that this empty category is a pure pronominal (pro), since English apparently lacks pro, as can be seen from the ungrammaticality of:

(120) *pro* left

and similar examples.

Completeness

Let us suppose, however, that at Logical Form (or, perhaps, some later level of representation which is semantically interpreted), elements that are in a verb's thematic grid must be realized. In particular, let us assume the existence of the following principle (see the principle of 'Full Interpretation' in Chomsky 1985):

(121)   *Completeness*
Predicates must be closed.

We interpret this completeness principle as requiring that implicit arguments must be realized at some level of representation and that, furthermore, these arguments must be bound. Such a principle would require that arguments that have been suppressed in the syntax, for example, the external thematic role in passive constructions, must be realized at some level of representation. For the sake of discussion, I will assume that this level of representation is LF. A passive S-Structure as in (122a) will be associated with an LF representation as in (122b):

(122)   a. $[_{CP} [_{IP} [_{NP}$ the thief$]_i$ was seen $t_i]]$
b. $[_{CP} [_{IP} [e]$ was $[_{VP} (\exists) [_{VP}$ seen $[_{NP}$ the thief$]] x]]]$

Notice that I further assume that NP traces may be covered in the sense that the head of an A-chain may be returned to its D-structure θ-position. Notice, finally, that the LF in (122b) contains an additional external argument-position. Assuming that Case marking is an S-Structure phenomenon, this induced argument need not receive Case, since it is not syntactically realized until LF. Thus, the position may be adjoined to VP and no insertion of a Case marker need be assumed.

The operator introduced by this process does not induce any scope ambiguities, as can be seen in examples like:

(123)   Every man is loved.

Example (123) is not ambiguous between a reading where some one individual loves every man and a reading where every man is the object of somebody's affections (not necessarily the same someone for each man). I will therefore assume that the existential quantifier is simply adjoined to some projection of the element that assigns the thematic role being realized, although I will return to this problem below (p. 200 and following). In the case of external thematic-roles, this category is, I will assume for the moment, VP. Thus, the purposive clause examples in (118) will have LF representations similar to those in (124) (leaving aside some details for later discussion):

(124) a. [$_{CP}$ [$_{IP}$ John [$_{VP}$ (∃x) [$_{VP}$ bought [$_{NP}$ these books]$_i$ x] [$_{CP}$ Op$_i$ [$_{IP}$ Op to read t_i to the children]]]]]
b. [$_{CP}$ [$_{IP}$ the school board [$_{VP}$ (∃x) [$_{VP}$ bought [$_{NP}$ these books]$_i$ x [$_{CP}$ Op$_i$ [$_{IP}$ Op to read t_i to the children]]]]]]

Finally, we need only assume that the empty element in the subject position of the purposive undergoes QR in the mapping to LF representation and may then be identified by the existential operator induced from the argument structure of the predicate of the superordinate clause, as in (125):

(125) [$_{CP}$ [$_{IP}$ the school board [$_{VP}$ (∃x) [$_{VP}$ bought [$_{NP}$ these books]$_i$ x [$_{CP}$ Op$_i$ [$_{IP}$ Op$_x$ [$_{IP}$ t_x to read t_i to the children]]]]]]]

A rough paraphrase of the above representation is: the school board has the property of there being some individual(s) such that the school board bought these books for the individual(s) and the individual(s) read(s) these books to the children.

Returning to the double-control cases, this type of sentence has the following representation:

(126) [$_{CP}$ [$_{IP}$ John [$_{VP}$ (∃x) [$_{VP}$ bought [$_{NP}$ these books]$_i$ x] [$_{CP}$ Op$_i$ [$_{IP}$ Op$_x$ [$_{IP}$ t_x to read t_i to the children]]]]]]

The above representation can be paraphrased as: John has the property of buying books for someone such that that someone reads the books to the children. The existential quantifier may range over the set of individuals who may benefit from the buying of books (presumably the set of humans). This set will, of course, possibly include John himself; thus, John is an individual who may benefit from the book-buying activity. The preference to take John as instantiating the benefactive argument could be stated as a pragmatic preference (determined at a postsyntactic level of representation); in example (118) above taking the subject as the benefactive is not simply a matter of logic, although this reading is a logical possibility. I will have occasion to extend this analysis of double control (see p. 221 and following), so I will delay any further discussion of these examples.

The result of the preceding discussion is that the so-called double-control readings in purposives do not follow from standard Control theory in the sense in which this theory is normally interpreted. This result should not be viewed as a purely negative one, since it is in accord with some facts about PRO that have been noted previously (see p. 178). That is, when the Spec of the Comp of the minimal CP containing a PRO is not null, then the PRO is subject to 'arbitrary interpretation':

(127) a. John$_i$ asked [$_{CP}$ [$_{IP}$ PRO$_i$ to shave himself$_i$]]
b. *John$_i$ asked [$_{CP}$ [$_{IP}$ PRO$_{arb}$ to shave oneself]]
c. John$_i$ asked [$_{CP}$ how [$_{IP}$ PRO$_{arb}$ to shave oneself]]

Examples similar to those in (127) have been taken as implying that control is blocked whenever Comp is not empty (see, for example, Manzini's (1983) treatment of control). Abstracting somewhat, we can identify the following as an environment for arbitrary control:

(128) NP may not control PRO in the environment:
... [$_{IP}$ ... NP ... [$_{CP}$ Spec C [$_{IP}$ PRO ...]] ...] ...
where Spec is non-null.

If the non-overt operator analysis of purposives is correct, then a purposive clause instantiates the schema in the following way:

(129) ... [$_{IP}$ ... NP ... [$_{CP}$ Op$_i$ [$_{IP}$ PRO ...]] ...] ...

The Spec of the minimal CP containing the PRO is non-null since it is occupied by the non-overt operator. Thus, we would not expect control to apply to the subject of a purposive clause, given the fundamental correctness of the schema in (128).

Let us consider the fate of an empty element (=PRO) under the analysis of PRO as a non-overt operator developed in this chapter. We begin with the following D-Structure:

(130) John bought these books [$_{CP}$ [$_{IP}$ [$_{NP}$ e] to read [$_{NP}$ e] to the children]]

where [$_{NP}$e] is taken to be an empty element at D-Structure that will ultimately be analyzed as a non-overt operator. As a first step, let us suppose that the empty element in the object position of *read* moves to the Spec of Comp of the purposive clause:

(131) John bought these books [$_{CP}$ [$_{NP}$ e]$_i$ [$_{IP}$ [$_{NP}$ e] to read t_i to the children]]

Now, suppose that the empty element in the subject position of the purposive clause undergoes 'move alpha'. From the results of the previous chapter, we are guaranteed that this empty element may only move to the Comp of the minimal CP containing it, since this CP does not satisfy any lexical requirements (see Chapter 3). Hence, the only possible S-Structure, given movement of the subject, is:

(132) John bought these books [$_{CP}$ [$_{NP}$ e]$_i$ [$_{NP}$ e]$_j$ [$_{IP}$ t_j to read t_i to the children]]

The representation in (132) is a classic example of a violation of superiority. If superiority effects are derived by means of the ECP, or some other form of head government, at LF, it is clear that (132) violates this condition, since the trace in the subject position of the purposive clause is not properly governed. Thus, I will assume that the only possible S-Structure for this example is:

(133) John bought these books [$_{CP}$ [$_{NP}$ e]$_i$ [$_{IP}$ [$_{NP}$ e] to read t_i to the children]]

I will return to the question of what prevents the empty element in the object position of *read* from remaining *in situ* in the syntax while the element in subject position moves to Comp. For the moment, let us note that the 'arbitrary' PRO in (133) is an element that remains *in situ* in the syntax.

Notice that an empty element, $[_{NP} e]$, is left in an A-position in (133). Let us suppose that this empty element has no inherent interpretation and is, furthermore, unbound at S-Structure. Since this element is unbound, it has no way of receiving an interpretation from some antecedent. I will take it as a given that an element that does not refer or, in the case of variables, does not receive a range over elements in domain D must be taken as an expletive. Thus, the empty element in the subject position of the purposive clause in (133), all things held equal, counts as an expletive. The subject position of the purposive, however, receives a thematic role under predication from the VP. Recall that (134) follows from the θ-Criterion as a well-formedness constraint on LF representations:

(134) Non-referential elements may not bear a thematic role.

A constraint like that in (134) has long been assumed in Government–Binding theory (see, for example, Chomsky 1981). If (134) is correct, then the representation in (133) is not well-formed; the empty element in the subject position of the purposive clause has no inherent reference, and so must be an expletive, but it bears a thematic role, and so may not be an expletive. The only way to circumvent this obvious contradiction is for the empty element to pick up a range from some other element.

QR may optionally apply to the empty element in the subject position of the purposive as in (135):

(135) John bought these books $[_{CP} [_{NP} e]_i [_{IP} [_{NP} e]_j [_{IP} t_j$ to read t_i to the children]]]]

The empty element now occupies an Ā-position and may be treated as a non-overt operator; meaning that this element is now treated as an Ā-anaphor which may pick up a range from some other operator in IP. Recall that we are also assuming that implicit arguments of the verb must be realized at LF (see the discussion of (121) above). The implicit benefactive argument of *buy* must, therefore, be realized and bound by an existential quantifier:

(136) $[_{CP} [_{IP}$ John $[_{VP} (\exists x) [_{VP}$ bought $[_{NP}$ these books$]_i x]$ $[_{CP} [_{NP} e]_i [_{IP} [_{NP} e]_j [_{IP} t_j$ to read t_i to the children]]]]]]

Consider the governing category and possible Ā-antecedents of the non-overt operator created in the mapping from S-Structure to LF. Notice that the purposive clause contains no accessible SUBJECT for this operator. The nearest accessible subject is the Infl of the superordinate clause, as we would expect, given our earlier discussion of non-overt operators. The representation in (136) contains two elements in Ā-positions which could act as a possible antecedent for the new non-overt operator. First, there is the non-overt operator in the Comp of the purposive. This element has received a range under predication of the purposive clause on *these books*. Let us suppose that the new non-overt operator is co-indexed with this element:

(137) $[_{CP} [_{IP}$ John $[_{VP} (\exists x) [_{VP}$ bought $[_{NP}$ these books$]_i x]$ $[_{CP} [_{NP} e]_i [_{IP} [_{NP} e]_i [_{IP} t_i$ to read t_i to the children$]]]]]]$

Notice that re-indexing the non-overt operator forces the variable that it binds to be re-indexed simply by convention. The variable in the subject position of the purposive now bears the same index as the variable in the object position of the purposive. As a result, the representation in (137) violates condition C (of the A-system) of binding. Since the Binding theory applies at least at LF (if not also at S-Structure), example (136) is filtered out. We conclude that the non-overt operator in the Spec of Comp is not a possible Ā-antecedent for the non-overt operator adjoined to IP.

There is another potential antecedent for the non-overt operator in the purposive. Namely, the existential operator induced from the argument structure of *buy* during the mapping from S-Structure to LF. Let us suppose that the non-overt operator is co-indexed with this existential operator:

(138) $[_{CP} [_{IP}$ John $[_{VP} (\exists x) [_{VP}$ bought $[_{NP}$ these books$]_i x]$ $[_{CP} [_{NP} e]_i [_{IP} [_{NP} e]_x [_{IP} t_x$ to read t_i to the children$]]]]]]$

No violation of condition C of the Binding theory occurs in representation (138), since every variable is A-free in the domain of its operator. Furthermore, every non-overt operator in (138) has picked up a range, as is indirectly required by convention (134);

the non-overt operator in the Spec of Comp of the purposive clause receives a range under predication with the object of *bought*, and the non-overt operator adjoined to the IP node of the purposive clause receives a range by virtue of being Ā-bound by the existential operator.

The above example should be contrasted with an example where an implicit argument may not be induced. Consider the contrast in (139):

(139) a. John$_i$ walked the dog [$_{CP}$ Op$_i$ [$_{IP}$ t_i to exercise it]]
b. *John$_i$ walked the dog$_j$ [$_{CP}$ Op$_j$ [$_{IP}$ Op to exercise t_j]]

In example (139a) there is only one non-overt operator which originates as the subject of the purposive at D-Structure. This non-overt operator will move to the Spec of Comp in the syntax and will be identified under predication with the subject of the matrix IP. Let us now consider the derivation of (139b); this example will have the following D-Structure:

(140) John$_i$ walked the dog$_j$ [$_{CP}$ [$_{IP}$ Op to exercise Op]]

The non-overt operator in object position moves to the Spec of Comp in the syntax and predication applies between the purposive clause and the subject of the matrix IP:

(141) John$_i$ walked the dog$_j$ [$_{CP}$ Op$_i$ [$_{IP}$ Op to exercise t_i]]

QR applies in the mapping from S-Structure to LF to the empty element in the subject position of the purposive clause, yielding the following structure:

(142) John$_i$ walked the dog$_j$ [$_{CP}$ Op$_i$ [$_{IP}$ Op$_k$ [$_{IP}$ t_k to exercise t_i]]

As shown, the representation in (142) is not well-formed, since the variable in the subject position of the purposive is not assigned a range by the non-overt operator that binds it. Since the non-overt operator is an Ā-anaphor, it may not be co-indexed with the subject of the matrix IP, *John*, since condition A of the Ā-system of binding would be violated. Furthermore, if indexing obtains between the subject of IP and the non-overt operator in question, condition C of the Binding theory will be violated since the variable in the subject position of the purposive will A-bind the variable in object position.

Similarly, suppose that the non-overt operator is co-indexed with the object of *walk*. If the object of *walk* c-commands the purpose clause, then it will A-bind the non-overt operator in question, which violates condition A of the Ā-system of binding; if the object of *walk* does not c-command the purposive clause, then the non-overt operator in question is free and, hence, lacks a range at LF and the representation is indirectly ruled out by principle (134). Since there is no additional argument that can be induced from the argument structure of *walk*, there is no Ā-element available to bind the non-overt operator. Hence, the non-overt operator may not provide a range to the variable in the subject position of the purposive clause. As a result, the subject position of the purposive must be interpreted as non-referential, in the sense of (134), and may not bear a thematic role. Since the subject position of the purposive does, in fact, receive a thematic role, the representation in (142) cannot be well-formed, since an expletive element bears a thematic role. Thus, under any assumptions about its indexing, the representation in (142) cannot be saved, which is the desired result.

Case and the distribution of non-overt operators

Further questions about the syntactic distribution of non-overt operators remain to be settled: What principle or principles restrict the distribution of non-overt operators which originate in non-subject position? What principle forces a non-overt operator originating in non-subject position to move in the syntax as opposed to undergoing QR in the mapping to LF?

Turning to the first question, it should be noted that non-overt operators originating in non-subject position have a very restricted distribution. Let us take the example of a non-overt operator in object position of a verb at D-Structure and consider the environments where the output is well-formed:

Control and non-overt operators

(143) a. [$_{NP}$ a book [$_{CP}$ Op$_i$ [$_{IP}$ PRO to read t_i]]] would be nice
b. [$_{NP}$ a well-qualified person [$_{CP}$ Op$_i$ [$_{IP}$ PRO to hire t_i]]] will not be easy to find around here
c. [$_{NP}$ some papers [$_{CP}$ Op$_i$ [$_{IP}$ PRO to send t_i to John]]] are on your desk

(144) a. This book is [$_{AdjP}$ hard [$_{CP}$ Op$_i$ [$_{IP}$ PRO to read t_i]]]
b. A well-qualified person is [$_{AdjP}$ easy [$_{CP}$ Op$_i$ [$_{IP}$ PRO to find t_i]]]
c. These papers will be [$_{AdjP}$ easy [$_{CP}$ Op$_i$ [$_{IP}$ PRO to send t_i to John]]]

(145) a. John bought a book [$_{CP}$ Op$_i$ [$_{IP}$ PRO to read t_i]]
b. John located a well-qualified person [$_{CP}$ Op$_i$ [$_{IP}$ PRO to hire t_i]]
c. Bill stacked some papers [$_{CP}$ Op$_i$ [$_{IP}$ PRO to send t_i to John]]

(146) a. Which book$_i$ did John buy t_i without [$_{CP}$ Op$_i$ [$_{IP}$ PRO reading t_i]]
b. Who$_i$ did the committee interview t_i without [$_{CP}$ Op$_i$ [$_{IP}$ PRO hiring t_i]]
c. Which papers$_i$ did Bill put t_i in an envelope without [$_{CP}$ Op$_i$ [$_{IP}$ PRO sending t_i to Bill]]

(147) a. A book is [$_{CP}$ Op$_i$ [$_{IP}$ PRO to read t_i]]
b. These papers are [$_{CP}$ Op$_i$ [$_{IP}$ PRO to send t_i to John]]
c. A shovel is [$_{CP}$ Op$_i$ [$_{IP}$ PRO to dig with t_i]]

The examples in (143) represent the case in which a non-overt operator may originate in object position and move to the Spec of a CP that modifies a noun. The examples in (144) are cases in which a non-overt operator moves to the Spec of Comp of a clause that is a complement to an adjective. The examples in (145) and

Control and non-overt operators

(146) are cases in which the non-overt operator moves to the Spec of Comp of a clause that is in an adjunct position. Finally, the examples in (147) are cases in which the non-overt operator moves to the Spec of Comp of a clause that is in a copular predicate structure.

The examples in (143–7) should be contrasted with the following structures:

(148) a. *[$_{CP}$ Op$_i$ [$_{IP}$ PRO to read t_i]] is a problem with this book
b. *[$_{CP}$ Op$_i$ [$_{IP}$ PRO to hire t_i]] is not so simple
c. *[$_{CP}$ Op$_i$ [$_{IP}$ PRO to send t_i to John]] may be difficult

(149) a. *The man wants [$_{CP}$ Op$_i$ [$_{IP}$ John {will/to} hit t_i]]
b. *This person tried [$_{CP}$ Op$_i$ [$_{IP}$ PRO to hire t_i]]
c. *These students asked [$_{CP}$ Op$_i$ [$_{IP}$ PRO to send t_i to John]]

(150) a. *The man worried [$_{PP}$ about [$_{CP}$ Op$_i$ [$_{IP}$ John's hitting t_i]]]
b. *The applicants were concerned [$_{PP}$ over [$_{CP}$ Op$_i$ [$_{IP}$ the committee's hiring t_i]]]

In the examples of (148–50) the clause containing the non-overt operator in question has a subject, an object, or an object of a preposition. Notice that each of the structures in (148–50) may take a non-overt operator in the Spec of Comp, just so long as that non-overt operator originates in the subject position of a non-finite clause:

(151) a. [$_{CP}$ Op$_i$ [$_{IP}$ t_i to read this book]] is a problem
b. [$_{CP}$ Op$_i$ [$_{IP}$ t_i to hire the right person]] is not so siimple
c. [$_{CP}$ Op$_i$ [$_{IP}$ t_i to send these papers to John]] may be difficult

(152) a. The man wants [$_{CP}$ Op$_i$ [$_{IP}$ t_i to hit John]]
b. The committee tried [$_{CP}$ Op$_i$ [$_{IP}$ t_i to hire the most qualified person]]

c. These students asked [$_{CP}$ Op$_i$ [$_{IP}$ t_i to be sent t_i to John]]

(153) a. The man worried [$_{PP}$ about [$_{CP}$ Op$_i$ [$_{IP}$ t_i hitting John]]]

b. The committee was concerned [$_{PP}$ over [$_{CP}$ Op$_i$ [$_{IP}$ t_i hiring the best aplicant]]]

We can place some organization on the above facts if we consider them in light of Case theory. Let us take the following simple form of Case theory as basically correct:

(154) a. A tensed Infl assigns Nominative Case to the position it governs;
b. V assigns Accusative Case to the position it governs;
c. P assigns Oblique Case to the position it governs.

Notice that nouns and adjectives do not assign Case and, furthermore, adjunct positions are not Case-marked. In the examples in (143–7), the CP containing the non-overt operator which originates in non-subject position is not in a Case-marked position, while the CP containing a similar non-overt operator in the examples in (148–50) are all in Case-marked positions. We will assume that the Case assigned to a CP can be associated with the Spec of CP (see Chomsky 1986 for some discussion of Case assignment to the Spec of a category). In particular, no principle requires that the CP bear the Case feature assigned to it. The entire set of data in (143–53) can be schematized in the following way:

(155) a. ... Op ... t ...
         [−Case]   [−Case]

b. ... Op ... t ...
         [+Case]   [−Case]

c. ... Op   ... t ...
      [−Case]   [+Case]
      ↑_____|

d. *... Op   ... t ...
      [+Case]   [+Case]
      ↑_____|

The schema in (155a) represents movement of a non-overt operator from a position that is not Case-marked to the Spec of a CP that is not Case-marked; thus, it corresponds to control of a subject in a clause that is in an adjunct position:

(156) a. John$_i$ left [$_{CP}$ Op$_i$ [$_{IP}$ t_i to go to the store]]
 b. Bill$_i$ ate the fondue [$_{CP}$ Op$_i$ [$_{IP}$ t_i to please Mary]]
 c. John$_i$ felt strange [$_{CP}$ Op$_i$ [$_{IP}$ t_i drinking all the beer]]

The schema in (155b) represents the movement of a non-overt operator from a position that is not Case-marked to the Spec of Comp of a CP which is assigned Case. This case corresponds to control of the subject of a clause in an A-position or one that follows a preposition:

(157) a. [$_{CP}$ Op$_i$ [$_{IP}$ t_i having his picture taken]] annoys John$_i$
 b. John$_i$ wanted [$_{CP}$ Op$_i$ [$_{IP}$ t_i to buy a new car]]
 c. John$_i$ became enraged [$_{PP}$ after [$_{CP}$ Op$_i$ [$_{IP}$ t_i reading the letter from the IRS]]]

The schema in (155c) represents movement of a non-overt operator from a Case-marked position to the Spec of Comp of a CP that is not in a Case-marked position. This schema represents tough-movement structures, infinitival relatives, purposive clauses, parasitic gaps, some sentential predicates, and, possibly, topicalization:

(158) a. John$_i$ is [$_{AdjP}$ easy [$_{CP}$ Op$_i$ [$_{IP}$ PRO to please t_i]]]
 b. [$_{NP}$ the one [$_{CP}$ Op$_i$ [$_{IP}$ PRO to see t_i]]] is John

Control and non-overt operators

    c. John bought the car$_j$ [$_{CP}$ Op$_j$ [$_{IP}$ PRO to fool around with t_j]]
    d. Which book$_i$ did Bill buy t_i without [$_{CP}$ Op$_i$ [$_{IP}$ PRO reading t_i]]
    e. A shovel$_i$ is [$_{CP}$ Op$_i$ [$_{IP}$ PRO to dig with t_i]]
    f. [this book$_i$ [$_{CP}$ Op$_i$ [$_{IP}$ I've read t_i a hundred times]]]

Notice that in the cases represented in (155a–c), there has been at most one Case-marked position in the link between the non-overt operator and the variable which it binds. The schema represented in (155d) differs from the previous one in that the link between the non-overt operator and its variable involves two Case-marked positions: the variable itself receives Case and the non-overt operator lands in the Spec of Comp of a clause that is Case-marked. This schema represents the ungrammatical structures in examples (148–50). It is interesting to observe that if the element in the Spec of Comp is lexicalized, the structures become grammatical (provided, of course, that we control for the lexical specifications of some of the verbs):

(159)   a. [$_{CP}$ what$_i$ [$_{IP}$ PRO to read t_i]] is always a problem
      b. [$_{CP}$ who$_i$ [$_{IP}$ PRO to hire t_i]] is not so simple
      c. [$_{CP}$ what$_i$ [$_{IP}$ PRO to send t_i to John]] may present some difficulties

(160)   a. the man wants [$_{CP}$ what$_i$ [$_{IP}$ John has t_i]]
      b. this person knows [$_{CP}$ who$_i$ [$_{IP}$ PRO to hire t_i]]
      c. the students asked [$_{CP}$ what$_i$ [$_{IP}$ PRO to send t_i to John]]

(161)   a. the man worried [$_{PP}$ about [$_{CP}$ what$_i$ [$_{IP}$ John said t_i]]]
      b. the applicants were concerned [$_{PP}$ over [$_{CP}$ who$_i$ [$_{IP}$ the committee would hire t_i]]]

These examples should be contrasted with (162), where it is not obvious that the operator in the Spec of Comp receives Case, due to the variation of the overt operator with a non-overt operator (Ken Safir, personal communication):

(162) a. a bigger margin than [$_{CP}$ what$_i$ [$_{IP}$ we expected t_i]]
 b. a bigger margin than [$_{CP}$ Op$_i$ [$_{IP}$ we expected t_i]]

The relevance of the examples in (162) will become evident below (see p. 194–198).

Given the near complementary distribution between non-overt operators and overt operators in the environments in (155), let us assume, provisionally, that the overt operators may be inserted as a phonological spell-out of a non-overt operator. We must now specify the conditions under which this spell-out occurs.

To come to some understanding of the above paradigm, let us take a definition of the notion 'chain' (from Chomsky 1981):[8]

(163) $C = (A_1, \ldots, A_n)$ is a chain if and only if
 a. A_1 is an NP
 b. A_i locally A-BINDS A_{I+1}
 c. for $i > 1$, A_i is a non-pronominal empty category, or A_i is A-free
 d. C is maximal, i.e. is not a proper subsequence of a chain meeting (a–c)

Notice that the above definition only holds for binding of A-positions, since clause (b) stipulates that a chain may only be formed if successive links in the chain are A-bound by their predecessors. In general, it would seem that a chain may only bear one Case-marked position. Consider a structure like:

(164) a. It seems to John that Bill is sick.
 b. *John$_i$ seems to t_i that Bill is sick.
 c. Bill$_j$ seems to John t_j to be sick.

(165) a. It struck John that Bill was sick.
 b. *John$_i$ struck t_i that Bill was sick.
 c. John$_i$ was struck t_i that Bill was sick.

The subject position in (164a) and (165a) is a $\bar{\theta}$-position, and so

Control and non-overt operators

should be available as a landing site for a moved NP, a hypothesis which is confirmed by the raising structure in (164c) and the passive in (165c). Notice that an NP originating in a Case-marked position may not land in subject position, as shown in (164b), where the NP receives Oblique Case from the preposition, and (165b), where the NP receives Accusative Case from the verb. It is reasonable to assume that the relationship between Case marking and a-chains is bi-unique: an A-chain may not contain two Case-marked positions.

It seems clear that a chain containing an overt NP must bear at least one Case, as shown in (166):

(166) *It is unclear [$_{CP}$ who$_i$ [$_{IP}$ t_i to die]]

In (166) the position bound by *who* is not Case-marked; furthermore, the CP dominating *who* is not in a position to receive Case since it is the complement of an adjective and adjectives do not, normally, assign Case.

Let us generalize the definition of chain to include both A-binding and Ā-binding:

(167) $C = (A_1, \ldots, A_n)$ is an X-chain if and only if
   a. A_1 is an NP
   b. A_i locally X-binds A_{i+1}
   c. C is maximal, i.e. is not a proper subsequence of a chain meeting (a–b)

We can say that a non-overt operator must be phonologically spelled-out if it occurs in a Case-marked Comp and heads an Ā-chain which bears Case. Assuming that an element that heads a Case-marked Ā-chain inherits (and, thus, bears) the Case of that chain, we can notate the restriction as follows:

(168) *[e   ]
         Comp [+Case]   where *e* is a non-overt operator
         [+Case]

The schema in (155) can be renotated as follows:

(169) a. ...   Op   ...   t   ...
                [−Case]   [−Case]

$$\begin{array}{ll} [& e \quad] \\ \text{Comp} & [-\text{Case}] \\ [-\text{Case}] & \end{array}$$

b. ... Op ... t ...
   [+Case]   [−Case]
   ↑_____|

$$\begin{array}{ll} [& e \quad] \\ \text{Comp} & [-\text{Case}] \\ [+\text{Case}] & \end{array}$$

c. ... Op ... t ...
   [−Case]   [+Case]
   ↑_____|

$$\begin{array}{ll} [& e \quad] \\ \text{Comp} & [+\text{Case}] \\ [-\text{Case}] & \end{array}$$

d. *... Op ... t ...
    [−Case]   [−Case]
    ↑_____|

$$\begin{array}{ll} *[& e \quad] \\ \text{Comp} & [+\text{Case}] \\ [+\text{Case}] & \end{array}$$

We would, therefore, expect that a non-overt operator can head a Caseless Ā-chain (as in 169a) and (169b)); hence, the subject of an infinitive may always be bound to a non-overt operator even if the clause containing this structure occurs in a Case-marked position. If the non-overt operator heads a Case-marked Ā-chain, then it must occur in a Caseless CP; we would thus expect that such a structure could occur only when governed by a noun or adjective or when it occurs in an adjunct position.

We can attribute the above restriction on the possible landing-sites for non-overt operators to the general tendency of phonologically null elements to avoid bearing Case. As a rule, the only null elements that may bear Case are variables and, possibly, pro. Other non-overt elements are systematically excluded from Case-marked positions. This insight underlies Bouchard's (1984) Principle of Lexicalization, which requires that Case-bearing empty categories be spelled-out phonologically. In order to make the Principle of Lexicalization work, Bouchard must assume that wh-elements, for example, carry their Case with them when they move to the Spec of Comp. This is because a Case-marked variable, under his assumptions, would have to be phonologically realized by virtue of its Case feature. This assumption is quite plausible, given a Case filter that applies to all phonologically overt NPs, regardless of their position; a wh-element might well have to carry its Case with it to the Spec of Comp in order to pass the Case filter. Suppose, following Safir (1985), that the Case filter is relativized to apply to A-positions; if this is so, then there is no need for an overt wh-element to bear Case when it occurs in an Ā-position in order to pass the Case filter. Adopting this modification of the Case filter along with the assumption that variables may have a Case feature (despite the Principle of Lexicalization), we can assume that elements moved to Ā-positions are Caseless, although they may head a Case-marked Ā-chain.

Our generalization is that a non-overt operator which heads a Case-marked Ā-chain may not appear in the Spec of a Case-marked CP. Given that the non-overt operator is phonologically null, by definition, the intuitive reason behind this restriction is that null elements avoid Case. The pairing of a Case-marked CP with a Case-marked Ā-chain is simply more than a phonologically null element can tolerate; in this environment, the non-overt operator must be lexicalized, as we have seen (examples (159–61) above). Notice that we immediately predict that 'tough' verbs cannot exist, because the non-overt operator would originate in a Case-marked position and then raise to the Spec of a Case-marked CP, creating an illegal chain. The relationship between Case and non-overt operators also sheds some light on another problem which we noted above.

We have been assuming, throughout the above discussion, that a non-overt operator in a Case-marked position obligatorily moves to the Spec of Comp in the syntax, taking precedence over a non-overt operator in the subject position of an infinitive. This assumption accounted for the interpretation of examples like:

(170) John$_i$ is [$_{AdjP}$ easy [$_{CP}$ Op$_i$ [$_{IP}$ [e] to please t_i]]]

where *John* obligatorily defines the range of the non-overt operator in the Spec of Comp under predication. We must, however, account for why the following S-Structure is impossible:

(171) *John$_i$ is [$_{AdjP}$ easy [$_{CP}$ Op$_i$ [$_{IP}$ t_i to please [e]]]]

In example (171) *John* again defines the range of the non-overt operator in Comp. The difference between (170) and (171) is that the non-overt operator in the Spec of Comp binds an empty category in the subject position of the complement clause in (171) but not in (170). In the mapping of the S-Structure in (171) to LF, we are assuming that the syntactically unrealized dative argument of *easy* is induced and bound by a universal (or generic) quantifier. Furthermore, the empty element in the object position of the complement clause would undergo QR and be interpreted as a non-overt operator:

(172) John$_i$ is [$_{AdjP}$ ($\forall$x) [$_{AdjP}$ easy x [$_{CP}$ Op$_i$ [$_{IP}$ [$_{IP}$ Op$_x$ t_i to please t_x]]]]]

Note that the new non-overt operator in (172) is an Ā-anaphor and must receive a range from some Ā-binder. The only possible Ā-binder is the quantifier induced from the argument structure of *easy*. As shown in (172), the non-overt operator takes on the index of the quantifier. Presumably, such a structure would have the sensible interpretation that it is easy for John to please people; hence, the structure in (172) cannot be ruled out purely on the basis of having an anomalous interpretation.

Thus, non-overt operators show an 'anti-superiority' effect; that is, a non-overt operator in a non-subject position systematically moves to the Spec of Comp in preference over a non-overt operator in subject position. Notice that the subject position in the relevant examples does not receive Nominative Case since it is not governed by a tensed Infl. The non-subject positions, on the other hand, are all environments of Case assignment (i.e. the non-overt operator occurs as object of a verb or a preposition at D-Structure). We have already seen, however, that non-overt operators are resistant to Case assignment; in general, the only empty category that may bear Case is a variable (or pro). The assumption throughout this work has been that Case assignment is a property of S-Structure, so the reason for the anti-superiority effect of non-overt operators is now apparent: an empty category that cannot be interpreted as a variable (for example, the empty category that will be interpreted as a non-overt operator) may not directly bear Case; if such an element appears in a position that will receive Case, it must evacuate that position in order to avoid receiving the Case feature. The S-Structure in (173) is, therefore, not well-formed:

(173)   John$_i$ is [$_{AdjP}$ easy [$_{CP}$ Op$_i$ [$_{IP}$ t_i to please [e]]]]

The empty category in the object position of the complement clause cannot be interpreted as a variable, since it is not Ā-bound. Since it is not a variable, this empty category may not bear a Case feature. It is, however, in a position of Case assignment. As a result, the S-Structure representation in (173) cannot be grammatical.

Summary

Before exploring this analysis of control any further, let us take a moment to summarize the approach advocated in this section. We began with the assumption that PRO, *per se*, does not exist. The element that has been taken to be PRO is, from this perspective, a pair consisting of a non-overt operator and the variable which it binds. We have adopted the standard distinction between obligatory control and non-obligatory ('arbitrary') control. In the former case, a superordinate head subcategorizes for a CP containing a non-overt operator, in much the same way that a head may subcategorize for a [+WH] Comp. The non-overt operator in obligatory control structures is assigned a range under predication which is lexically specified by the head; in the case of adjunct clauses, the non-overt operator is assigned a range under predication with the subject of IP. In both cases, the control is obligatory, although it is lexically specified only in the former instance.

Arbitrary control has been reanalyzed as a case of binding at LF; the non-overt operator may remain *in situ* in the syntax (under certain circumstances) and undergo QR in the mapping to LF. In this instance, the empty element is analyzed as an operator without a range; in order for the representation to be well-formed, the operator must be Ā-bound. Only then may the non-overt operator be interpreted as having a range. One result of this analysis of arbitrary control is that we must assume that LF representations are richer than has been standardly assumed in previous works. In particular, syntactically unrealized arguments (by this I mean slots in a head's thematic grid which have not been associated with an argument position in the syntax) may be realized in LF representations. These newly realized argument positions are operator-bound at LF; the nature of the operator that binds these positions is, presumably, a lexical property of individual heads. Thus, a universal (or, possibly, generic) quantifier is specified by *easy* in:

(174) a. John$_i$ is [$_{AdjP}$ easy [$_{CP}$ Op$_i$ [$_{IP}$ [e] to please]]]
b. John$_i$ is [$_{AdjP}$ ($\forall$x) [$_{AdjP}$ easy [$_{CP}$ Op$_i$ [$_{IP}$ Op$_x$ [$_{IP}$ t_x to please t_i]]]]]

while an existential operator is involved in:

(175) a. John$_i$ [$_{VP}$ bought the book$_j$ [$_{CP}$ Op$_j$ [$_{IP}$ [e] to read t_j to the children]]]
b. John$_i$ [$_{VP}$ ($\exists$x) [$_{VP}$ bought the book$_j$ x [$_{CP}$ Op$_j$ [$_{IP}$ Op$_x$ [$_{IP}$ t_x to read t_j to the children]]]]]

There will be a more extended discussion of arbitrary control and properties of LF representations in the next section.

The surface distribution of non-overt operators is regulated by Case theory. Non-overt operators may not appear in a Case-marked position at S-Structure. Hence, a non-overt operator in a non-subject position must move to the Spec of Comp in the syntax, while a non-overt operator in the subject of a non-finite clause may remain *in situ* until LF. Furthermore, a non-overt operator which heads an Ā-chain bearing Case may not land in the Spec of a CP which receives Case. These assumptions accounted for the distribution of tough constructions, infinitival relatives, parasitic-gap constructions, purposive clauses, environments of obligatory and optional control, and certain sentential predicates.

Finally, the analysis of control proposed in this chapter has unified the type of binding found in all of the above constructions. In every case, a non-overt operator, which must be identified in order for the structure to receive an interpretation, is involved.

4.4 LF representations and the interpretation of arbitrary control

The LF representations we have been assuming so far in this chapter are more articulated than the LF representations assumed in many of the standard works of generative grammar (see, for example, May 1977). It has generally been assumed that LF is the level of representation at which scope relationships are disambiguated (compare this, however, with the discussion of LF in May 1985). The term 'scope relationships' is intended to cover the relationships between quantified NPs, negation, and any other operators (e.g. adverbials) which may contribute to the interpretation of a sentence. To take a concrete example, the sentence

(176)   Every student read some book.

is taken as ambiguous between the reading where every student read a book, but not necessarily the same book (wide scope on *every student*, i.e. *every student* has scope over *some book*) and the reading where some book is read by every student, where each student reads the same book. In the latter case, *some book* is said to have scope over *every student*.

In order to disambiguate the readings, we assume that QR may adjoin operators to IP (or, to state the rule in its most general form, QR may adjoin operators to any maximal projection, including IP as a special case). We may then define the scope of an operator as the set of nodes which it c-commands (see Reinhart 1983 for a somewhat different account of the syntax of scope).[9] Returning to the above example, wide scope on *every student* implies an LF representation like that in (177):

(177) $[_{IP}$ every student$_i$ $[_{IP}$ some book$_j$ $[_{IP}$ t_i read t_j]]]

where *every student* c-commands, and hence has scope over, *some book*. The LF representation where *some book* has scope over *every student* would have the following form:

(178)   [$_{IP}$ some book$_j$ [$_{IP}$ every student$_i$ [$_{IP}$ t_i read t_j]]]

where *some book* c-commands *every student*. The structural differences between (177) and (178) result from differences in the application of QR. In (177) QR first chomsky-adjoins *some book* to IP and then chomsky-adjoins *every student* to the newly created IP node. In (178) the order of application has been reversed; QR first chomsky-adjoins *every student* to IP and then adjoins *some book* to the newly created IP node.

The approach sketched out above is purely syntactically driven; that is, quantified NPs and other operators are present in the syntax – they must, in fact, be base-generated and, therefore, are present at D-Structure. S-Structure representations feed the mapping to LF and only overt operators present at S-Structure are assigned scope. LF itself is taken to be a level of pure representation of scope.

In this chapter we have made different assumptions about the role that LF plays in the theory of grammar, although our assumptions are very much in the spirit of the idea that LF is a disambiguated language from which semantic interpretation may take place. In very rough terms, we have taken LF to be a level of complete disambiguation (we must, of course, make the sense of 'complete' much more precise). To say that LF is a level of disambiguation implies, of course, that scope relationships be represented in an unambiguous way. It also has a number of other consequences; in particular, we have required that certain positions that are present in the argument structure of a head, but syntactically unrealized, may come to be represented explicitly at LF.

The role of implicit arguments

The idea that syntactically unrealized arguments play a role in the interpretation of sentences is by no means a new one. One example of this sort of phenomenon is control by an implicit argument (see Keyser and Roeper 1984 for an extensive discussion of the following facts).[10] Adopting a standard analysis of passivization (see, for example, Chomsky 1981 or Jaeggli 1986), we can say that passive morphology blocks assignment of an external thematic role to the subject of IP; while this thematic role is syntactically suppressed, it is not absent from the argument structure of the verb. The external thematic role may act as a controller of PRO, as the following examples show:

(179) a. The ship was sunk [PRO to win the war]
b. The building was burned [PRO to collect the insurance]
c. The ice was melted [PRO to provide water]

In each of the examples in (179) the implicit agent of the verb is understood as the controller of the PRO in the adjunct clause. Thus, in (179a) the implicit agent who is responsible for the sinking of the ship is the winner of the war; in (179b) the party responsible for the burning of the building is the one who wants to collect the insurance; in (179c) the melter of the ice is also the provider of the water.

The examples in (179) should be contrasted with ergative constructions. Ergative morphology in English destroys the external thematic role completely; meaning that the external thematic role comes to be completely absent from the argument structure of the verb that bears the ergative morphology. In short, there is no implicit argument available for the control of PRO:

(180) a. *The ship sank [PRO to win the war]
b. *The building burned [PRO to collect the insurance]
c. *The ice melted [PRO to provide water]

(I am ignoring cases of sentient ships and buildings or animate snowmen.) It is fairly easy to see how the analysis of control in this chapter accounts for the above examples. In the case of the passive examples, the empty element in the subject position need not move to the Spec of Comp until the mapping to LF, since the subject position is Caseless and no selectional restrictions are placed on the adjunct clause. During the mapping to LF. Furthermore, the suppressed external thematic role may be realized syntactically, presumably as a variable in an A-position with an existential quantifier adjoined to the category that would assign the external

Control and non-overt operators

thematic role. We may, thus, posit the following LF representation for the examples in (181):

(181) a. $[_{IP} [e] [_{Infl'} (\exists x)$ was $[_{Infl'} [_{VP}$ sunk the ship$] x] [_{CP}$ Op$_x [_{IP} t_x$ to win the war$]]]]$
b. $[_{IP} [e] [_{Infl'} (\exists x) [_{Infl'}$ was $[_{VP}$ burned the building$] x] [_{CP}$ Op$_x [_{IP} t_x$ to collect the insurance$]]]]$
c. $[_{IP} [e] [_{Infl'} (\exists x) [_{Infl'}$ was $[_{VP}$ melted the ice$] x] [_{IP}$ Op$_x [_{IP} t_x$ to provide water$]]]]$

(Note that in each of the above cases, the S-Structure subject is returned to its D-Structure position, leaving a null expletive in subject position.) the non-overt operator must pick up a range from some Ā-binder at LF. The only available element is the 'implicit' argument, which we are assuming is bound by an existential quantifier; hence, the non-overt operator picks up its range from this existential quantifier and the interpretation of the non-overt operator is obligatorily related to the 'implicit argument'.

The LF representations in (181) should be contrasted with those in (182):

(182) a. *$[_{IP} [e] [_{VP}$ sank the ship$] [_{CP}$ Op$_\emptyset [_{IP} t_\emptyset$ to win the war$]]]$
b. *$[_{IP} [e] [_{VP}$ burned the building$] [_{CP}$ Op$_\emptyset [_{IP} t_\emptyset$ to collect the insurance$]]]$
c. *$[_{IP} [e] [_{VP}$ melted the ice$] [_{CP}$ Op$_\emptyset [_{IP} t_\emptyset$ to provide water$]]]$

Recall that the ergative morphology completely eliminates the external thematic role of the verb it attaches to. Thus, in the mapping to LF, none of the examples in (182) have an additional thematic role that may be realized as an argument position. If this is the case, the non-overt operator in the adjunct clause has no potential Ā-binder. Therefore, the non-overt operators in (182) have no range at LF and the variables which they bind must be interpreted as expletives. Expletive elements may not bear a thematic role, however; since each of the variables in (182) occupies a θ-position, despite being obligatorily interpreted as expletives, the examples are ruled out.

Control and non-overt operators

A cautionary note is in order at this point. We have so far been treating the relationship between implicit arguments and non-overt operators as cases of pure structural binding in the sense that once an operator binding an implicit argument has been spelled out, it may bind a non-overt operator just so long as the newly spelled out operator occupies a structural position which c-commands the non-overt operator. Empirically, it would appear that other factors must be taken into account in order to adequately capture the complete array of facts. Let us return to the case of ergative constructions in English and consider a wider range of facts:

(183) a. *Every naval vessel sank [PRO to win the war]
b. *Some building burned [PRO to collect the insurance]
c. *Some ice cube melted [PRO to provide water]

The examples in (183), unlike the parallel examples in (180), have quantified NPs in the surface subject-position. Therefore, in the mapping to LF, the NPs in surface subject-position should undergo QR. Assuming that the empty element in subject position undergoes QR and is analyzed at LF as a non-overt operator, we should have LF representations similar to (184) (I will continue to assume that an empty expletive occupies the matrix subject-position in these examples and the true variable is in object position):

(184) a. $[_{IP}$ every naval vessel$_i$ $[_{IP}$ [e] $[_{VP}$ sank $t_i]$ $[_{CP}$ Op$_i$ $[_{IP}$ t_i to win the war]]]]
b. $[_{IP}$ some building$_i$ $[_{IP}$ [e] $[_{VP}$ burned $t_i]$ $[_{CP}$ Op$_i$ $[_{IP}$ t_i to collect the insurance]]]]
c. $[_{CP}$ some ice cube$_i$ $[_{IP}$ [e] $[_{VP}$ melted $t_i]$ $[_{CP}$ Op$_i$ $[_{IP}$ t_i to provide water]]]]

Since each of the quantified NPs in (184) occupies an Ā-position which c-commands the non-overt operator, it should be possible for the quantified NP to assign the non-overt operator a range. Nevertheless, the above examples are not measurably better than the examples in (180), which were ruled out on purely structural grounds.

The examples in (183) could be ruled out on the grounds of selectional restrictions or because the semantic reading is simply anomalous. In all of the examples in (183) the predicates in the adjunct clauses assign an agent thematic-role to their subjects and, presumably, have an animate selectional restriction on the subject position. The range assigned by the quantified NPs, however, is strictly inanimate – naval vessels, buildings, and ice cubes. Hence, the sets over which the variables in the adjunct clauses will systematically violate the selectional restrictions placed upon the variable position. Similarly, one could argue that the adjuncts in (183) predicate an intention on the part of the quantified NPs in the matrix clauses. Since vessels, buildings, and ice cubes are not normally taken to be capable of having intent, the resulting semantic representations are odd.

The above problem, I think, falls under a rather different generalization. Compare the examples in (183) with the following example (see Lasnik 1988):

(185)   *The ship was sunk [PRO to become a hero]

Since the matrix verb in the example is a passive, it contains a syntactically suppressed external thematic-role as part of its argument structure. This thematic role, under our assumptions, may be realized at LF, resulting in the following representation:

(186) $[_{IP} [e] [_{Infl'} (\exists x) [_{Infl'}$ was $[_{VP}$ sunk the ship$] x] [_{CP}$ Op$_x [_{IP} t_x$ to become a hero$]]]]$

In (186) the existential quantifier should be in a position to identify the range of the non-overt operator. Presumably, the existential quantifier ranges over the set of humans, so there should be no problem either with the selectional restrictions placed on the variable in the adjunct clause or with the presupposition of intent on the part of the lexically induced agent of the verb *sink*. Clearly, an individual may perform an act with the intent of being glorified as a hero:

(187)   The sailor$_i$ sank the ship $[_{CP}$ Op$_i [_{IP} t_i$ to become a hero$]]$

The example in (186) is, nevertheless, odd. Such examples indicate that the relationship between implicit arguments and non-overt

205

operators is constrained by factors other than purely structural relations, selectional restrictions, and presuppositions of intent.

Lasnik (1988) has pointed out that examples like that in (185) have been used to support the argument that control of PRO may involve control by a VP or IP. In particular, (185) is ungrammatical because the entire IP, *the ship was sunk* controls the PRO; *the ship was sunk*, however, is not a possible subject for the predicate *become a hero* and, therefore, the example is filtered out on the basis of selectional restrictions placed on its subject by *become a hero*. It should be noted that VPs (or IPs) may be antecedents; consider an example like:

(188)   John jumped around, which was a stupid thing to do.

In (188) it would appear that *jumped around* is the antecedent for *which* since *be a stupid thing to do* seems to be predicated of *jump around*.

Let us assume, for the sake of argument, that the above analysis of (185) is correct and that we can uncover some mechanism that determines whether an NP or a VP (or IP) controls a particular PRO. Notice, now, that *become* does allow an IP in its subject position, depending on the complement following *become*. Consider the following, for example:

(189)   Smoking marijuana became illegal in the 1930s.

Example (189) is, to my ear, perfectly grammatical. Now, compare example (185) with:

(190)   *Marijuana was smoked [to become illegal in the 1930s]

Example (190) is ungrammatical, despite the fact that an IP is a possible subject for the predicate *become illegal*. It would appear, then, that appealing to control by IP or VP to explain example (185) will not solve our problem since ungrammaticality remains constant even if an IP is a possible subject for the predicate in the adjunct clause. Let us look for another mechanism that will help us to explain these examples.

Thematic roles and controls

Whatever constrains the interpretation of arbitrary PRO at LF is over-ridden in environments of obligatory control, as shown in (187). We might suppose, therefore, that LF interpretation is subject to some additional constraint that is not imposed on binding relations in the syntax. We have already seen that this additional constraint does not make reference to structural position, although it does work in tandem with the Binding theory, so that a potential antecedent for a non-overt operator must obey certain structural conditions. Let us suppose, then, that this additional constraint on binding at LF makes reference to logical relations between the antecedent operator and the non-overt operator. To be more explicit, let us suppose that this constraint makes reference to thematic roles (see Nishigauchi 1984 for some precise proposals on the interaction between control and thematic roles):

(191) *Thematic compatibility*

An element A is a possible antecedent for an element B at LF if the thematic role assigned to the chain headed by A is compatible with the thematic role assigned to the chain headed by B.

We can assume that the examples in (184) and (186) are ruled out because the operator which we have taken as the antecedent for the non-overt operator is not a possible antecedent; if so, then the non-overt operators in these examples simply lack a range at LF and are, as a result, ruled out. If this assumption is correct, then it must be the case that the thematic role assigned to the Ā-chain headed by the operator (which binds the implicit argument) is not compatible with the thematic role assigned to the Ā-chain headed by the non-overt operator.

Let us return to our examples. The first case is that of the ergative verbs:

(192) a. [$_{IP}$ every naval vessel$_i$ [$_{IP}$ [e] [$_{VP}$ sank t_i] [$_{CP}$ Op$_i$ [$_{IP}$ t_i to win the war]]]]
b. [$_{IP}$ some building$_i$ [$_{IP}$ [e] [$_{VP}$ burned t_i] [$_{CP}$ Op$_i$ [$_{IP}$ t_i to collect the insurance]]]]

c. [$_{CP}$ some ice cube$_i$ [$_{IP}$ [e] [$_{VP}$ melted t_i] [$_{CP}$ Op$_i$ [$_{IP}$ t_i to provide water]]]]

The variable in the object position of the matrix clause is assigned the theme role, while the variable in the subject position of the adjunct is assigned the agent role. The fact that the Ā-chain headed by the putative antecedent of the non-overt operator receives the theme role eliminates it as a real antecedent, since the Ā-chain headed by the non-overt operator bears the agent thematic-role. Hence, because of the functioning of (191), the non-overt operator in these examples cannot find an antecedent. As a result, it lacks a range and the variable it binds must be treated as non-referential which, we have already seen, is impossible.

The next example is the case in (186) (repeated here):

(193) [$_{IP}$ [e] [$_{Infl'}$ (∃x) [$_{Infl'}$ was [$_{VP}$ sunk the ship] x] [$_{CP}$ Op$_x$ [$_{IP}$ t_x to become a hero]]]]

The existential operator binds an argument that is the realization of the agent thematic-role of the verb *sink*; hence, the existential operator heads an Ā-chain that bears an agent thematic-role. The non-overt operator, on the other hand, heads an Ā-chain that receives whatever thematic role the predicate *become a hero* assigns. It seems quite likely that the thematic role assigned to the subject position of the adjunct is distinct from the agent thematic-role and it is equally likely that the two thematic roles are not sufficiently compatible for the existential operator to act as a potential antecedent for the non-overt operator. If this is correct, then the non-overt operator lacks an antecedent at LF and its variable must, once again, be treated as a non-referential element.

The constraint in (191) bears some conceptual similarity to transparency, discussed in Chapter 3. In both cases, thematic theory narrows the range of *a priori* possible structural relationships. Notice, however, that (191) must make reference to particular thematic roles and calls a metric (i.e. compatibility) into play. The general tendency in generative grammar has been to make reference to thematic roles in only the most general way. Thus, the θ-Criterion requires that all arguments bear a thematic role, but has nothing to say about the specific nature of the thematic roles. Similarly, the constraint developed in Chapter 3 makes no reference to particular thematic roles, but, rather, quantifies over thematic roles.

For the Thematic Compatibility Constraint to be completely useful, we must, of course, give a coherent definition of the notion of *compatibility*. We could either give an exhaustive list of the possible thematic roles available to natural languages plus all the pairs of thematic roles that we will call compatible or we could give a set of propositions from which we could derive the compatibility of any two thematic roles. The former approach would present us with some enormous difficulties. The list of possible thematic roles is of unknown length and some have argued (see, for example, Marantz 1984) that it could not be given for the simple reason that external thematic-roles are defined on the basis of the compositional semantics of the predicate that assigns them. If this is correct, then the list of thematic roles is potentially infinite. Assuming that we could give a finite listing of the set of possible thematic roles, we would then have to provide a listing of all the possible combinations of thematic roles taken two at a time. This final list of compatible thematic-roles would, in all likelihood, be quite large and, in the final analysis, taxonomic in the sense that it provides no explanation as to why any two thematic roles are compatible. I will, therefore, not pursue this line of analysis.

The idea of deriving thematic compatibility from some set of principles seems the more promising approach, since it circumvents the combinatorial difficulties of the previous method and it is likely to deliver a more satisfying account of the phenomenon. Let us continue with the assumption that LF is not a level of semantic interpretation but is, rather, a level of disambiguation which is then mapped to a semantic representation. In the spirit of Keenan and Faltz (1984), I will assume that part of the task of semantic theory is to provide an account of *predicate formation*, where I assume that a predicate is a semantic unit that maps some argument onto a value. We can take a value to be a truth-value, a set of individuals, or any other entity defined in the semantic system (see Keenan and Faltz 1984 for discussion).

In general, the relationship between syntactic constituency and predicate structure is so close as to be virtually isomorphic; for example, in a sentence like:

(194)   [$_{IP}$ [$_{NP}$ John] [$_{VP}$ tossed the book to Bill]]

the VP can be treated as mapping directly onto a one-place predicate that takes *John* as its argument to give a proposition (which, in turn, maps onto a truth-value, depending on whether John is a member of the set of things that tossed the book to Bill). The argument structure of a head (i.e. the set of thematic roles associated with the head) may be viewed as a set of instructions to the syntax on how to form predicate/argument structures.

The mapping between syntactic constituents and the semantic units that correspond to predicates is not necessarily so simple as described in the preceding paragraph. The role of adjuncts in this approach is to form new predicates from those predicates that can be mapped by the syntax directly from the argument structure of a head. To take a particularly extreme example of this approach, consider the case of purposive clauses, as in:

(195) Bill bought the old car$_i$ [$_{CP}$ Op$_i$ [$_{IP}$ [e] to fool around with t_i]]

Keenan (personal communication) treats the predicate/argument structure of the example in (195) as:

(196) Bill [bought to fool around with] the old car

where *bought to fool around with* is a two-place predicate that takes *the old car* as argument to yield the one-place predicate *bought to fool around with the old car*. If this is correct, then the relationship between syntactic constituency and the formation of predicates in the semantics may be relatively indirect.[11] Notice that the non-overt operators act as an interface between the syntactic structure and the more remote level of semantic representation in that they keep an account of the relationship between the arguments (in the syntactic sense) of syntactic elements and the arguments (in the semantic sense) of the predicates.

Underlying this approach is the attempt to give an account of the formation of possible predicates so that all and only the possible predicates of a natural language would be formed. In order to give a complete account of this phenomenon, one must be able to describe the set in which such predicates take their denotation and, related to this, the type of denotation that the arguments of these predicates must have. While I will not pretend to have such a theory of possible predicates, it is possible to make some observations. Let us return to the following set of contrasts:

(197) a. The sailor$_i$ sank the ship [$_{CP}$ Op$_i$ [$_{IP}$ t_i to become a hero]]
b. *[$_{IP}$ [e] [$_{Infl'}$ ($\exists$x) [$_{Infl'}$ was [$_{VP}$ sunk the ship] x] [$_{CP}$ Op$_x$ [$_{IP}$ t_x to become a hero]]]]
c. [$_{IP}$ [e] [$_{Infl'}$ ($\exists$x) [$_{Infl'}$ was [$_{VP}$ sunk the ship] x] [$_{CP}$ Op$_x$ [$_{IP}$ t_x to win the war]]]]

The contrasts in (197) would seem to be based both on the referential properties of the element that the complex one-place predicates may take as an argument and on the denotations of the complex one-place predicates. On the one hand, the subject of (197a) takes its denotation in the denotation set of definite descriptions, while the 'subjects' (arguments that receive the external thematic-role of *sink*) in (197b) and (197c) are examples of unrestricted existential quantification. We also have a contrast between (197a) and (197b), on the one hand, and (197c), on the other. The former examples involve the predicate 'become *y*' which involves a relation between possible situations (or points in time) while the latter example involves the predicate 'win the war'. We may, therefore, hypothesize that higher-order one-place predicates such as *sink the ship to become a hero* may not take an element under unrestricted quantification (such as the LF realization of an implicit argument) as an argument. The somewhat simpler predicate *sink the ship to win the war* may, however, take an element under unrestricted quantification as its argument.

The approach outlined above would maintain our theory of control, subject to filtering by an interpretive component that forms semantic predicates from complex syntactic structures. This latter component involves a theory of the denotation sets for predicates and arguments (see Keenan and Faltz 1984 for some discussion). We will, therefore, allow the syntax to generate examples like (197b), since such structures are subject to filtering by the interpretive component.

Unselective quantification and control

We have so far investigated some of the ramifications of realizing syntactically suppressed arguments at LF and the inter-relationship between these implicit arguments and the theory of control. Let us now turn to some further examples of elements that are present at LF but absent from the syntax, and explore how such elements interact with the theory of control.

One suggestive piece of evidence for the presence of operators at LF which are not, strictly speaking, visible in the syntax comes from the work of Heim (1982), in which she investigated the interpretation of indefinite NPs. The basic form of the puzzle is exemplified by the following contrast:

(198) a. A man won a prize.
       b. If a man wins a prize, he displays it in his trophy case.

The sentence in (198a) contains two indefinite NPs, *a man* and *a prize*. Both of these NPs apparently have the force of existential quantification; that is, the following seems to be a fair paraphrase of (198a):

(199) (for some x : x a man (for some y : y a prize (x won y)))

The sentence in (198b) also contains two indefinite NPs, *a man* and *a prize*; in contrast to (198a), the indefinite NPs in (198b) do not seem to have the force of existential quantification but, rather, universal quantification. Thus, (200) seems to be a close paraphrase of (198b):

(200) (for any x : x a man (for any y : y a prize (if x wins y then x displays y in x's trophy case)))

Since the indefinite NPs in (198a) are formally the same as the indefinite NPs in (198b) – in both examples the NPs have an indefinite article – how are we to account for the drastic difference in the interpretation of the indefinite NPs in the two examples?

One popular approach to this problem has been to give a number of rules for transforming existential quantification to universal quantification in certain environments (see Heim 1982 for details). Heim argues quite persuasively that such a system of rules can be little more than taxonomic and that they obscure the correct generalization completely (see Heim 1982 for discussion). Her approach to the puzzle is quite different. Following the work of Lewis (1975), she develops a theory of unselective quantifiers.

Lewis (1975) notes sentences like the following (from Heim 1982):

(201) a. If a man owns a donkey he always beats it.
       b. In most cases, if a table has lasted for 50 years, it will last for another 50.
       c. Sometimes, if a cat falls from the fifth floor, it survives.
       d. If a person falls from the fifth floor, he or she will very rarely survive.

Lewis treats the adverbs in the above sentences as quantifiers which have the property of binding an unlimited number of variables simultaneously, unlike the more familiar 'selective' quantifiers (e.g. *some*, *all*, etc.). These 'unselective' quantifiers have interpretations like those shown in (202). Note that in the following interpretations, A and B are variables quantifying over propositions. An assignment to free variables in a proposition *satisfies* that proposition if the assignment yields the value 'true' to the interpretation of that proposition:

(202) a. 'Always(A, B)' is true if and only if every assignment to the free variables in A which satisfies A also satisfies B.
       b. 'In most cases(A, B)' is true if and only if most assignments to the free variables in A which satisfy A also satisfy B.
       c. 'Sometimes(A, B)' is true if and only if some assignments to the free variables in A which satisfy A also satisfy B.
       d. 'Very rarely(A, B)' is true if and only if very few assignments to the free variables in A which satisfy A also satisfy B.

Heim argues that we will derive the correct interpretation for examples like those in (198) and (201) if the indefinite NPs are not taken as having quantificational force but, rather, if they contribute nothing but their status as variables to the interpretation of the sentences they occur in. Thus, she argues that an example like (201a) has a representation like (I have simplified her representations somewhat):

(203) (always x : a man, y : a donkey)(if x owns y then x beats y)

Given the interpretation for 'always' in (202a), (203) is equivalent to:

(204) (for every x : x a man (for every y : y a donkey (if x owns y then x beats y)))

The interpretation of (201a) should be contrasted with a sentence like:

(205) A man very rarely kisses a strange woman.

The interpretation of (205) should be true if the kissing relation contains very few pairs consisting of a man and a strange woman, just as the interpretation of *very rarely* given in (202d) would predict:

(206) (very rarely x : x a man, y : y a strange woman)(x kisses y)

Let us take it as a given, then, that certain operators may be unselective in that they may bind any (unbound) variable in their scope (i.e. in the set of nodes which they c-command). We may now reconsider the original puzzle of why some indefinites seem to have existential force while other indefinites have universal force:

(207) a. A man won a prize.
       b. If a man wins a prize, he displays it in his trophy case.

Heim's hypothesis that indefinites have no inherent quantificational force seems to be counterexemplified by the examples in

(207). Unlike the examples in (201), neither of the sentences in (207) contain an overt unselective operator (like *always*) to bind the variables left by the indefinite NPs. The fact remains, however, that the quantificational force of the indefinite NPs in (207) is not a constant, as pointed out above.

Heim eliminates the counterexample in (207a) by developing a rule of Existential Closure; I will have little to say about this rule here, but see Heim (1982) for a formulation of the rule and extensive discussion. Existential Closure is a rule of sentence grammar that inserts an unselective existential quantifier in LF representations. Application of Existential Closure to the LF representation of (207a) would yield:

(208)   (there exists $x : x$ a man, $y : y$ a prize)(x won y)

Since the operator inserted by Existential Closure is unselective, it may bind as many free variables as are in its scope.[12] Hence, in the absence of any other unselective operators, indefinite NPs will be interpreted as having existential force.

Existential Closure cannot be responsible for the interpretation of the indefinite NPs in (207b) for the simple reason that these NPs are interpreted as having the force of universal quantification. The binding of an indefinite NP by means of Existential Closure is, of course, a default case, since the binding transpires only when no other operator is available to bind the indefinite. By surface appearances, there is no other operator available in (207b) to bind the indefinite NPs. In order to account for examples like (207b), Heim rejects the hypothesis that the conditional is true material-implication. Instead, she develops the following two hypotheses: first, conditionals express a form of conditional necessity with the *then* clause read as under the scope of a necessity operator which is restricted by the *if* clause; second, the invisible necessity-operator is an unselective operator which may bind any number of variables.

The necessity operator involved in the interpretation of conditionals involves quantification over a restricted set of possible worlds. The details of this quantification over possible worlds need not concern us here (see Heim 1982 for the formal definition of this operator); it suffices to observe that this quantification will give the indefinite NPs in (207b) the force of universal quantification. Example (207b) will be associated with the following LF representation (I notate the necessity operator with 'N'):

(209) (N$x : x$ a man, $y : y$ a prize)(if x wins y then x displays y in x's trophy case)

In (209) the necessity operator, being unselective, may bind the indefinite NPs, parallel to the example in (208). The representation in (209) will ultimately be interpreted in a way that requires for any man and any prize, if the man wins the prize in any possible world, then the man puts the prize in his trophy case in that world.

If Heim's treatment of the interpretation of indefinite NPs is correct, then LF representations contain 'syntactically invisible' operators that may bind null elements. We have so far seen cases of invisible necessity-operators associated with conditionals, and invisible existential-operators which are introduced by Existential Closure. We have also seen that certain implicit arguments must be realized and operator-bound at LF under the assumption that LF is a level of disambiguation. Under the framework developed in Lewis (1975) and Heim (1982), we have also seen that certain adverbs count as quantifiers at LF. Finally, we may assume, following Jackendoff (1972) and Safir (1985), to name only a few examples, that modals count as operators at LF.

Given the relative richness of the LF representations we are assuming, it should come as no surprise that the various operators listed in the previous paragraph are available for binding non-overt operators. The binding relation between these operators and non-overt operators is constrained by the fact that the binding conditions apply at LF and non-overt operators are treated as pure Ā-anaphors by the binding conditions. It follows that a non-overt operator may only be Ā-bound by a 'syntactically invisible' operator (hereafter, the 'induced operator') if that operator is in the governing category of the non-overt operator. As we have seen above, this means that the induced operator must be no farther away than the CP that is superordinate to the CP containing the non-overt operator.

To make the discussion more concrete, let us turn to some examples. We can begin with an adverb of quantification (see above), as in:

(210) a. It is always easy to annoy John.
b. It is very rarely easy to please John.

If the analysis developed up to this point is correct, then the 'arbitrary PROs' in the examples in (210) should differ as to quantficational force. In the mapping to LF, the adverbs of quantification in these examples will be assigned scope; I will assume that these adverbs take matrix scope. Furthermore, the empty category in the subject position of each of the complement clauses will be moved to an Ā-position. Finally, we may assume that the implicit argument of the adjective *easy* may also be realized. The sentences will have the following representations (prior to assignment of indices):

(211) a. [$_{IP}$ always [$_{IP}$ it is [$_{AdjP}$ easy [$_{CP}$ Op$_\emptyset$ [$_{IP}$ $t_\emptyset$ to annoy John]] $x_\emptyset$]]]
b. [$_{IP}$ very rarely [$_{IP}$ it is [$_{AdjP}$ easy [$_{CP}$ Op$_\emptyset$ [$_{IP}$ $t_\emptyset$ to please John]] $x_\emptyset$]]]

Prior to assignment of indices, the non-overt operator, the variable which it binds, and the induced argument of *easy* have no inherent reference and no range; I have noted this by using a special index, '$\emptyset$'. Notice, however, that the non-overt operator and the implicit argument of *easy* are within the scope of the adverbs of quantification, *always* and *very rarely*. These adverbs, furthermore, occupy Ā-positions in the governing category of the non-overt operators. Thus, the adverbs of quantification may act as antecedents for the non-overt operators (and for the implicit argument of *easy*). The only indexation which leads to well-formed LF representations of these examples is:

(212) a. [$_{IP}$ always$_i$ [$_{IP}$ it is [$_{AdjP}$ easy [$_{CP}$ Op$_i$ [$_{IP}$ t_i to annoy John]] x_i]]]
b. [$_{IP}$ very rarely [$_{IP}$ it is [$_{AdjP}$ easy [$_{CP}$ Op$_i$ [$_{IP}$ t_i to please John]] x_i]]]

Although the derivations leading to the two LFs in (212) are very similar, the non-overt operator in each of the examples is bound by a different adverb of quantification. A review of the informal interpretations assigned to these adverbs (given in (202)) shows that these adverbs of quantification have different truth conditions. The readings of the examples in (212) should differ accordingly. The elements bound by *always* in example (212a) should have the force of universal quantification; roughly, every individual should find it easy to annoy John. This is so because the interpretation of *always* given in (202) makes it equivalent to a universal quantifier. The example in (212b), however, should not have the same quantificational force, since the non-overt operator is bound by *very rarely*; roughly, (212b) should be true only if, at any given time, the predicate *easy to please John* is satisfied by very few individuals in domain D. This reading is in accord with the interpretation given *very rarely* in (202d) and it accurately reflects the quantificational force of the variables in (212b).

Notice that this interpretation of (212b) is somewhat different from the expected interpretation, given the reading normally associated with universal quantification; there are two possible ways to assign scope with respect to the adverb of quantification and the putative universal quantifier:

(213) a. (for every *x* (very rarely (it is easy for *x* to please John)))
b. (very rarely (for every *x* (it is easy for *x* to please John)))

Let us assume that *very rarely* in the examples of (213) quantifies over points of time only, perhaps with the interpretation that there are very few points of time at which the proposition over which it has scope is true. Example (213b) implies that there are very few points in time at which everyone finds it easy to please John. This interpretation seems to be fairly remote from intuitions about the meaning of the example at hand.

Example (213a) is closer to matching the intuitions; we can paraphrase the reading with 'for every *x* there are very few points of time at which it easy for *x* to please John'. This reading seems, however, to allow for the situation where some individual always finds it easy to please John, but for any one individual the points of time at which that individual finds it easy to please John are few and far between; thus, although John is always pleased, he is always being pleased by a different individual. This situation does not seem to match up very well with the meaning of the sentence.

Assuming that we could provide an analysis of the interaction between the universal quantifier and the adverb of quantification to eliminate this problem, we would still have to provide an account of why the universal quantifier always seems to take scope over the adverb of quantification in examples like (213a). The account given here of the interaction between the adverb of quantification and the non-overt operator faces no such difficulties, since it is precisely the adverb of quantification which provides the range of the non-overt operator. Since the non-overt operator is contingent on the adverb of quantification in order to receive an interpretation, there can be no scope ambiguity between the two; the non-overt operator must be in the scope of the adverb of quantification in order to receive an interpretation.

Linked readings

Let us turn, now, to a phenomenon first discussed in Lebeaux (1984). For purposes of exposition, I will include an adverb of quantification in the example before generalizing the analysis to include examples that do not contain an adverb of quantification. The examples in question involve two non-finite clauses, as in:

(214) $[_{CP} [_{IP} [e]$ to be famous]] is seldom $[_{CP} [_{IP} [e]$ to be happy]]

Lebeaux points out that the two arbitrary PROs in the above example must be interpreted as co-varying. In other words, the example in (214) may not be taken as meaning that for someone to be famous is seldom for someone else to be happy. We can paraphrase the example in (214) more closely with:

(215) For any individual x, for x to be famous is seldom for x to be happy.

Loosely speaking, in performing Fregean substitution on individuals that may satisfy the above example, one must always select the same individual to satisfy the famous property and the happy property.

Let us assume that *seldom* is an adverb of quantification with an interpretation that is equivalent to the interpretation given to *very rarely* in (202d):

(216) 'Seldom(A, B)' is true if and only if very few assignments to the free variables in A which satisfy A also satisfy B.

Given our assumptions that adverbs of quantification are assigned scope and that arbitrary PRO involves movement of non-overt operator to an Ā-position in the mapping to LF, (214) will have the following structure prior to indexation:

(217) [$_{IP}$ seldom [$_{IP}$ [$_{CP}$ Op$_\emptyset$ [$_{IP}$ $t_\emptyset$ to be famous]] is [$_{CP}$ Op$_\emptyset$ [$_{IP}$ $t_\emptyset$ to be happy]]]]

The adverb of quantification, *seldom*, will take scope over the entire proposition and both of the embedded non-finite clauses will have a non-overt operator (with no inherent range or reference) in their Comps. Each non-overt operator binds a variable in the subject position of the non-finite clauses over which it has scope. The non-overt operators are taken as pure Ā-anaphors and, in order for the variables that they bind to bear a thematic role, they must be assigned a range at LF. Both non-overt operators have the superordinate S̄ as their governing category. The only well-formed indexation of the above example is:

(218) [$_{IP}$ seldom$_i$ [$_{IP}$ [$_{CP}$ Op$_i$ [$_{IP}$ t_i to be famous]] is [$_{CP}$ Op$_i$ [$_{IP}$ t_i to be happy]]]]

Roughly, (218) should be true only if there are few individuals who are both famous and happy. This follows from the interpretation of *seldom* and the fact that *seldom* binds the non-overt operators in the Comps of the embedded clauses.

It should be noted that adverbs of quantification may apparently supersede the operator induced to bind an implicit argument. Consider an example like:

(219) In most cases, ships were sunk to annoy hostile countries.

In (219) the adverb of quantification, *in most cases* (see the interpretation in (202b), may bind the suppressed external argument of *sink* and the non-overt operator in the Comp of the adjunct clause:

(220) [$_{IP}$ in most cases$_i$ [$_{IP}$ [e] [$_{Infl'}$ were [$_{VP}$ [$_{VP}$ sunk ships] x_i] [$_{CP}$ Op$_i$ [$_{IP}$ t_i to annoy hostile countries]]]]]

Example (220) is true if there are many individuals of whom the predicate *sink ships to annoy hostile countries* holds. This seems to be an intuitively correct interpretation of (219), although, unlike other cases we have seen of implicit arguments, it does not involve existential quantification.

The LF of linked readings

We have so far been able to give a fairly simple account of the interaction between adverbs of quantification and non-overt operators in fixing the interpretation of structures involving 'arbitrary control'. We have also considered how a number of 'syntactically invisible' operators contribute to LF representations. As a rule of thumb, we have proposed that syntactically suppressed elements of a head's thematic grid be realized in the mapping to LF and that these newly realized arguments be bound by operators at LF. The nature of these 'induced' operators bears some investigation; in some cases, particularly with verbs, the implicit argument seems to be bound by an existential quantifier, although this existential operator may be superseded by an adverb of quantification, as shown in (221c):

(221) a. [$_{IP}$ John [$_{VP}$ ($\exists$x) [$_{VP}$ bought the book$_i$ x] [$_{CP}$ Op$_i$ [$_{IP}$ Op$_x$ [$_{IP}$ t_x to read t_i to the children]]]]]
       b. [$_{IP}$ [e] [$_{Infl'}$ ($\exists$x) [$_{Infl'}$ was [$_{VP}$ sunk the ship] x] [$_{CP}$ Op$_x$ [$_{IP}$ t_x to win the war]]]]
       c. [$_{IP}$ in most cases$_i$ [$_{IP}$ [e] [$_{Infl'}$ were [$_{VP}$ [$_{VP}$ sunk ships] x_i] [$_{CP}$ Op$_i$ [$_{IP}$ t_i to annoy hostile countries]]]]]

We have also seen that implicit arguments of adjectives are often bound by universal quantifiers, although the universal quantifier may again be superseded by an adverb of quantification:

(222) a. [$_{IP}$ ($\forall$x) [$_{IP}$ it is [$_{AdjP}$ easy [$_{CP}$ Op$_x$ [$_{IP}$ t_x to please John]] x]]]

b. [$_{IP}$ seldom$_i$ [$_{IP}$ it is [$_{AdjP}$ fun [$_{CP}$ Op$_i$ [$_{IP}$ t_i to annoy a gorilla]] x]]]

It would seem that constructions involving predicative *be* often involve a sort of universal quantification which may be over-ridden by an adverb of quantification. This becomes clear if we reconsider the example in (214):

(223) a. [[e] to be famous] is [[e] to be happy]
       b. [[e] to be famous] is seldom [[e] to be happy]

The examples in (223) will have LF representations similar to those in (224):

(224) a. [$_{IP}$ ($\forall$i) [$_{IP}$ [$_{CP}$ Op$_i$ [$_{IP}$ t_i to be famous]] is [$_{CP}$ Op$_i$ [$_{IP}$ t_i to be happy]]]]
       b. [$_{IP}$ seldom$_i$ [$_{IP}$ [$_{CP}$ Op$_i$ [$_{IP}$ t_i to be famous]] is [$_{CP}$ Op$_i$ [$_{IP}$ t_i to be happy]]]]

In the absence of an adverb of quantification, example (223a) seems to require that all (or almost all) individuals who are famous are also happy. Thus, the class of examples illustrated above shares the property that, in the absence of other unselective operators, its non-overt arguments are bound by an apparently universal quantifier with the predicate adjective examples.

Heim (1982) points out the similarity in meaning between the following examples:

(225) a. If a cat has been exposed to 2,4-D it goes blind.
       b. A cat that has been exposed to 2,4-D goes blind.

Example (225a) is another example of the invisible necessity-operator associated with conditionals. Example (225b), while not a conditional in the sense that example (225a) is, has a generic NP as its subject and seems to be a close paraphrase of example (225a). It would appear, then, that the invisible necessity-operator is present in both examples:

(226) a. (Nx : x a cat) (if x has been exposed to 2,4-D then x goes blind)

b. (**N**x : x a cat that has been exposed to 2,4-D)(x goes blind)

Heim points out, however, that conflating the operator in (226a) with the operator in (226b) is a very rough cut indeed. The necessity operator has the force of universal quantification, while the quantification found with generics is somewhat weaker. To illustrate this, consider the following:

(227)   A human is bipedal.

Following Heim, we will assume that bipedalness is a property that holds of an individual by virtue of its membership in the class of humans. Example (227) is not falsified if I produce a monopedal human, however. Let us suppose that the operator in these cases ranges over a set of worlds that are ordered in terms of some ideal of normality (see Heim 1982 for some discussion) and that a proposition 'an X is Y' is true if some significantly large subset of the set of individuals in the set X have the property Y. Thus, this operator, call it '**G**', will bear some similarity to the necessity operator; its quantificational force will be somewhat weaker.

The question now becomes one of explaining how it is that this operator is induced from S-Structure representations in the mapping from S-Structure to LF. We have grounds for believing that this operator is generally present in constructions involving predicative *be* (see Safir 1985 for some discussion of predicative *be*) insofar as generics (like example (227)), constructions involving the predication of an adjective (or some other predicate, see examples like those in (222)), and constructions involving 'linked' non-overt operators (as in (224)) all seem to involve this form of quantification. We have also seen that adverbs of quantification can modify the force of this quantification (for example the contrast exemplified by (224a) and (224b)). We can assume, then, that this operator is induced by making reference to properties of Infl – the tense of the Infl and possibly the presence of predicative *be* – along with any adverbial modification of Infl – adverbs of quantification like *seldom*, *often*, or *never*.

Having identified a plausible source for the induced operator found in many predicative sentences, we can go on to consider further evidence that control involves a non-overt operator that must be Ā-bound in its governing category. Consider the following contrast, first noted in Lebeaux (1984):

(228) a. [[e] having relatives in the Old World] makes [[[e] winning the West] difficult]
 b. [[e] having relatives in the Old World] makes [[stories about [[e] winning the West] implausible]

Let us assume that the Infl in the examples of (228) is such that we can induce the operator 'G', perhaps as a function of the aspect of the matrix clause. The sentence in (228) has a sentential subject with an empty category in its subject position. In the mapping to LF, this empty category may be moved to an Ā-position and identified as a non-overt operator. Given that we have induced G in the matrix clause, this non-overt operator will have the matrix clause as its governing category. Furthermore, a small clause occupies the object position of *make* in (228a). This small clause has a sentential subject which, like the matrix subject, has an empty category in its subject position; this empty category will move to an Ā-position in the mapping to LF and also be identified as a non-overt operator. Since the small clause does not contain a SUBJECT accessible to this non-overt operator, its governing category will be the matrix clause. The following approximates the LF representation of example (228a):

(229) $[_{IP}\ G_i\ [_{IP}\ [Op_i\ [t_i$ having relatives in the Old World]] makes $[[Op_i\ [t_i$ winning the West]] difficult]]]$

The non-overt operators in (229) are identified in their governing category by the operator, G, as required by condition A of the Ā-system of binding and by the requirement that operators assign a range to the variables which they bind. Notice that we have derived the linked interpretation of the non-overt operators as a consequence of these requirements.

While (228a) is yet another case of the linked interpretation of non-overt operators, the non-overt operators in example (228b) do not have the linked interpretation. The people who have relatives in the Old World are not necessarily the people responsible for winning the West. Superficially, this interpretation of (228b) may seem surprising; example (228b) differs in structure from

(228a) in that one of the embedded clauses is a nominal complement, but this nominal does not, on the surface, contain a SUBJECT accessible to the non-overt operator. If this is indeed the case then the two non-overt operators in (228b) should have the same governing category and, hence, should have the same Ā-antecedent (namely, the induced operator, **G**). How are we to account for the difference in interpretation between (228a) and (228b)?

The solution to the puzzle of the non-linked reading for (228b) is best approached by considering the question of the governing categories for the non-overt operators. Our account of (228a) crucially relied on the fact that the non-overt operator contained in the subject had the same governing category as the non-overt operator contained in the complement; the governing category for non-overt operators was the superordinate IP. Given this, it is reasonable to suppose that the non-overt operators in (228b) do not share the same governing category, and so must find their antecedents in distinct syntactic domains. It would, then, come as no surprise that the non-overt operators in (228b) have an 'unlinked' interpretation.

The standard definition of 'governing category for some element' appeals to the notion of accessible SUBJECT – the most prominent element in some syntactic domain that both bears ϕ features and is a potential antecedent for the element in question. 'Potential antecedent' means that co-indexation of the SUBJECT with the element is, in principle, well-formed. It has often been assumed that well-formed indexings obey the *i-within-i* condition, which bars a node from being co-indexed with another node when the latter dominates the former. Consider, however, the following:

(230) a. they$_i$ thought [that [[$_{NP}$ pictures of themselves$_i$] Infl would be on sale]]
       b. they$_i$ thought [that [[$_{NP}$ pictures of them$_i$] Infl would be on sale]]

The classical analysis of (230a) is that the tensed Infl of the embedded clause cannot act as an accessible SUBJECT for the anaphor, *themselves*, because co-indexation of the Infl with the anaphor would violate the *i-within-i* condition. In general, we would expect the governing category for an element properly contained in the subject of a tensed clause to be a superordinate clause (if one exists).

The above analysis fails to account for (230b); the governing category for the pronoun, *them*, in the embedded clause in (230b) should be the matrix IP. We would incorrectly expect that the pronoun is obligatorily disjoint from the matrix subject. Huang (1982) and Aoun (1986) have argued that, in general, the governing category of a pronoun contained inside an NP is that NP and not a category superordinate to the NP; hence, pronouns and anaphors are not in complementary distribution in (231):

(231)   a. John$_i$ heard [$_{NP}$ a story about himself$_i$]
        b. John$_i$ heard [$_{NP}$ a story about him$_i$]

Huang (1982) argues that the head noun of an NP can act as a SUBJECT for a pronoun but not for an anaphor. If this is correct, then there is an asymmetry between the notions 'accessible SUBJECT for an anaphor' and 'accessible SUBJECT for a pronoun'. The latter notion makes no appeal to the *i-within-i* condition on well-formed indexings, while the former notion does make an appeal to such a condition.

There is some evidence that the *i-within-i* condition is not relevant in determining the governing category for other types of elements. This can be seen by considering relational nouns like *mother* (and, in one of its interpretations, *stories*). Consider, by way of illustration, the following contrast:

(232)   a. [$_{NP}$ no one's mother] called him
        b. [$_{NP}$ the mother of no one] called him

In example (232a) *no one* may take wide scope; it has the interpretation that for no individual x is it true that x's mother called him. Example (232b) does not have this interpretation; *no one* must have NP-internal scope. It requires that some individual, who is the mother of no one, called him. This NP-internal scope for *no one* is forced if the head noun can act as a SUBJECT for the variable bound by *no one*; if the NP is the governing category for this variable, then QR cannot raise *no one* outside of this NP.[13] It appears to be the case that Ā-anaphors class with pronouns; the *i-within-i* condition is irrelevant for determining the governing category of Ā-anaphors.

This predicts that the governing category for a non-overt operator contained in a clausal subject does, in fact, have a governing category (as noted above) – the superordinate clause. Thus, the non-overt operators in the Comp of the sentential subjects of (233) have the matrix clause as their governing category and the linked interpretation of the operators follows naturally:

(233) a. $[_{IP}$ ($\forall$i) $[_{IP}$ $[_{CP}$ Op$_i$ $[_{IP}$ t_i to be famous]] is $[_{CP}$ Op$_i$ $[_{IP}$ t_i to be happy]]]]

b. $[_{IP}$ seldom$_i$ $[_{IP}$ $[_{CP}$ Op$_i$ $[_{IP}$ t_i to be famous]] is $[_{CP}$ Op$_i$ $[_{IP}$ t_i to be happy]]]]

Furthermore, a non-overt operator contained in the Comp of a nominal complement will have the NP as its governing category, since the head noun will act as its accessible SUBJECT. This is exactly the case represented by (228b). The head noun, *stories*, acts as a SUBJECT accessible to the non-overt operator in its complement. Consider, in this light, the structure:

(234) [Op$_i$ [t_i having relatives in the Old World]] Infl makes [$_{NP}$ stories about [Op$_j$ [t_j winning the West]]] implausible

The non-overt operator contained inside the subject, Op$_i$, will have the matrix IP as its governing category because the matrix Infl acts as a SUBJECT accessible to this operator. The non-overt operator inside the postverbal NP, however, will have this NP as its governing category because the head noun, *stories*, acts as an accessible SUBJECT. Since the two non-overt operators are contained in distinct governing categories, we have every reason to expect an unlinked reading, since a proper antecedent for the one operator will not be a proper antecedent for the other non-overt operator, as the reader can verify.

We have not, as yet, provided an account for the antecedent of the non-overt operator properly contained in the NP headed by *stories*. As yet, we can only speculate about how this operator receives an interpretation. Recall that we are allowing syntactically unrealized arguments of heads to be overtly represented at LF. These arguments may be bound by an already existent unselective operator or by an existential operator (perhaps as a result of

Heim's rule of Existential Closure, see p. 215). If we extend this analysis to nouns, then the solution to the puzzle posed by the reading for this non-overt operator may become more transparent. In particular, let us suppose, as is reasonable, that some nouns have an articulated argument structure and that these arguments may be realized at LF as bound, in the unmarked case, by an existential operator. The noun, *story*, for instance, may have a syntactically unrealized argument (perhaps corresponding to the storyteller) so that (233) is analogous to (235):

(235) [[*e*] having relatives in the Old World] makes [[someone's stories about [[*e*] winning the West]] implausible]

An operator binding this implicit possessor may be realized in the mapping to LF. If this is so, then the non-overt operator inside the sentential complement to the noun, *stories*, will have a possible antecedent contained inside its governing category:

(236) $[_{IP} G_i [_{IP} [Op_i [t_i$ having relatives in the Old World]] makes $[[_{NP} (\exists x) [_{NP} x$ stories about $[Op_\emptyset [t_\emptyset$ winning the West]]]] implausible]]]

The induced existential-operator in the subject position of the small clause in (236) acts as a possible antecedent for the non-overt operator in the clausal complement to the noun, *stories*. Let us suppose that the non-overt operator in the clausal complement takes on the index of the induced existential-operator at LF as shown in (237):

(237) $[_{IP} G_i [_{IP} [Op_i [t_i$ having relatives in the Old World]] makes $[[_{NP} (\exists x) [_{NP} x$ stories about $[Op_x [t_x$ winning the West]]]] implausible]]]

In (237) the induced subject of the NP headed by *stories* locally A-binds the non-overt operator. This state of affairs violates the conditions we have placed on the distribution of non-overt operators at LF. Since the induced subject of the NP is not present at S-Structure, the clausal complement may not be predicated of this subject in the syntax. The only viable way to identify the non-overt operator is by Ā-binding at LF.

While I have been able to account for the fact that the interpretation of the non-overt operator inside the NP in example (237) is not linked with the interpretation of the non-overt operator in the sentential subject of the matrix IP, I still need to discuss in greater detail what assigns the non-overt operator a range at the level of LF representation. There remains, then, the task of outlining a possible solution to this apparent contradiction.

Again, a possible solution may be found by developing Heim's (1982) rule of Existential Closure. This rule inserts an unselective existential-quantifier in LF representations by adjoining this operator to IP. Heim invokes this rule in order to account for the existential force associated with indefinite NPs in sentences like:

(238) a. A man walked into the room.
 b. A dog bit a cat.
 c. A bureaucrat gave a form to an applicant.

After applying QR to each of the indefinite NPs in (238) and then applying Existential Closure to the result, the examples in (238) will have LF representations like:

(239) a. $(\exists x \; x : x \text{ a man})(x \text{ walked into the room})$
 b. $(\exists x, y \; x : x \text{ a dog}, y : y \text{ a cat})(x \text{ bit } y)$
 c. $(\exists x, y, z \; x : x \text{ a bureaucrat}, y : y \text{ a form}, z : z \text{ an applicant})(x \text{ give } y \text{ to } z)$

The immediate problem posed by Existential Closure is one of constraining its operation. In general, the existential operator will be unable to license unbound gaps in the syntax (i.e. levels of representation prior to and including S-Structure) but it may license variables at LF. Thus, the modular character of the theory of grammar that we are assuming here restricts the operation of Existential Closure to the interpretation of indefinites, implicit arguments that have been induced at LF, and the interpretation of 'arbitrary PRO'. Let us assume that Existential Closure adjoins an operator in one of two environments: a tensed IP, or a 'relational NP' such as an NP headed by *story, mother, destruction,* etc.[14] We can assume, in fact, that Existential Closure is responsible for providing a range to the induced subject of *story* in (240) (if such exists, notice that this account does not rely on the existence of an implicit argument). Since the operator inserted by Existential Closure is unselective, it may bind any number of distinct positions; hence, the non-overt operator may bind the non-overt operator in (240) just so long as the index assigned to the non-overt operator under this binding is disjoint from the index associated with the induced subject of the NP headed by *story*:

(240) $[_{IP}$ **G**$_i$ $[_{IP}$ [Op$_i$ [t_i having relatives in the Old World]] makes $[[_{NP}$ ($\exists$x, y) $[_{NP}$ x stories about [Op$_y$ t_y winning the West]]]] implausible]]

Thus, the interpretation associated with (240) follows from the interaction of the Binding theory, the assumption that implicit arguments are realized in LF, and the functioning of the independently motivated rule of Existential Closure, which is required by the interpretation of indefinites. The empty element in the subject position of the non-finite clause is moved to an Ā-position by QR and, as a result, is treated as a non-overt operator. It is an Ā-anaphor that must be locally Ā-bound in order to receive an interpretation. In essence, the account given of so-called 'arbitrary control' in this chapter claims that the same mechanisms involved in the interpretation of indefinites also constrains the interpretation of arbitrary PRO. I claim that arbitrary PRO is simply the creation of an operator/variable pair during the mapping to LF (forced by the θ-Criterion) and that the operator is a pure Ā-anaphor, subject to condition A of the Ā-system of binding. It may, therefore, receive a range only if it is locally Ā-bound by an operator (e.g. an unselective quantifier) contained in its governing category. Returning to examples like (240), note that the presence of an unselective quantifier (in this case *seldom*) has no impact on the interpretation of 'arbitrary PRO' if the quantifier is not contained in the proper governing category:

(241)   [having relatives in the Old World] *seldom* makes $[_{NP}$ stories about [Op$_i$ [t_i winning the West]]] believable

In (241) the unselective quantifier, *seldom*, is outside of the governing category of the non-overt operator (the NP headed by *stories*); my judgement is that *seldom* does not limit the set over which the non-overt operator ranges. That is, (241) means, very roughly, that few individuals who have relatives in the Old World find stories about anyone's winning the West believable. This is as we would expect, given the locality constraint on finding an antecedent for the non-overt operator.

Before concluding this section, I will consider some examples that are, at least on the surface, more problematic for the analysis of control developed in this chapter. We have been assuming that arbitrary control involves syntactically invisible operators that often result from the realization, in the mapping to LF, of so-called implicit arguments. This analysis gave us a fairly simple account of the 'double control' found in many purposive clauses. I have so far ignored cases where all the possible arguments of a verb are realized, as in (242) and (243) (see the discussion of the 'On binding' analysis of double control in connection with examples (104–19) above):

(242) a. John bought a book for Mary.
b. Bill cooked an artichoke for Mary.
c. Bill read a book to the children.

(243) a. John bought Mary a book.
b. Bill cooked Mary an artichoke.
c. Bill read the children a book.

Prima facie, we would not expect the 'double-control' phenomenon, since no implicit argument will be induced in such examples. Nevertheless, in some examples, the 'double-control' reading is still possible:

(244) a. John bought a book for Mary to read.
b. John bought Mary a book to read.

We can eliminate (244a) as a counterexample, since the PP headed by *for* is not necessarily a complement of the verb *buy*; we could assign the following structure to (244a):

(245) $[_{IP}$ John $[_{VP}$ bought a book$_i$] $[_{CP}$ Op$_i$ for $[_{IP}$ Mary to read t_i]]]

where *for* is a complementizer and *Mary* is in the subject position of the adjunct clause. If (245) is the S-Structure for (244a), then we can assume that the implicit benefactive of *buy* is induced in the mapping to LF and Existential Closure then applies:

(246) $[_{IP}$ John $[_{VP}$ ($\exists$x) $[_{VP}$ bought a book$_i$] x] $[_{CP}$ Op$_i$ for $[_{IP}$ Mary to read t_i]]]

At some level of interpretation after LF, *Mary* could be identified with the argument bound by the existential quantifier, thus accounting for the tendency to identify *Mary* as the benefactive argument of *buy* as well as the agent of *read*. There is some evidence for identifying (245) as the S-Structure of (244a). Notating a major intonational break with 'II', it appears that a major intonational break may be placed between *a book* and *for Mary* but such a break is unnatural between *for Mary* and *to read*:

(247)   a. John bought a book II for Mary to read.
            b. ?John bought a book for Mary II to read.

If intonation breaks correspond to syntactic constituency, then it is natural that an intonational break may occur between a VP and a CP (which corresponds to the S-Structure in (245)) rather than occurring in the middle of VP (which corresponds to an analysis that treats *for Mary* as a complement of the verb *buy*). If this analysis is correct, then examples like (244a) do not contain an 'arbitrary PRO' in the subject position of the adjunct clause, and so do not constitute a counterexample to the analysis of control structures presented in this chapter.

The example in (244b) is more problematic; in this case the S-Structure must be as shown in (248):

(248) $[_{IP}$ John $[_{VP}$ bought Mary a book$_i$] $[_{CP}$ Op$_i$ $[_{IP}$ [e] to read t_i]]]

In (248) the benefactive NP, *Mary*, is undoubtedly dominated by VP, so the counteranalysis we exploited for (244a) is unavailable to us here. On the face of it, we cannot appeal to the realization, at LF, of an implicit argument that will be bound under Existential Closure; but then the empty category in the subject position of the adjunct clause cannot be bound by a non-overt operator, since the non-overt operator will have no Ā-antecedent to assign it a range. We would therefore predict that the empty category in the subject position of the adjunct should be treated as an expletive and the entire representation should be ruled out, given that an expletive may not occupy a θ-position.

Let us investigate the status of the putative benefactive NP in the representation of (244b). Recall that this NP obeys very strong Subject-Condition effects; that is, the NP in question is an island to extraction. Kayne (1984) has provided persuasive evidence that the benefactive NP in examples like (244b) is a subconstituent of the subject of a small clause:

(249) $[_{IP}$ John $[_{VP}$ bought $[_{SC}$ Mary a book$_i]]$ $[_{CP}$ Op$_i$ $[_{IP}$ $[e]$ to read $t_i]]]$

If this analysis of dative-shift constructions is correct, then the benefactive NP is not, strictly speaking, a complement of the verb; we might plausibly assume that the benefactive receives its thematic role internally to the small clause. There is some support for this idea insofar as such constructions may easily take a second benefactive; compare the following:

(250) a. John bought Mary a book for Bill.
       b. ?John bought a book for Mary for Bill.

This suggests that the verb, *buy* in this case, still has an implicit benefactive argument which may be realized, and bound under Existential Closure, during the mapping to LF. The LF representation of (244b) may very well be like the following:

(251) $[_{IP}$ John $[_{VP}$ ($\exists$x) $[_{VP}$ bought $[_{sc}$ Mary a book$_i]$ $x]$ $[_{CP}$ Op$_i$ $[_{IP}$ Op$_x$ $[_{IP}$ t_x to read $t_i]]]]]$

The 'true' benefactive argument of the verb in (251) has been realized and bound in the mapping to LF. This, in turn, makes an antecedent available for the non-overt operator associated with the subject position of the adjunct clause.

It should be noted that the entire problem probably disappears if we adopt the analysis of dative shift found in Stowell (1981). He

Control and non-overt operators

argues that the 'dative-shifted' NP is in fact cliticized onto the verb; it is then plausible to treat this cliticized NP as an Ā-binder which could plausibly bind the non-overt operator in question at LF. Thus, the analysis of control presented in this chapter seems to be independent of the analysis of dative-shift constructions.

The analysis accorded to the counterexamples in (244) is, of course, largely speculative in nature and there are, no doubt, many other potential counterexamples to this analysis. the direction of research is, however, clear; properties of control follow from the interaction of the Binding theory with argument structure. In explicating the argument structure of particular lexical items, many, if not all, of the properties of control will follow naturally. From this perspective, there is no independent module of grammar that is concerned exclusively with control, but rather an interaction of binding and argument structure.

As a final illustration, consider examples of the following form:

(252) a. John knows [what [[e] to eat]]
b. John explained [how [[e] to solve the problem]]
c. John discovered [how [[e] to make fire]]

Not all of the matrix verbs in (252) are lexical-control verbs:

(253) a. John knows [[e] to eat apples]
b. *John explained [[e] to solve the problem using diagonalization]
c. *John discovered [[e] to make fire using two sticks]

(Note that (253a) seems to have a modal sense: 'John knows that he should eat apples'.) In (253b) and (253c) a 'PRO' subject is only possible if the Comp of the embedded clause contains an overt wh-element. According to standard judgements, each of the empty subjects in (252) is an instance of 'arbitrary PRO'. Thus, (252a) means that, in general, John knows what one ought to eat; (252b) means that John explained how one generally goes about solving a problem like the one at hand; and (252c) means that John discovered how one could go about making fire. The crucial observation here is that all of the examples in (252) involve essentially modal notions of obligation (see (252a)) or possibility (see (252b-c)).[15]

Given that each of the Comps of the embedded clauses in these examples contains an overt operator at S-Structure; movement of a non-overt operator to Comp in the syntax is blocked. Thus, the examples in (252) class with the analysis of other 'arbitrary-control' structures insofar as the movement of the non-overt operator must take place in the mapping to LF. This entails that the non-overt operator is identified under Ā-binding and not under predication (as would be the case with 'obligatory control'). The question now is what element Ā-binds the non-overt operator at LF. Recall that the verbs have the lexical property that when they take a [+WH] complement, they take on a modal reading of obligation or possibility; it is reasonable to assume that this lexical property is ultimately what assigns a range to the non-overt operator. For example, taking *OB* to be an operator of obligation, we might map (252a) onto the following LF representation:

(254) $[_{IP}$ John $[_{VP}$ OB$_x$ $[_{VP}$ knows $[_{CP}$ what$_i$ $[_{IP}$ Op$_x$ $[_{IP}$ t_x to eat t_i]]]]]]

That is, John knows what one (including himself) ought to eat. While this analysis is very rough, it does suggest that a careful analysis of lexical semantics will contribute greatly to our theorizing about LF representations.

A brief comment on bound pronouns

I have assumed throughout this discussion that the Binding theory applies freely both to S-Structure and LF representations. Assuming that implicit arguments are realized in the mapping to LF and that certain operators may be induced during this mapping, there is a possible undesirable interaction between these processes and the interpretation of bound pronominals.

To illustrate this point, consider an example like:

(255) It is easy for Mary to please him.

If we assume that *easy* may take an implicit argument and that *Mary* is the subject of the embedded IP, then the following LF representation is a logical possibility:

(256) $[Gx$ [it is easy x [for Mary to please him$_x$]]]

In (256) the pronoun is bound by the implicit argument of *easy* and, as a result, may be interpreted as a bound variable at LF.

Clearly, (255) cannot mean that it is easy for Mary to please people generically, so the representation in (256) must be ruled out by some independent means. The solution to this puzzle follows if we exploit the differences between levels of representation in the syntax. Notice that the implicit argument is inactive prior to the level of LF representation. Following Reinhart (1983, 1984) and Williams (1986), let us suppose that S-Structure is the exclusive level at which bound pronouns are licensed; that is, a bound-pronoun rule operates only at S-Structure and no pronoun may be interpreted as bound if this relation has not been so licensed.

Under this assumption, example (255) does not present a problem. A bound pronoun must enter into a particular structural relation with its antecedent at S-Structure; since the putative antecedent of the pronoun in (256) is inactive at S-Structure, it cannot be an antecedent for that pronoun. Hence, (256) is not licensed by the grammar.

4.5 Conclusions

We can return, now, to the puzzle of the 'PRO gate' (see p. 141). Examination of cases of weak cross-over led to the conclusion that pronominals may not be directly Ā-bound. Pronominals may be treated as bound variables just in case they are, in turn, A-bound by a variable. If PRO has a pronominal feature, however, then we must weaken this restriction, since PRO may be directly Ā-bound at LF:

(257) a. [PRO_i kissing his_i mother] annoys every boy_i
b. [$_{IP}$ every boy_i [$_{IP}$ [PRO_i kissing his_i mother] annoys t_i]]

This direct Ā-binding of PRO by operators at LF also implies that empty categories must have inherent features; if the properties of empty categories are derived solely with reference to the structure in which they occur in the manner discussed in Chomsky (1982), then the PRO in (257b) will be identified as a variable, since it occurs in an A-position and is locally Ā-bound by *every boy*. But a variable in the position of the PRO in (256b) is not head-governed, and so violates the ECP. Thus, we must simply stipulate that this empty category is a PRO and put aside the idea that empty categories may be contextually defined. I would argue that, whatever conceptual deficiencies the contextual definition of empty categories may have, it did force a tight correlation between properties of empty categories and properties of syntactic representations. While we will undoubtedly wish to abandon the hypothesis that empty categories have no inherent features (see Brody 1984; Safir 1985), we may still maintain that there is a strong correlation between the inherent properties of empty categories and properties of syntactic representations. Allowing a [+pronominal] empty category to be locally Ā-bound represents a weakening of the theory, with or without the contextual definition of empty categories.

In order to circumvent these problems, I have argued that PRO should be replaced by a non-overt operator/variable pair. Notice that the conclusion that a variable occupies the subject position of the embedded IP in (257b) is exactly what is predicted by the contextual definition of empty categories: an empty category that is locally Ā-bound is a variable. The difference is that the relationship between *every boy* and the variable is mediated by a non-overt operator; thus, the ECP is not violated, since the variable is governed by the non-overt operator. In this framework, the PRO gate comes as no surprise, since non-overt operators are anaphors which must pick up a range from some Ā-binder.

The hypothesis that control involves a non-overt operator led us to the conclusion that control is simply another instance of the type of binding found in other constructions which involve a non-overt operator, like tough movement, parasitic gaps, infinitival relatives, and so on. The analysis of these latter constructions and obligatory control was as follows: syntactic movement of an empty element to an Ā-position was forced either by subcategorization features (obligatory control) or by the fact that the empty element occupies a Case-marked position. In both cases, the distribution is regulated by Case theory. Once it has moved to an appropriate Ā-position, the empty element is identified as a non-overt operator and must be assigned a range so that the variable which it binds will not be taken as an expletive. In the syntax there are two ways to identify a non-overt operator: predication or Ā-binding. Predication identifies the non-overt operator in obligatory control structures, while Ā-binding identifies the non-overt operator in parasitic-gap constructions. Since predication is an S-Structure property, it follows that 'obligatory control' is also an S-Structure property.

In cases of arbitrary (or non-obligatory) control, syntactic movement is not forced by either subcategorization or Case theory. If the empty category remains *in situ*, however, it will be taken as an expletive element and may not bear a thematic role. If the empty element moves to an Ā-position, it will be taken as a non-overt operator. There is only one way to identify a non-overt operator at LF, however: Ā-binding. This last assumption led us into a consideration of properties of LF. I concluded that LF is a very rich level of representation, where operators that are induced from tense and mood, or operators associated with adverbs of quantification are realized and assigned scope.

Furthermore, I argued that syntactically unrealized arguments may be realized at LF. I view LF as a completely unambiguous level, where argument structure is realized in its purest form. We can therefore contrast LF with D-Structure. In this framework, D-Structure is a level where syntactically obligatory thematic positions like 'subject' or 'direct object' are represented; from our perspective, D-Structure is thematically pure with respect to the syntax. LF differs from D-Structure in that suppressed arguments are realized and scope is assigned unambiguously to various operators. Thus, LF is the thematically pure level of representation. My assumptions about LF, in turn, provided an account of how the realization and binding of implicit arguments interacts with 'control'. Along the way I noted an interaction between 'control' and, for example, adverbs of quantification. In general, the assumption that 'control' involves non-overt operators not only allowed the elimination of Control theory as an independent module of grammar, but also leads to a unification of apparently diverse types of binding, and uncovered a variety of interesting interactions, as was the case with adverbs of quantification. All this provides evidence of the robustness of the hypothesis that control is a special case of a non-overt operator. The entire approach, finally, crucially assumes a grammar made up of interactive modules (see the relationship between Case theory and binding assumed in this chapter) which apply at different levels of representation (see the distinction between obligatory control – which is captured at S-Structure – and non-obligatory control – which is captured at LF).

The relatively optimistic picture painted in the previous paragraph should, however, also be a reminder of the amount of work that remains. The framework developed in this chapter, and, indeed, throughout this book, requires a theory of argument structure and predicate formation; this theory, however, is still in its infancy. The conclusion is that argument structure is a fundamental ingredient in explicating the mental representation of syntactic structure.

Finally, there is a last puzzle; I have focused my attention in this chapter on the reduction of PRO in the subject position of IP to a non-overt operator. I have not looked at the problem of PRO inside an NP, although I argued in Chapter 2 that PRO could, in fact, occur in the Spec of NP. By my logic, the non-overt operator in the structure shown in (258a) will move to the Spec of NP in order to avoid Case assignment by the preposition and in order to receive some referential content which will allow the gap after the preposition to bear a θ-role, as shown in (258b):

(258) a. ... need [$_{NP}$ a good [$_{N'}$ -ing [$_{V'}$ talk [$_{PP}$ to Op]]]] ...
b. ... need [$_{NP}$ Op$_i$ a good [$_{N'}$ -ing [$_{V'}$ talk [$_{PP}$ to t_i]]]] ...

Drawing on this parallelism between retroactive nominals and obligatory-control structures, retroactive nominals involve identification of a non-overt operator under lexical specification of the governing verbal. The apparent problem with this analysis is that, as I noted in Chapter 2, the retroactive-nominal construction never involves successive-cyclic movement:

(259) *John$_i$ needs some thinking [$_{CP}$ that [$_{IP}$ Mary likes e_i]]

Under the analysis adopted in Chapter 3, the CP complement is transparent because it is θ-marked by *think*, which is morphologically indistinguishable from a verb at D-Structure.

Consider the structure of (259):

(260) John$_i$ needs [$_{NP}$ Op$_i$ some [$_{N'}$ -ing [$_{V'}$ think [$_{CP}$ t_i that [$_{IP}$ Mary likes t'_i]]]]]

The intermediate CP dominates a trace which counts as a pure Ā-anaphor (Aoun 1986) in contrast to an Ā-bound element in an A-position which is subject to condition A of the Ā-binding system and condition C of the A-binding system. Recall that Ā-anaphors do not obey the *i-within-i* condition (see the discussion of examples (228b) and (232b), above). We may assume, then, that the [+N] affix ('0-*ing*') acts as an accessible SUBJECT in (259). Since the domain of this element is N', we might assume that N' acts as the governing category for the trace in the Spec of Comp. This interpretation also accounts for the ultra-narrow scope interpretation of *no one* in (232b):

(261) [$_{NP}$ the mother of no one] called him

(where *mother* is interpreted as having scope over *no one*). It is easy to see that if the non-overt operator is adjoined to the Spec of NP, it will not be dominated by the minimal subtree containing the trace in Comp and its accessible SUBJECT. Examples like (259) violate condition A of the Ā-binding system.

This analysis solves a final puzzle. I noted in Chapter 2 that retroactive nominals marginally license parasitic gaps:

(262) ?This problem$_i$ is worth some thinking about t_i without losing any sleep over e_i

While (262) is quite marginal, it is not as bad as:

(263) *Which paper t_i was read without filing e_i

If both examples are ruled out due to A-binding of the parasitic gap, we would expect them to be equally bad. Some dialects seem to allow (262) relatively freely, but not (263). I speculated that some of the discomfort associated with (262) was due to the presence of a sentential adjunct on the object NP, which may be stylistically marked in many dialects.

Under the non-overt operator analysis of control, the difference in acceptability between (262) and (263) follows more naturally;

to the extent that elements in an Ā-position license parasitic gaps, the non-overt operator in (264) may license one:

(264)   ... [Op$_i$ some [$_{N'}$ -ing [$_{V'}$ think [$_{PP}$ about t_i]]]
        [without losing any sleep over e_i]] ...

In (264), the non-overt operator will locally Ā-bind the parasitic gap, which is sufficient for treating the gap as a variable. The construction in (264) is thus well-formed, to the degree that parasitic-gap constructions are ever well-formed.

The preceding comments make clear what direction research on the distribution of non-overt operators inside nominals should take. Many details of the exact nature of the internal structure of nominals remain to be investigated. The preceding discussion implies, for example, that nominals can contain an internal Ā-position that may be present to receive a non-overt operator where needed (contrary to my assumptions in Chapter 2); such a position could be created by adjunction or may be pre-existent. I will leave the investigation of this question for future research. It should be clear that syntactic investigation can profitably be undertaken if we consider the interaction of lexical argument structure and independent syntactic conditions. Thus, extraction seems to be contingent on the structure of lexical predicates (Chapters 2 and 3) and many of the factors involved in so-called control phenomena rely on the argument structure of predicates.

Notes

1 Introduction

1. For a discussion of lexical semantics, see Levin (1985) and Jackendoff (1983). The importance of the lexicon in language acquisition is discussed in Grimshaw (1981) and Pinker (1984, 1987) and the references cited in these works.
2. The influence of Kayne's important work is evident here (see Kayne 1984). The analysis developed here differs from Kayne's insofar as I have attempted to downplay the role of tree geometry (direction of branching in phrase markers, for example). It should be kept in mind, however, that tree geometry is, to a great extent, a function of the argument structure of lexical items. It is difficult, but crucial, to determine the interplay between argument structure, the geometric form of structural descriptions, and locality. Much of the current research in generative grammar has been an investigation of just this problem.
3. Infl is not associated with a lexical item but, rather, contains abstract grammatical information regarding tense, aspect, mood, and agreement.
4. I will assume that the empty string in subject position comes to be covered by the expletive element, *it*, which does not refer, despite having a phonological realization.
5. A further possibility is that the empty element in (21c) is PRO. This possibility is independently ruled out by the Binding theory, for reasons that would take us far afield. See the discussion of PRO in Chapter 4.
6. It is not possible to give a detailed account of Case theory in this limited space. The following examples appear to be problematic, but have received extensive attention in the literature:

(i) John gave Mary a book.
(ii) Bill believes [$_S$ John to be innocent]

Example (i) is an instance of Dative shift and it appears that two NPs must receive Case. For discussion, see Kayne (1984) and the references cited there. Example (ii) is an instance of Exceptional Case Marking; see Chomsky (1981) and the references cited there.

7. On the definition of c-command, see Reinhart (1983). For the moment, I will say that a node c-commands all those nodes dominated by its sister. Again, the definition is meant to give the informal effect and not to be a precise characterization of c-command. We will have occasion to discuss the c-command relation on page 22.

2 On a certain class of nominals

1. The term 'retroactive' is taken from Jespersen (1940) who applied it to certain infinitives. Hantson (1984) uses the term with reference to gerunds. Hantson arrives at an analysis of a gerundive construction that is parallel to the nominal construction examined here. His analysis, insofar as it involves passivization, is similar to my analysis of the nominal construction.
2. An element is *bound* if it is c-commanded by a co-indexed category; *A* is *locally bound* by *B* if *A* is bound by *B* and there is no element *C* such that *C* binds *A* but does not bind *B*. On the definition of c-command and government, see Aoun and Sportiche (1983).
3. *See* is taken, here, in its transitive sense only. Notice that it is insufficient to say that the child fails to construct well-formed representations for structures like (9a) simply because such examples are not included in the child's primary linguistic data. The child does, in fact, have evidence of phonetically null subjects of tensed sentences in relative-clause structures: 'the man that John said *e* saw him'. The question that needs to be answered is why the child acquiring English fails to generalize from relative-clause structures to tensed sentences in general. This question is of even greater interest given the data from Chinese in example (10).
4. For discussion of the definition of local domain and government, see Chomsky (1981) and the references cited there. If we assume that Genitive Case is assigned configurationally rather than on the basis of government then, *a priori*, one might expect an overt NP with the features [+anaphor, +pronominal] could occur in this position. Some proposals made in Huang (1982) and Aoun (1986) may circumvent this problem. Notice that if configurational Case is available in some structural position, we would expect [+anaphor, +pronominal] elements to be in free variation with other elements here, all things being equal.

243

Notes

5. For a rather different approach to PRO, see Bouchard (1984) and Sportiche (1983) where it is argued that PRO may be either a pure anaphor or a pure pronominal but not [+anaphor, +pronominal]. See page 134 for arguments that the distribution of PRO is not limited to the subject position of infinitives and gerunds. In Chapter 4, we will have occasion to reconsider the entire framework for PRO, although along different lines from those assumed by Bouchard and Sportiche.
6. Recent research (e.g. Brody 1984 and Safir 1984b) indicates that empty categories do have inherent properties that cannot be determined on the basis of structural properties alone. Nevertheless, since the basic points that interest us here will not be significantly altered, I will assume that the functional definition of empty categories provides a set of diagnostics for determining the inherent features of the empty category in question.
7. An element is in an A(rgument)-position if that position is a subject or receives a θ-role; otherwise, it is in a non-argument (A-bar) position.
8. For the moment, I will exclude pro, the empty pure pronominal, from the discussion.
9. An element A is the SUBJECT of a projection X if A is the most prominent nominal element within X. A is accessible to B only if co-indexing A with B does not violate the *i-within-i* condition. For discussion, see Chomsky (1981) and the references cited there.
10. On A-chains, see Chomsky (1981) and Safir (1985).
11. One might imagine the case of a verb analogous to *want* which subcategorizes for an infinitival clause which obligatorily passivizes:

    (i) a. John$_i$ *tnaws* [PRO$_i$ to be examined]
        b. *John$_i$ *tnaws* [PRO$_i$ to examine him]

    I am not aware of any verb which has this property: a significant fact, if true. It is likely that a verb could not select for a morphological property of a verb embedded in a clausal complement due to the fact that the matrix verb could not govern the embedded verb. This would rule out the case in (i), although one might imagine a verb which subcategorizes for a small-clause complement could select such a morphological property of the head of the small-clause predicate. Again, I am unaware of such a case. The behavior of retroactive nominals is somewhat puzzling in this light. The most plausible assumption is that this property of retroactive nominals must follow from core principles of grammar. I am grateful to Ken Safir for this observation.
12. Chomsky (1982) assumes that pro may be identified by a sufficiently rich inflection or by a clitic. Huang (1984) hypothesizes that, in some languages, pro may also be identified by means of co-indexation with a topic. English, however, lacks a sufficiently rich inflection, has no clitics, and does not allow pro to be co-indexed with a topic; hence, it

is commonly assumed that English lacks pro.
13. See also the discussion in Safir (1986). Note that these examples may involve adjunction to the fronted NP. This adjunction might be consistent with the assumptions about adjunction in May (1985) and Chomsky (1986) both of whom rule out adjunction to elements in A-positions. Note that example (37a) involves movement of the NP to Comp, the canonical Ā-position; a simple analysis would be that the wh-operator may adjoin to the fronted element in the syntax. The analysis is somewhat more difficult for the polarity *so* in (37b) since the NP occupies an A-position. A full analysis of the properties of *so* would take us well beyond the scope of the present discussion. One might extend on the work of Abney (1986), who hypothesizes that determiners may head NPs.
14. See van Riemsdijk (1978) on the existence of a Comp-like non-argument position in certain prepositional phrases in Dutch.
15. Let us quickly dispense with the matter of weak cross-over, which involves the binding of two A-positions by a single operator. The question is whether or not a representation with the correct structural properties for testing weak cross-over can be built for retroactive nominal constructions. Recall that, for possibly independent reasons, the retroactive nominal construction shows a strong SSC effect; thus the environment where the nominal contains a subject which, in turn, contains a pronominal is ruled out for reasons which are independent of cross-over. Hence, we cannot construct a representation entirely on a par with example (43).

Furthermore, a pronominal immediately contained in the NP will be in the same governing category as the subject of S, which is, itself, co-indexed with the empty category in the nominal; this configuration is already ruled out by condition B of the Binding theory. Finally, a pronominal contained in a restrictive relative will be locally bound by the trace left by the non-overt operator, since the trace will c-command the restrictive relative. As a result, this case is irrelevant for weak cross-over since the local binding relation will still be bijective.

I will note, in passing, the existence of examples like those in (i) which involve adjuncts:

(i) a. John$_i$ could always use some comforting t_i after his$_i$ sessions with the psychiatrist.
b. John$_i$ could use a good talking to t_i about his$_i$ many annoying habits.

These examples are, at first blush, an embarrassment for the operator analysis of retroactive nominals, since the pronoun should be subject to weak crossover. These facts are far from conclusive and need not detain us, given other evidence to be developed.
16. The analysis of parasitic gaps relies on that of Chomsky (1981). More recently (see Chomsky 1986, and the references cited there) it has

Notes

been argued that the parasitic gap is itself generated by movement. Since licensing of the parasitic gap still involves a wh-trace, we need not linger over the details of the more recent analysis. Suffice it to say that the crucial property for our purposes – the presence of a licensing variable formed by Ā-movement – remains constant.

17. We will consider a construction more congruent to retroactive nominals – 'Mary is pretty to look at' – below.
18. We may assume, following Keyser and Roeper (1984), that the absorption of Accusative Case and the blocking of the subject's θ-role are not, in fact, two independent operations, but, rather, they follow from Burzio's Generalization (1986) to the effect that the subject position does not receive a θ-role if Accusative Case is not assigned to the object.
19. See Chomsky (1981) for some discussion of compositional θ-role assignment. The famous 'broken arm' example might serve to establish the point:

    (i) John broke his arm.

    If *John* is disjoint from the pronoun *his*, then *John* must be interpreted as the AGENT of the breaking. If, on the other hand, *John* binds *his*, then *John* need not be interpreted as the AGENT, but may receive the PATIENT θ-role. Thus, facts about the reference of NPs internal to the predicate are crucial in determining the nature of the θ-role assigned to the subject. In brief, θ-role assignment to the subject is compositional.
20. The systematic gaps in nominal paradigms discussed here and below (p. 45) have received attention in a number of places; see, for example, Chomsky (1970), Postal (1974), Williams (1982), and Kayne (1984).
21. But compare (76) with:

    (i) the consideration of Bill as a threat . . .

    The addition of *as* to the predicate seems to improve the NP. In itself, however, this fact should not be taken as an indication that nouns admit a particular type of small clause (i.e., those including an *as*).
22. In order for this analysis to work out completely, we must adopt Kayne's analysis of Datives. Kayne assumes that *give Mary the book* has the following bracketing:

    (i) [give [$_X$ [$_{NP}$ Mary] [$_{NP}$ the book]]]

    i.e., that *Mary the book* is a small clause and that the node labeled X in (i) is a maximal projection.
23. But see Safir (1984a) where it is argued that at least one adjective,

namely *worth*, may assign Case. Safir also points out that adjectives may assign Case in German. For more on *worth*, see Safir (1984a), Hantson (1984), and p. 76. Notice also that if Case assignment were crucial for government across a maximal projection, then passive participles should be incapable of governing across such a projection. This would predict that Exceptional Case-Marking verbs should not allow passive when the complement clause is infinitival. This is counterexemplified by (i):

(i) John is believed to have been abducted.

24. Cinque (1984) argues that parasitic gaps are impossible in Italian when the adjunct clause is introduced by the preposition *per*:

(i) *Questo libro$_i$ è troppo di parte per adottare e_i
     'Which book is too biased to adopt?'
(ii) Questo libro$_i$ è troppo di parte per adottar*le*$_i$
     'Which book is too biased to adopt it?'

If the generation of parasitic gaps involves non-overt operators, then this fact indicates that the non-overt operator is not properly governed. Notice, however, that prepositions are not proper governors in Italian independently of their ability to govern across maximal projections.

25. I have not included examples of Dative shift, tough movement, and raising simply because I could not find any examples that were semantically plausible. The inability to govern into Comp and the absence of small-clause complements are sufficient to demonstrate the point.

Notice that these observations should be taken as applying to the core case. Tim Stowell (p.c.) points out that there is at least one preposition in English that does allow small clauses:

(i) a. With John out of the way, we can safely continue our conversation.
     b. With the alarm system broken, anyone could just walk in.

My judgement is that *with* only takes a small clause when it occurs in an adjunct position. The relevance of this fact should be apparent shortly.

26. This hypothesis should be read with the proviso in note 24 kept in mind; that is, in the core case, prepositions do not independently assign a θ-role to their complements. Some prepositions like *on, over, above*, etc. can assign a θ-role to their objects directly. Notice that the ability of these prepositions to assign a θ-role may be over-ridden when the preposition occurs as the complement of a verb, as can be seen in the ambiguity of:

Notes

(i) They decided on the boat.

where *on the boat* may occur as a locative PP or as a complement of the verb *decide*. The θ-role assigned to *the boat* differs across these two cases.

27. An interpretive approach to the thematic roles associated with nominal complements would provide a research strategy for investigating the range of interpretations found for the subject of NP, as observed in Williams (1982).
28. Here, we assume, following Kayne (1984), that a potential binder of a trace must be of the same category as the trace. He observes that this accounts for the contrast in (i):

    (i) a. $[_{N'}$ Poland's$]_i$ invasion $[_{N'} e]_i$ by Germany ...
        b. *the $[_{Adj}$ Polish] invasion $[_{N'} e]$ by Germany ...

    In (ia) the trace in the object position is A-bound by the Genetive NP. In (ib) the trace is A-free because the adjective, *Polish*, cannot bind the trace of an NP. Example (ib), therefore, violates the Binding theory.

29. J. Aoun (p.c.) and T. Hoekstra (p.c.) have observed that under the assumption that governed PRO is a pure anaphor, the SSC facts may still be made to follow. We will not discuss this hypothesis here, leaving any detailed discussion of Control theory to Chapter 4. We will, however, be able to eliminate the assumption made in this chapter that government is directional. This result follows from the reanalysis of PRO given in Chapter 4.
30. There is a great deal of similarity between (125) and Chomsky's recent work on government (Chomsky 1986). See Chapter 3 for a more detailed comparison.
31. Higginbotham (1985) develops other means of θ-role assignment, including θ-identification, which is involved in modification, and autonymous θ-marking. Both processes are relevant to the formation of complex predicates. These forms of θ-role assignment need not concern us here, although they are clearly relevant to material discussed in Chapter 4.
32. The analysis of retroactive nominals presented in this section differs markedly from the analysis found in Clark (1984 and 1985b), due to some insightful work on the construction by Safir (1986); note, however, that the present analysis differs from Safir's in many respects – any errors are, therefore, not to be attributed to him.
33. I owe a great debt to Ken Safir, whose comments on this chapter led me to assimilate retroactive nominals more fully to passive constructions.

Notes

3 Thematic domains and bounding

*The work presented in this chapter is an adaptation and extension of work in Clark (1984, 1985b).

1. A small clause consists of a predicate, of any major grammatical category, and a subject, as in the bracketed portion of (i):

    (i) John considers [it obvious that Bill will be late]

    I will assume that the head of the predicate is the head of the small clause (see Stowell 1983). Thus, the small clause in (i) is an adjective phrase. Note that the subject of the small clause in (i) is pleonastic *it*. Thus, the subject of the small clause cannot be a complement of the verb that governs the small clause or the θ-Criterion will be violated. For a different approach see Williams (1980, 1983), Emonds (1985), and the references cited in those works.

2. I have no account for the impossibility of (18b). Notice that *see* does admit passive:

    (i) $Mary_i$ was seen t_i

    so it cannot be because *see* does not have a passive participle. Nor is the impossibility of passive a general property of perception verbs, as example (18c) shows. The example in the text should be contrasted with:

    (ii) $Mary_i$ was seen [t_i to leave]

    which is fully grammatical.

3. Chomsky (1986), following observations of Adriana Belleti, observes that the following violations of the Adjunct-Island Condition are relatively minor:

    (i) a. ?He is the person to whom they left [before speaking t]
         b. ?He is the person who they left [before speaking to t]

    with (ib) being slightly better than (ia). The account developed here does not distinguish between the examples in (i) and those in (ii); both sets are ruled out by transparency.

    (ii) a. *He is the person who they felt bad [because they insulted t]
         b. *He is the person who they left [(in order) to speak t]

    The barriers framework, in fact, allows well-formed derivations for both sets of examples. For further discussion of the contrast between the barriers framework and the transparency framework, see section 3.3. I will continue to assume that the transparency should degrade

Notes

both sets of examples and will put aside questions of distinguishing between them.

4. Lightfoot (1979) notes that extraposition from the subject of NP was not always ruled out in English; Middle English allowed the following sort of construction:

   (i) a. kyng Priamus sone of Troy
          'king Priamus of Troy's son'
       b. the Prolog of the Clerkes tale of Oxenford
          'the prolog of the clerk of Oxford's tale'

   I have, as yet, no principled analysis of why the examples in (i) were grammatical. Notice that extraposition from subject position cannot be derived via movement under the transparency account; the subject will always be non-transparent. Hence, cases normally treated as extraposition (see (ii)) will have to be base-generated:

   (ii) A book arrived which I ordered last month

   It is possible to treat the extraposed element as a predicate which may be applied to the subject under mutual c-command. This derives the impossibility of extraposing from a nominal complement, as in (iii):

   (iii) [a picture [of a man *t*]] was stolen who I knew well

   See May and Gueron (1984) and the references cited there for a discussion of extraposition and a more complete analysis. We will return to cases like (iv), which involve extraposition from a complement, below (p. 119–24):

   (iv) [a picture *t*] was taken of John

5. Notice that we cannot rule out chomsky-adjunction to an adjunct, if Chomsky's approach to parasitic gaps is correct (Chomsky 1986: 54–68). Crucially, on this account, chomsky-adjunction to adjuncts must be possible. If only NPs are allowed to adjoin to phrases (Chomsky 1986) then (66b) is ruled out, but not (66a). One might try to force all phrases to pass through Comp (this is independently forced for sentential complements). In this case, (66a) would violate the Minimality Condition.

6. The hypothesis that 'move alpha' does not preserve superscripting entails that a moved phrase is an island to extraction; 'move alpha' may not extract a subpart of a moved phrase out of that phrase. This result recalls the Raising Principle (RP) of Wexler and Culicover (1980). The RP prevents a transformation from analyzing a subpart of a raised node. Wexler and Culicover wanted to demonstrate that a rather simple learning device could converge on the adult grammar

(in their case the transformational component of the adult grammar) in bounded time. They achieved this result by restricting the class of possible grammars (in particular, they restricted the ways in which transformations could operate). Given restrictions like the RP, they were unable to impose a bound on the relative complexity of input data; the learner need not be exposed to input data that required a parse tree with a depth of embedding greater than 3 (this is 'degree 2 learnability'). Given a finite lexicon, then, the input data required for the learner to converge on the adult grammar would also be finite.

The recent shift of emphasis from rule-based systems to principles found in much recent syntactic theory (see, e.g., Berwick 1985) does not negate the importance of the result in Wexler and Culicover. We must still show that the learner can arrive at the adult parameter-settings in bounded time given plausible input data. We would expect that many of the constraints discussed in Wexler and Culicover would have analogues in a 'principles and parameters' approach. It is therefore of some interest that our result mimics the RP.

4 Control and non-overt operators

1. Strictly speaking, an element could escape the governing category requirement by not having an accessible SUBJECT in any domain that contains it. To my knowledge, this possibility has been ignored in the literature. The notion of 'accessible SUBJECT' is relevant to determining local syntactic domains in which an element must be bound or free. A is an accessible SUBJECT for B if A is the most prominent element bearing agreement features in a subtree which contains B and co-indexing A and B does not violate the *i-within-i* condition. The latter condition rules out co-indexing one node with a node that properly contains it. Thus, (i) violates the *i-within-i* condition:

    (i) $[_{NP}$ a picture of itself$_i]_i$

    Intuitively, the *i-within-i* condition rules out certain cases of circular reference where a constituent is referentially dependent on itself. Thus, the referent of *a picture of itself* cannot be established until the referent of *itself* is established but the latter cannot establish a referent until the reference of the former is established. See Chomsky (1981) and Hornstein (1984) for some discussion.
2. One could, of course, assume that there are several non-overt operators, each with its own lexical entry and its own inherent range. This approach is completely uninteresting insofar as it merely stipulates the properties of non-overt operators rather than attempting to derive these properties from independent principles.
3. 'Implicit' should not be taken as implying syntactically unrealized.

Epstein requires the 'implicit' argument to be syntactically realized as a pro. Others, for example Keyser and Roeper (1984), place no such requirement on implicit arguments, which they take as present in a head's argument structure, but not necessarily syntactically realized. See, especially, the next section.

4. As Lasnik and Saito (1984) demonstrate, these requirements are not checked at S-Structure universally. In particular, Chinese and Japanese lack syntactic movement so that all wh-elements are *in situ* at S-Structure in these languages. nevertheless, these languages have verbs which obligatorily take embedded interrogatives (see Huang 1982, and Lasnik and Saito 1984 for details). In these languages the requirement must be checked at LF rather than at S-Structure. This raises interesting possibilities for the analysis of PRO developed in this chapter. In particular, I would expect that languages could differ with respect to the level of representation at which obligatory control is determined.

5. Intuitively, the subject of the predication in the case of psych verbs seems to be the object of the verb. This fact indicates that the notion 'subject of a predication' does not necessarily correspond with the notion 'grammatical subject'. 'Subject of a predication' more closely corresponds to the notion of 'subject' developed in, for example, Geach (1962). It is a matter of some interest that the two notions have a rather close correlation, although they may diverge in instances like psyche-verb constructions. A complete exploration of the matter would take us well off the topic of this chapter and will be left as a matter for future research.

6. Chomsky (1980) did not have recourse to the Binding theory in ruling out *a dog* as a possible controller. Instead, he stipulates a bijective relation between controllers and controlled elements. Once an NP has been identified as a possible controller, it is no longer available as a controller for some other element. The effect of this stipulation, along with the top-down ordering of the algorithm and the minimal-distance principle, is to arrange possible controllers in a push-down stack, where only the topmost NP on the stack is an available controller and where each controller is popped off the stack when it has been identified as a controller. The feature [±SC] is necessary to get around this push-down stack arrangement in examples like:

(i)   John$_i$ promised Bill$_j$ [PRO$_{(i,*j)}$ to leave]

7. Notice the similarity in this part of the definition of 'nearest controller' and the definition of a predication structure given in Williams (1980), where mutual c-command between the subject and the predicate is assumed.

8. Note that this definition bears some similarity to the definition of θ-chain in Safir (1985) where, among other things, the notion of BIND is eliminated. 'BIND' in the definition refers to both subscripting

and superscripting, while 'bind' covers subscripting only. The notion of 'BIND' was required to cover certain cases of rightward movement where the trace left by movement c-commands the landing site. See Safir (1985) for discussion.

9. For present purposes, I will assume the following definition of *c-command*:

   (i) A node A c-commands a node B if and only if the first branching node dominating A also dominates B.

   This definition makes c-command into a reflexive relation. In the examples in (177) and (178) the c-command relation will guarantee that the operators are in an asymmetrical c-command relation.

10. Control by an implicit argument was, to my knowledge, first noted by Manzini (in a talk).

11. Keenan (personal communication) and Stowell (personal communication) have advocated a similar treatment of small-clause structures. Namely, the predicate of the small clause may form a complex predicate with the verb in the matrix clause. Thus, an example like (i) would, at some level, be mapped onto a representation like (ii):

    (i) John considers [Bill ugly]
    (ii) John [considers ugly] Bill

    Again, the relationship between syntactic constituency and predicate structure is fairly remote in these examples.

12. We still require some mechanism for attaching the lexical content of indefinite NPs as a restriction on the unselective operator. There are many ways to do this: see, for example, Heim's treatment (Heim 1982). For present purposes I will assume that the indefinites undergo QR and then may undergo a form of Absorption (see Higginbotham and May 1981).

13. We are restricting our attention here to nominal complements. An adjunct on a noun may not have the head noun as its SUBJECT for structural reasons.

14. In other words, a relational noun is a noun that denotes a relation between two or more individuals. For example, *mother* denotes a relation between an individual and her progeny. I include in this class derived nominals and other nouns with a θ-grid with multiple entries.

15. Hagit Borer (personal communication) has noted that in Hebrew the literal translation of (252a) involves an explicit modal and that this modal is obligatory.

References

Abney, S. (1987) 'The English noun phrase in its sentential aspect', PhD dissertation, MIT.
Anderson, M. (1985) 'Prenominal genitive NPs', *The Linguistic Review* 3: 1–24.
Anderson, S. (1982) 'Where's morphology?', *Linguistic Inquiry* 13: 571–612.
Aoun, J. (1979) 'A short note on cliticization', ms., MIT.
Aoun, J. (1981) 'The formal nature of anaphoric relations', PhD dissertation, MIT.
Aoun, J. (1985) *A Grammar of Anaphora*, Cambridge, MA: MIT Press.
Aoun, J. (1986) *Generalized Binding*, Dordrecht, The Netherlands: Foris.
Aoun, J. and Clark, R. (1985) 'On non-overt operators', *Southern California Occasional Papers in Linguistics*, University of Southern California, 17–36.
Aoun, J. and Sportiche, D. (1983) 'On the formal theory of government', *The Linguistic Review* 2: 211–36.
Aoun, J., Hornstein, N., Lightfoot, D., and Weinberg, A. (1987) 'Two types of locality', *Linguistic Inquiry* 18, 4: 537–95.
Bach, E. (1976) 'Comments on the paper by Chomsky', in P. Culicover, T. Wasow, and A. Akmajian (eds.) *Formal Syntax*, New York: Academic Press, 133–56.
Bach, E. (1980) 'In defense of passive', *Linguistics and Philosophy* 3, 3.
Bach, E. (1982) 'Purpose clauses and control', in P. Jacobsen and G. Pullum (eds) *The Nature of Syntactic Representation*, Dordrecht, The Netherlands: Reidel, 35–57.
Bach, E. and G. Horn (1976) 'Remarks on "Conditions on transformation"', *Linguistic Inquiry* 7: 265–99.
Baker, C.L. (1981) 'Learnability and the English auxiliary system', in C.L. Baker and J.J. McCarthy (eds) *The Logical Problem of Language Acquisition*, Cambridge, MA: MIT Press 296–323.
Baker, M. (1988) *Incorporation: A Theory of Grammatical Function Changing*, Chicago: The University of Chicago Press.

References

Berwick, R. (1985) *The Acquisition of Syntactic Knowledge*, Cambridge, MA: MIT Press.
Borer, H. (1984) *Parametric Syntax*, Dordrecht, The Netherlands: Foris.
Borer, H. and Wexler, K. (1987) 'The maturation of syntax', in T. Roeper and E. Williams (eds) *Parameter Setting*, Dordrecht, The Netherlands: Reidel, 123–72.
Bouchard, D. (1984) *On the Content of Empty Categories*, Dordrecht, The Netherlands: Foris.
Brody, M. (1984) 'On contextual definitions and the role of chains', *Linguistic Inquiry* 15, 3: 355–80.
Burzio, L. (1986) *Italian Syntax: A Government Binding Approach*, Dordrecht, The Netherlands: Reidel.
Chierchia, G. (1985) 'Formal semantics and the grammar of predication', *Linguistic Inquiry* 16: 417–43.
Chomsky, N. (1957) *Syntactic Structures*, The Hague: Mouton.
Chomsky, N. (1965) *Aspects of the Theory of Syntax*, Cambridge, MA: MIT Press.
Chomsky, N. (1970) 'Remarks on nominalization', in R. Jacobs and R. Rosenbaum (eds) *Readings in English Transformational Grammar*, Waltham, MA: Ginn.
Chomsky, N. (1973) 'Conditions on transformations', in S. Anderson and P. Kiparsky (eds) *A Festschrift for Morris Halle*, New York: Holt, 232–86.
Chomsky, N. (1977) 'On WH-movement', in P. Culicover, T. Wasow, and A. Akmajian (eds) *Formal Syntax*, New York: Academic Press, 71–132.
Chomsky, N. (1980) 'On binding', *Linguistic Inquiry* 11: 1–46.
Chomsky, N. (1981) *Lectures on Government and Binding*, Dordrecht, The Netherlands: Foris.
Chomsky, N. (1982) *Some Concepts and Consequences of the Theory of Government and Binding*, Cambridge, MA: MIT Press.
Chomsky, N. (1985) *Knowledge of Language: Its Nature, Origin and Use*, New York: Praeger.
Chomsky, N. (1986) *Barriers*, Cambridge, MA: MIT Press.
Chomsky, N. and Lasnik, H. (1977) 'Filters and control', *Linguistic Inquiry* 8: 425–504.
Cinque, G. (1984) 'Ā-bound *pro* vs. variable', ms., Università di Venezia.
Clark, R. (1984) 'Control into NP', in *Proceedings of the West Coast Conference on Formal Linguistics* 3: 40–7.
Clark, R. (1985a) 'The syntactic nature of Logical Form: evidence from Toba Batak', *Linguistic Inquiry* 16, 4: 663–9.
Clark, R. (1985b) 'Boundaries and the treatment of control', unpublished PhD dissertation, UCLA.
Contreras, H. (1984) 'A note on parasitic gaps', ms., University of Washington.
Davidson, D. (1980) *Essays on Actions and Events*, London: Oxford University Press.
Di Sciullo, A.M. and Williams, E. (1987) *On the Definition of Word*, Cambridge, MA: MIT Press.

References

Emonds, J. (1976) *A Transformational Approach to English Syntax*, New York: Academic Press.
Emonds, J. (1985) *A Unified Theory of Syntactic Categories*, Dordrecht, The Netherlands: Foris.
Epstein, S.D. (1984) 'Quantifier-PRO and the LF representation of PRO_{arb}', *Linguistic Inquiry* 15, 3: 499–505.
Fabb, N. (1984) 'Syntactic affixation', PhD dissertation, MIT.
Faraci, R. (1974) 'Aspects of the grammar of infinitives and *"for"*-phrases', PhD dissertation, MIT.
Farmer, A. (1984) *Modularity in Syntax: A Study of Japanese and English*, Cambridge, MA: MIT Press.
Fiengo, R. (1980) *Surface Structure*, Cambridge, MA: Harvard University Press.
Geach, P.T. (1962) *Reference and Generality*, Ithaca, NY: Cornell University Press.
Grimshaw, J. (1981) 'Form, Function, and the Language Acquisition Device', in C.L. Baker and J.J. McCarthy (eds) *The Logical Problem of Language Acquisition*, Cambridge, MA: MIT Press, 165–82.
Guéron, J. and May, R. (1984) 'Extraposition and Logical Form', *Linguistic Inquiry* 15, 1: 1–31.
Hale, K. and Keyser, S.J. (1987) 'Some transitivity alternations in English', Lexicon Project, Center for Cognitive Science, MIT.
Hantson, A. (1984) 'Towards an analysis of retroactive gerunds', in W. de Geest and Y. Putseys (eds) *Sentential Complementation*, Dordrecht, The Netherlands: Foris, 95–103.
Heim, I. (1982) 'The semantics of definite and indefinite noun phrases', PhD dissertation, University of Massachusetts, Amherst.
Higginbotham, J. (1980) 'Pronouns and bound variables', *Linguistic Inquiry* 11: 679–709.
Higginbotham, J. (1983) 'Logical Form, binding, and nominals', *Linguistic Inquiry* 14, 3: 395–420.
Higginbotham, J. (1985) 'On semantics', *Linguistic Inquiry* 16, 4: 547–93.
Higginbotham, J. (1987) 'Elucidations of meaning', Lexicon Project, Center for Cognitive Science, MIT.
Higginbotham, J. and May, R. (1981) 'Questions, quantifiers and crossing', *The Linguistic Review* 1, 1: 41–80.
Hornstein, N. (1984) *Logic as Grammar*. Cambridge, MA: MIT Press.
Hornstein, N. and Lightfoot, D., eds (1981) *Explanation in Linguistics*, New York: Longman.
Hornstein, N. and Weinberg, A. (1981) 'Case theory and preposition stranding', *Linguistic Inquiry* 12, 1: 55–91.
Horvath, J. (1981) 'Aspects of Hungarian syntax and the theory of grammar', PhD dissertation, UCLA.
Huang, C.-T.J. (1982) 'Logical relations in Chinese and the theory of grammar', PhD dissertation, MIT.
Huang, C.-T.J. (1984) 'On the distribution and reference of empty pronouns', *Linguistic Inquiry* 15, 4: 531–74.

Jackendoff, R. (1972) *Semantic Interpretation in Generative Grammar*, Cambridge, MA: MIT Press.
Jackendoff, R. (1977) *X̄-Syntax: A Study of Phrase Structure*, Cambridge, MA: MIT Press.
Jackendoff, R. (1983) *Semantics and Cognition*, Cambridge, MA: MIT Press.
Jaeggli, O. (1982) *Topics in Romance Syntax*, Dordrecht, The Netherlands: Foris.
Jaeggli, O. (1986) 'Passive', *Linguistic Inquiry* 17, 4: 587-622.
Jespersen, O. (1940) *A Modern English Grammar*, Copenhagen: E. Munksgaard.
Kayne, R. (1984) *Connectedness and Binary Branching*, Dordrecht, The Netherlands: Foris.
Keenan, E. and Faltz, L. (1984) *Boolean Semantics for Natural Language*, Dordrecht, The Netherlands: Reidel.
Keyser, S.J. and Roeper, T. (1984) 'On the middle and ergative constructions in English', *Linguistic Inquiry* 15, 3: 381–416.
Koopman, H. and Sportiche, D. (1981) 'Variables and the Bijection Principle', ms presented at 1981 GLOW Conference, Göttingen.
Koopman, H. and Sportiche, D. (1983) 'Variables and the Bijection Principle', *The Linguistic Review* 2, 2.
Lapointe, S. (1980) 'A theory of grammatical agreement', PhD dissertation, University of Massachusetts, Amherst.
Lasnik, H. (1988) 'Subjects and the θ-Criterion', *Natural Language and Linguistic Theory* 6, 1: 1–17.
Lasnik, H. and Saito, M. (1984) 'On the nature of proper government', *Linguistic Inquiry* 15, 2: 235–89.
Lebeaux, D. (1984) 'Anaphoric binding and the definition of PRO', *Proceedings of NELS* 14: 253–74.
Lees, R.B. (1960) *The Grammar of English Nominalizations*, PhD dissertation, MIT. Published 1970, The Hague, The Netherlands: Mouton.
Levin, B. (1985) 'Lexical semantics in review: an introduction', in B. Levin (ed.) *Lexical Semantics in Review*, Lexicon Project, Center for Cognitive Science, MIT, 1–62.
Levin, B. and Rappaport, M. (1986) 'The formation of adjectival passives', *Linguistic Inquiry* 17, 4: 623–61.
Lewis, D. (1975) 'Adverbs of quantification', in E. Keenan (ed.), *Formal Semantics of Natural Language*, Cambridge: Cambridge University Press, 3–15.
Lightfoot, D. (1979) *Principles of Diachronic Syntax*, Cambridge: Cambridge University Press.
Longobardi, G. (1985) 'Connectedness, scope and c-command', *Linguistic Inquiry* 16, 2: 163–92.
Manzini, M.R. (1983) 'On control and Control theory', *Linguistic Inquiry* 14, 3: 421–46.
Marantz, A. (1984) *On the Nature of Grammatical Relations*. Cambridge, MA: MIT Press.

References

May, R. (1977) 'The grammar of quantification', PhD dissertation, MIT.
May, R. (1985) *Logical Form: Its Structure and Derivation*. Cambridge, MA: MIT Press.
May, R. and Guéron, J. (1984) 'Extraposition and logical form', *Linguistic Inquiry* 15, 1.
Muysken, P. and Riemsdijk, H. van, eds (1985) *Features and Projections*, Dordrecht, The Netherlands: Foris.
Nishigauchi, T. (1984) 'Control and thematic domain', *Language* 60, 2: 215-50.
Pesetsky, D. (1982a) 'Complementizer-trace phenomena and the Nominative Island Condition', *The Linguistic Review* 1, 3: 297-343.
Pesetsky, D. (1982b) 'Paths and categories', PhD dissertation, MIT.
Pinker, S. (1984) *Language Learnability and Language Development*, Cambridge, MA: Harvard University Press.
Pinker, S. (1987) 'Resolving a learnability paradox in the acquisition of the verb lexicon', Lexicon Project, Center for Cognitive Science, MIT.
Postal, P. (1974) *On Raising*. Cambridge, MA: MIT Press.
Reinhart, T. (1983) 'Coreference and bound anaphora: a restatement of the anaphora question', *Linguistics and Philosophy* 6, 1: 47-88.
Reinhart, T. (1984) *Anaphora and Semantic Interpretation*, London: Croom Helm.
Riemsdijk, H. van (1978) *A Case Study in Syntactic Markedness*, Dordrecht, The Netherlands: Foris.
Rizzi, L. (1982) *Issues in Italian Syntax*, Dordrecht, The Netherlands: Foris.
Roeper, T. (1986) 'Implicit arguments, implicit roles, and subject/object asymmetry in morphological rules', ms., University of Massachusetts, Amherst.
Rosenbaum, P.S. (1967) 'The grammar of English predicate complement constructions', PhD dissertation, MIT.
Ross, J.R. (1967) 'Constraints on variables in syntax', PhD dissertation, MIT.
Ross, J.R. (1973) 'Nouniness', in O. Fujimura (ed.) *Three Dimensions of Linguistic Theory*, Tokyo: TEC.
Rouveret, A. and Vergnaud, J.R. (1980) 'Specifying reference to the subject', *Linguistic Inquiry* 11, 1.
Safir, K. (1984a) 'Worth', ms., Rutgers University.
Safir, K. (1984b) 'Multiple variable binding', *Linguistic Inquiry* 15, 4: 603-38.
Safir, K. (1985) *Syntactic Chains*, London: Cambridge University Press.
Safir, K. (1986) 'Evaluative predicates', ms., Rutgers University.
Scalise, S. (1984) *Generative Morphology*, Dordrecht, The Netherlands: Foris.
Schachter, P. (1976) 'A non-transformational account of gerundive nominals in English', *Linguistic Inquiry* 7, 2.
Selkirk, E. (1982) *The Syntax of Words*, Cambridge, MA: MIT Press.
Sportiche, D. (1981) 'Bounding nodes in French', *The Linguistic Review* 1, 2: 219-46.

References

Sportiche, D. (1983) 'Structural invariance and symmetry in syntax', PhD dissertation, MIT.
Stowell, T. (1981) 'Origins of phrase structure', PhD dissertation, MIT.
Stowell, T. (1983) 'Subjects across categories', *The Linguistic Review*, 2: 285–312.
Stowell, T. (1985) 'Null operators and antecedent government', ms., UCLA.
Visser, F.T. (1973) *An Historical Syntax of the English Language; part Three, Second Half.* Brill, Leyden.
Wexler, K. and Culicover, P. (1980) *Formal Principles of Language Acquisition.* Cambridge, MA: MIT Press.
Williams, E. (1980) 'Predication', *Linguistic Inquiry* 11, 1: 203–38.
Williams, E. (1982) 'The NP cycle', *Linguistic Inquiry* 13, 2: 277–95.
Williams, E. (1983) 'Against small clauses', *Linguistic Inquiry* 14, 2.
Williams, E. (1985) 'PRO and the subject of NP', *Natural Language and Linguistic Theory* 3: 297–315.
Williams, E. (1986) 'A reassignment of functions of LF', *Linguistic Inquiry* 17, 2: 265–99.

Index

A-binding 32, 55-7
A-bar binding 39, 133
A-bar position 34-5
Abney, S. 245
Absorption 253
A-chain 28, 38, 42, 43, 55, 193, 252
   generalized 194
Accusative Case 12-13, 75, 246
Adjunct-Island Condition 94-101, 111-13, 114, 118, 131, 132, 249
Adverbs of quantification 213, 219-20, 221, 222, 223, 238
Anderson, M. 42, 43
Anderson, S. 21
Anti-superiority 197
Aoun, J. 56, 58, 130, 133, 151, 153, 156, 169, 226, 240, 243, 248
Argument structure (*see* lexical argument structure)

Bach, E. 32, 98, 147
Baker, C. L. 126
Baker, M. 21, 74
Barrier 101, 103, 104, 107, 112
Belleti, A. 249
Berwick, R. 251
Bijection Principle 145, 146, 154
Binding Theory 6, 19, 26, 27, 32, 71, 73, 79, 130, 134, 153-6, 185, 234, 235-6, 242, 243
Condition A 55, 134, 154, 155, 156
Condition B 134
Condition C 32, 33, 148, 154, 155, 176, 185, 187
Blocking category 103
Borer, H. 4, 253
Bouchard, D. 24, 134, 177, 196, 244
Bound 243
Bound pronouns 235-6
Bounding Theory 6
Bridge verbs 116-18, 135-6
Brody, M. 143, 237, 244
Burzio, L. 75, 122
Burzio's Generalization 75, 122, 246

Case Filter 42, 46, 75, 76, 196
Case Theory 6, 12-14, 24-5, 41, 46, 51, 58, 71, 190, 237, 238, 242-3
   and non-overt operators 187-98
C-command 15, 22, 243, 253
C-domain 138
Chierchia, G. 167, 171
Chinese 23, 243
Chomsky, N. 1, 3, 6, 9, 12, 15, 17, 21, 24, 25, 32, 36, 37, 40, 41, 46, 62, 80, 82, 83, 84, 87, 90, 91, 94, 97, 98, 99, 100, 101-10,

114, 116, 119, 133, 134, 138–9, 141, 143, 144, 147, 148, 149, 150, 153, 154, 155, 159, 163, 165, 166, 172–3, 174, 177, 179, 180, 184, 190, 193, 202, 243, 244, 245, 246, 248, 249, 250, 251, 252
Chomsky-adjunction 104, 200–1
Cinque, G. 247
Clark, R. 17, 151, 248, 249
Clitic 234, 244
Complement 7–9
Completeness 179–87
Complex NP Constraint 113–14, 118
Contreras, H. 148, 149
Control Theory 6, 133
  and adjuncts 171–3
  arbitrary control (*see* non-obligatory control)
  Double control 133, 181–7, 231
  Linked readings 219–35
  Non-obligatory control 133–4, 137, 182, 200–36, 238
  Obligatory control 133–4, 136, 137, 163–87, 237
  and unselective quantification 217–19
  (*see also* PRO)
Culicover, P. 250, 251

Dative shift 44–5, 233–4, 243, 246
Davidson, D. 127
Deverbalizing Schema 67
DiSciullo, A. 68
Domain-Governing Category 138
D-Structure 4–5, 9–13
Dutch 245

Emonds, J. 5, 249
Empty Categories 22, 24–5
Empty Category Principle 15–18, 45, 61, 70–1, 72, 73, 80, 81–2, 88, 97, 100, 105–9, 112, 113, 114, 115, 118, 121, 144, ,149, 155, 183, 237
Epstein, S. 161–2, 252

Ergative Construction 124, 202
Exceptional Case Marking 44–5, 90–3, 103, 110–11, 165, 243, 247
Exclusion 104–5
Existential Closure 215–16, 228, 229, 230, 232, 233
Extended Projection Principle 3–4, 11, 21, 26, 76, 106, 122
Extraposition 119–22, 250

Fabb, N. 74
Faltz, L. 209, 211
Faraci, R. 133
Farmer, A. 9
Fiengo, R. 147
Functional determination of empty categories 143

Gamma-marking 106, 107, 109, 112
Geach, P. 252
Generalized Binding 153–6
Genitive 53, 97
Government-Binding theory 3, 19
Government theory 6, 56–7, 82–4, 105
  proper government 105
Grimshaw, J. 242
Gueron, J. 119, 250

Hale, K. 124
Hantson, A. 243, 247
Hebrew 253
Heim, I. 65, 212, 213, 214, 215, 216, 222–3, 228, 229, 253
Higginbotham, J. 50, 63–4, 126, 128, 133, 141, 143, 159, 248, 253
Hoekstra, T. 248
Horn, G. 98
Hornstein, N. 18, 58, 62, 94, 251
Horvath, J. 56
Huang, J. 23, 226, 243, 244, 252

Identification 160–1
Implicit arguments 162, 201–6, 235–6, 238, 251–2, 253

261

Indefinite NPs 212, 214–15, 253
Infinitival relatives 173–4
ing nominals 20, 52–3, 57, 59–60, 69–70, 74, 75, 77, 80, 97, 131, 240
Italian 119, 247
i-within-i condition 138, 225, 226, 227, 240, 251

Jackendoff, R. 6, 41, 46, 60, 67, 68, 69, 216, 242
Jaeggli, O. 48, 50, 58, 74, 122, 202
Japanese 252
Jespersen, O. 243

Kayne, R. 36, 44, 45, 51, 58, 82, 88, 89, 90, 94, 120, 144, 149, 233, 242, 243, 246, 248
Keenan, E. 209, 211, 253
Keyser, S. J. 122, 124, 201, 246, 252
Koopman, H. 144, 145, 154

Lapointe, S. 100
Lasnik, H. 15, 106, 124, 166, 172–3, 205, 206, 252
Learnability 4, 18, 250–1
Lebeaux, D. 161–2, 177, 219, 224
Lees, R. 41
Left-Branch Condition 89
Levels of representation 4–5, 106, 166–7
Levin, B. 122, 242
Lewis, D. 213, 216
Lexical argument structure 1, 4
Lexicon 1
Lightfoot, D. 18, 250
Linked readings 219–35
L-marking 102, 103, 112, 113
Longobardi, G. 157
Logical Form 4–5, 15–18, 50, 133, 179–80, 200–1, 221–36

Manzini, M.-R. 133, 134, 135, 138, 139, 140, 141, 146, 177, 182, 253
Marantz, A. 209
May, R. 15, 17, 104, 119, 141, 200, 245, 250, 253
M-command 105
Middle construction 124, 129
Middle English 250
Minimal Distance Principle 136, 175, 252
Minimality Condition 108–9, 155, 250
Modularity 4, 11
Move alpha 5–6, 13–14, 41, 43, 104, 122, 173
Muysken, P. 6

Nishigauchi, T. 3, 133, 134, 136, 207
Nominalizations 96–100, 113–14
Nominative Case 12–13, 129, 165
Non-overt operators 32–9, 133, 144, 146, 147–61
  relationship with PRO 161–200
NP-trace 24–5, 29–31, 42

Oblique Case 12–13, 94
of insertion 45
Operators 31–41

Parameters 4
Parasitic gaps 32, 36–40, 144, 148–50, 152–3, 158, 240, 245–6, 250
Passive 13–14, 26, 41–3, 48–9, 76, 122–4, 129, 202–3, 244, 249
  (*see also* pseudo-passive)
Pesetsky, D. 15, 88
Phonetic Form 4–5
Pinker, S. 242
Pleonastics 28, 91
Postal, P. 246
Predicate Formation 209–10, 239
Predicates of requirement 34
Prediction 158–61, 167–71
Preposition stranding 72–3, 85–6, 96
Principle of Lexicalization 196
pro 25, 166
PRO 2–3, 19, 24–5, 26, 29, 31, 56, 57, 58, 71–2, 79, 103, 131, 133, 242, 243, 248

Arbitrary PRO 135, 161–3, 182, 183, 229, 230, 232, 234
  Distribution of 134–5
  PRO gate 133, 134, 141–7, 236–7
  Linked readings of 133
Pseudo-passive 44, 59, 96–7, 100 (*see also* passive)
Psych verbs 169–71
Purposives 32, 174–9

Quantifier Raising 15, 142, 181, 200–1, 204, 229, 230, 253

Raising 30, 93–4
Raising Principle 250–1
Rappaport, M. 122
Reanalysis 58–9
Reciprocals 153
Reflexives 153
Reinhart, T. 200, 236, 243
Retroactive nominals 26, 38–9, 62, 67, 76, 79, 97, 239–41, 245
van Riemsdijk, H. 6, 58, 245
Rizzi, L. 116
Roeper, T. 53, 54, 122, 124, 201, 246, 252
Rosenbaum, P. 136
Ross, J. R. 60, 98
Rouveret, A. 12

Safir, K. 64, 74, 77, 121, 143, 193, 196, 216, 237, 244, 245, 246, 247, 248, 252, 253
Saito, M. 15, 106, 124, 166, 252
Scalise, S. 68
Schachter, P. 60
Scope 200–1
Selkirk, L. 68
Small clauses 44–5, 48, 88–90, 91, 249, 253
Specifier 7–9
Sportiche, D. 56, 116, 134, 144, 145, 154, 177, 243, 244
SSC 40–1, 52, 53, 54, 57, 77, 79, 248
S-Structure 4–5, 12–15, 133, 236
Stowell, T. 9, 41, 47, 56, 58, 83, 117, 120, 125, 127, 129, 147, 163, 233, 247, 249, 253
Subcategorization 35, 49, 124–8, 163–4
Subjacency 94, 105–9, 111, 113, 114, 115–9, 124, 132, 150
  bounding nodes 116
Subject 27, 54, 155, 225, 226, 227, 240, 244, 251, 253
Subject Condition 36, 88–94, 110–11, 114, 118, 131, 132, 233
Superiority effects 183

Thematic Compatibility 207, 209
Thematic roles 1–2
Theta Binding 64, 66, 81
Theta-chain (*see* A-chain)
Theta Criterion 3–4, 10, 11, 13, 19, 28, 33, 36, 37, 49, 50, 55, 65, 74, 76, 106, 123, 166, 184, 208, 230, 249
Theta-government 102, 113, 155
Theta Theory 6, 11, 19–20, 51, 62–3
Tough movement 32, 33–4, 44–5, 196–7, 247
Tough verbs 196
Transparency 51, 82–3, 91, 111, 114, 117, 122, 124, 128, 129, 130, 131
  extraction-transparency 84, 85–6, 87, 90, 95, 128, 132
  government-transparency 83, 132

Universal Grammar 18
Unselective quantification 212–19
  and control 217–19

Variable 24–5, 148
Vergnaud, J.-R. 12
Visser, F. 75

Weak cross-over 134, 141–3, 236, 237, 245
Weinberg, A. 58, 62, 94
Wexler, K. 4, 250, 251

263

Index

Williams, E. 42, 68, 159, 167, 168, 172, 236, 246, 248, 249, 252
worth 76–9

X' Theory 5–6, 6–9, 11, 41, 67, 84

For Product Safety Concerns and Information please contact our EU representative GPSR@taylorandfrancis.com
Taylor & Francis Verlag GmbH, Kaufingerstraße 24, 80331 München, Germany

www.ingramcontent.com/pod-product-compliance
Lightning Source LLC
Chambersburg PA
CBHW071814300426
44116CB00009B/1312